Linux® Game Programming

PRIMA TECH'S

GAME DEVELOPMENT

Check the Web for Updates

To check for updates or corrections relevant to this book and/or CD-ROM, visit our updates page on the Web at **http://www.prima-tech.com/updates**.

Send Us Your Comments

To comment on this book or any other PRIMA TECH title, visit our reader response page on the Web at **http://www.prima-tech.com/comments**.

How to Order

For information on quantity discounts, contact the publisher: Prima Publishing, P.O. Box 1260BK, Rocklin, CA 95677-1260; (916) 787-7000. On your letterhead, include information concerning the intended use of the books and the number of books you want to purchase. For individual orders, turn to the back of this book for more information.

LINUX® GAME PROGRAMMING

MARK "NURGLE" COLLINS

PRIMA TECH'S

GAME DEVELOPMENT

PRIMA TECH

A DIVISION OF PRIMA PUBLISHING

A Division of Prima Publishing

Prima Publishing and colophon are registered trademarks of Prima Communications, Inc. PRIMA TECH and the Game Development series are trademarks of Prima Communications, Inc., Roseville, California 95661.

Publisher: Stacy L. Hiquet
Associate Marketing Manager: Jennifer Breece
Managing Editor: Sandy Doell
Acquisitions Editor: Jody Kennen
Project Editor: Heather Talbot
Technical Reviewer: Zach Slater
Copy Editor: Alice Martina Smith
Interior Layout: Bill Hartman
Cover Design: Prima Design Team
Indexer: Johnna VanHoose Dinse
Proofreader: Fran Blauw

Linux is a registered trademark of Linus Torvalds.

OpenGL is a registered trademark of Silicon Graphics, Inc.

Loki and OpenAL are registered trademarks of Loki Software, Inc.

Important: Prima Publishing cannot provide software support. Please contact the appropriate software manufacturer's technical support line or Web site for assistance.

Prima Publishing and the author have attempted throughout this book to distinguish proprietary trademarks from descriptive terms by following the capitalization style used by the manufacturer.

Information contained in this book has been obtained by Prima Publishing from sources believed to be reliable. However, because of the possibility of human or mechanical error by our sources, Prima Publishing, or others, the Publisher does not guarantee the accuracy, adequacy, or completeness of any information and is not responsible for any errors or omissions or the results obtained from use of such information. Readers should be particularly aware of the fact that the Internet is an ever-changing entity. Some facts may have changed since this book went to press.

ISBN: 0-7615-3255-2

Library of Congress Catalog Card Number: 00-110735

Printed in the United States of America

00 01 02 03 04 II 10 9 8 7 6 5 4 3 2 1

CONTENTS AT A GLANCE

CONTENTS

CHAPTER 2

LINUX DEVELOPMENT TOOLS ················11

CHAPTER 3

THE STRUCTURE OF A GAME ···············23

CHAPTER 4
2D GRAPHICS UNDER LINUX 29

CHAPTER 5

INPUT WITH SDL ■■■■■■■■■■■■■■■■■■■■■■■■■■■■■59

CHAPTER 6
3D GRAPHICS FOR LINUX GAMES 87

CHAPTER 7
USING OPENGL IN GAMES ■■■■■■■■■■■■■■■■117

CHAPTER 8
SOUND UNDER LINUX 147

CHAPTER 9

NETWORKING ■■■■■■■■■■■■■■■■■■■■■■■■■■■■■■■■■169

CHAPTER 10

ARTIFICIAL INTELLIGENCE 197

CHAPTER 11

OPENSOURCE! FRIEND OR FOE? 225

APPENDIX A

OpenSource License Agreements ...243

APPENDIX B
PORTING •••••••••••••••••••••••••••••••••••273

APPENDIX C
REFERENCES 299

ACKNOWLEDGMENTS

First of all, I'd like to thank my co-authors, Steve Baker, Ben Campbell, and Martin Donlon, for taking time out of their busy lives to help complete this book on time. If it weren't for their support, this book may not have happened at all. I'd also like to thank all the guys and gals at Prima Publishing, namely Jody Kennen and Heather Talbot, as well as André LaMothe (who may one day forgive me for not speaking at the XGDC).

A big shout goes to all the staff and regulars at GameDev.Net for putting up with my ever-inflating ego and for not banning me from the message boards. (Although if they did, who'd run the Linux forum?) In the same breath, I'd like to say "hi" to all the lame software pirates in the Syndicate of London, namely Paris, Llama, Comrade, and Cronus (I shall enjoy watching you die, Mr. Anderson), and to all the l33t people at #hackerzlair on DALnet.

A big thanks to my ex-ex-ex-ex-ex-ex-ex-ex-ex-ex-girlfriend, Sima, for supporting me throughout this little adventure (when we weren't arguing), and to all my friends from Bath, many of whom owe me large quantities of alcohol.

In true hacker fashion, these acknowledgments wouldn't be complete without a list of shouts. So in no particular order, shouts to: ShinyEyedMermaid, JerryLee, TheHermit, Nurse, Mistress Demonica, nes8bit, pouya, Myopic Rhino, jhky, TANSTAAFL, JadeFalcon, Dulie, Paris, Comrade, Llama, ^cronus^, Infinity Matrix, Fwaggle, Dysfunksi0n, Trax, Lockpick, Laura^, MaryJayne, all the guys and gals at Silicon Dreams (especially Lara, she's hot), Gumby, Trev, Ruth, Puppy, Mike, Lil' Chris, Roper, Amy, Jonsey—and last, but not least, Invisible Bob (the unofficial Indrema mascot).

——The Infamous Mark "Nurgle" Collins, **me@thisisnurgle.org.uk**
Lead Author, *Linux Game Programming*

AUTHOR BIO

The Infamous **Mark "Nurgle" Collins**, the teenager with an ego that dwarfs Texas, has worked in just about every area of the IT industry, from Web design to network consultancy, but one field has repeatedly attracted his expertise and outside-the-box thinking. That area is game development.

In addition to all his hobbyist involvement, Mark has worked for one of the largest developers in Europe, and he acts as a freelance consultant to various commercial developers all over the globe. Having skills in networking, AI, and graphics, he believes that games should be fun, rather than yet another Quake clone.

LETTER FROM THE
SERIES EDITOR

Dear Reader,

A long time ago, in a cubicle far, far away, UNIX was created. UNIX has shown itself to be a reliable and robust platform for workstations, mainframes, and even PCs. But, UNIX had never really gained much momentum on the PC platform for anyone other than the power user or technically minded. However, the time has come when the PC version of UNIX, named Linux, has begun to make major in-roads into the average user's home, and game programmers are taking notice! Now is the time that gamers and developers alike want to play and develop games for Linux. However, Linux, like UNIX, wasn't a simple platform to learn to program games for—until now...

Linux Game Programming is without a doubt one of the most ambitious game programming books ever written. There are so many aspects to basic Linux programming, it boggles the mind to even begin to think about writing 2D/3D games for Linux. But, I can say that *Linux Game Programming* does it all. The author, Mark "Nurgle" Collins, starts from square one setting up the compiler, explaining the tools and libraries of Linux, and covering general game programming theory.

This book is not just a bridge for Windows game programmers who want to learn how to port to Linux, but an entire treatise on game programming on the Linux platform. This book covers it all! And I mean everything–from 2D and the SDL (Simple DirectMedia Layer) to open GL and full 3D game programming.

In conclusion, this book sets the standard for Linux game programming and will definitely be a jewel in your game programming library.

André LaMothe
March 2001

INTRODUCTION

Well, it's been a long time coming, but now there is finally a book on Linux game programming. With the growing interest in both the commercial and desktop uses of the free Linux operating system, it was only a matter of time until people started thinking about writing games for it. Sure, many people have written little games in the past, such as *xbill* and *xboing* (and a plethora of titles starting with the letter *x*), but only in recent years have games that are almost commercial quality been available for Linux.

With companies such as Loki porting successful titles such as *Descent 3* and *SimCity 3000*, it's only a matter of time until software houses start developing original titles for the Linux platform. With the imminent launch of the Indrema console, a Linux-based system, that future is set to become a reality.

But what is Linux? In 1991, a student in some country in Scandinavia made an announcement on a message board with this immortal line: "I'm working on a minix-based operating system; it won't be as big as the GNU project, though." (I'm paraphrasing here.) Since then, the "small" operating system that was never going to be as big as the GNU project has grown to several million users worldwide, with uses ranging from enterprise Web servers to games consoles.

Linux is a semi-POSIX-compatible, UNIX-like operating system that runs on almost every platform available today, ranging from i386s to PalmPilots. Until the past few years, however, few people considered using Linux as a desktop environment, but with projects such as KDE and Gnome paving the way, more and more people are wiping out Windows and switching to one of the many Linux distributions available.

MY JOYS WITH LINUX

I first played with Linux in 1994, running an old version of *Slackware* on a CD-ROM. After finding that the version of *Doom* included with that program refused to get past the title screen, I started looking for other games on the CDs (I couldn't get XWindows working back then). That's when I discovered *Abuse*, the classic side-scrolling platform game with a rather innovative feature: You aim with the mouse while moving with the keyboard. I was impressed with this feature but knew it wasn't going to last.

After a few weeks, I tried to install a few things from the CD, but horror struck! I was running on a UMSDOS partition, co-existing with Chicago (later renamed Windows 95). A broken installation program wiped out all the partitions on my hard disk completely, without even having the courtesy to ask first.

A few years later (and after the phenomenal success of *Spong*, a really bad *Pong* clone for DOS, which everyone in my school became addicted to), I decided to try Linux again. So I popped down to the shop and bought a RedHat boxed set, and I was away. After a few problems getting XWindows running in anything higher than standard VGA, everything ran perfectly. I was happily playing around with stuff, reconfiguring files here and there, setting up security, and so on. But I never actually used it. Why? Because there was nothing to do. Every time I wanted to play *Dungeon Keeper*, I would reboot into Windows and load it from there.

After some time, I did start playing some of the Linux games that were in existence, but none of them really impressed me. So I started looking for ways to write my own games. I downloaded SDL and started playing around with it. Then the worst thing in the world happened: I got a job. Working on server-side Java for Web sites, I had no time for personal projects. Soon I moved up to network consultancy and still had no time for games. About a year after that, however, things changed.

I was looking for a career change, and boy did I find one. Within a week after sending my curriculum vitae to an agency, I had an interview at Silicon Dreams. And I got the job. I stayed in that job until December 2000, at which point I decided to write this book full time. (I was fired.)

While I was at Silicon Dreams, I learned many things (one of which was to not annoy Microsoft; they'll complain to your boss if you do). One of the most important things I learned is this: No one in the "professional" industry cares about Linux development—at least officially, that is. Many of my co-workers at Dreams were closet die-hard Linux fans; as soon as they found out that I was writing this book, I had the sudden urge to kill many of them.

As unlikely as it may seem, the small project that was never destined for big things may actually become a hardcore gaming platform. I, for one, would like to see that happen.

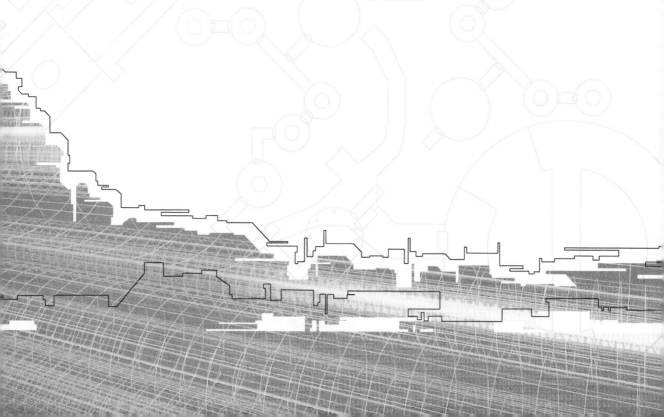

CHAPTER I

INTRODUCTION TO GAME DEVELOPMENT

Listen my children, for I will tell a tale of a quest for glory, an adventure most heroic. A long time ago, in a place far away, a young man sat in front of a magic box and decided to give something to the world. He spent many moons working on his creation. And when it was complete, he looked upon his creation and saw that it was good. This creation was a computer game. (After this he went down to the pub for a few drinks because he really needed a good night out.)

WHAT MAKES A GAME?

Why is a game different from any other type of application? There are several major differences: Games generally use more input and output devices than other applications. Games generally run faster than normal applications and make use of a lot of CPU time. The differences between games and other software are recognized by large software developers such as Microsoft and have forced these companies to create additional tools to allow developers to access the hardware directly.

Let's compare a game to a word processor. What do you do in a word processor? You type stuff in, add a bit of formatting, stick in some random comments for your editor to have a chuckle over, and save the file. But in a game, a lot more is involved. You have to update the screen as many times as possible during a single second. You need enemies reacting to the player's actions, you need a goal to achieve, and most important, the game has to be fun.

DIFFERENT GAME GENRES

There are many different types of games on the market, ranging from shoot-em-ups to strategy, from card games to simulations. Although some genres are generally more popular than others (such as first-person shooters), others have much more playability (such as card games).

SHOOT-EM-UPS

The shoot-em-up type of game is probably one of the most popular game genres at the moment. This category includes games such as *Quake* and *Unreal Tournament*. There are several types of shoot-em-up, ranging from first-person perspective to scrolling games such as *Defender*. Most games in this genre have but one goal: to kill anything that moves, from a shotgun to space ship.

Many newer shoot-em-ups have multiplayer capabilities, while others are written only for use as multiplayer games (for example, *Quake III: Arena*). These games have come under a lot of fire from the media in recent years and have been blamed for the Columbine shootings.

Games of this genre generally have very little in the way of a storyline—who needs an excuse to kill the alien invaders? Although some games make an effort to craft a story, original stories are harder to come up with these days.

Many games based on films fall into this category, such as *Die Hard Trilogy* and *Alien versus Predator*.

STRATEGY GAMES

There are two types of strategy games: real-time and turn-based. Games such as *Command and Conquer*, *StarCraft*, and *Dune* are real-time, whereas the hugely successful *Civilization* series is turn-based.

Real-time strategy games generally consist of two or more sides battling it out for an area of land. These games usually require the mining of raw materials to build new structures and units. These games are nearly as popular as shoot-em-ups but require a lot more time to play (a single level of *Command and Conquer* can take several hours of playing before it's completed). Consequently, it takes a lot of patience to play these games, and they can become very frustrating.

Games that require the building of a civilization, such as *Sid Miers Civilization*, tend to be turn based. Turn-based games can be played for days on end with only regular cups of coffee to keep you going. Turn-based games allow a player to move all of their units before allowing the other players to have their turns.

SIMULATIONS

Any game that attempts to simulate a real event is a simulator, be it a flight simulator or a fishing game. These games are designed to emulate real life as much as possible, allowing the users to gain experience in areas they wouldn't normally get a chance to experience.

Some simulators are used for training, such as the Concorde simulator at British Aerospace Filton in the United Kingdom. This multimillion-dollar computer game emulates the real behavior of the aircraft exactly (except that they won't let you barrel roll it). A few years ago, I had the opportunity to browse through the source code for the simulator (written in Assembler)—all several million lines worth of code! Accurate simulators are big projects and are not suited for the weekend programmer.

PLATFORM GAMES

Some of the most successful games ever have been platform games, such as the *Mario* series. This genre consists of a character moving around on a level that usually scrolls from side to side, but that in more recent years has become a full three-dimensional environment, with the character jumping around like a hyperactive frog on anti-depressants.

Many people new to games development choose a platform game as one of their earlier projects (usually after a few puzzle games). This is because platform games are generally uncomplicated from the developer's point of view and can result in hours of entertainment for the player.

PUZZLE GAMES

There are probably more puzzle games in the world than any other type of game. Puzzle games are very easy to code and can be very addictive for the player. This type of game requires very little in the way of artificial intelligence and tends to be relatively small compared to games from other genres that require large numbers of external data files to run.

Examples of puzzle games include *Tetris* and *Minesweeper*. These games require patience and planning to win. Like strategy games, puzzle games can get very frustrating over time.

ADVENTURE GAMES

Adventure games run the gamut of complexity, from the text-based *Zork* to the full 3D *Tomb Raider*.

This genre usually consists of the main character interacting with various NPCs (Non-Player Characters) to achieve a goal, whether that goal is rescuing a lost artifact or hooking up with a sexy babe (as in *Leisure Suit Larry*, by Sierra). These games tend to be highly immersive and can suck away many days of life from a dedicated adventurer.

ROLE-PLAY GAMES

Similar to adventure games, role-play games often involve going on a quest of some description, but tend to be a lot more open ended. Players can spend years building up a character, giving it a personality, and collecting a large stash of cash.

Some of the earlier RPGs (Role-Play Games), such as *Ultima*, used very simple graphics but proved highly successful, and some are still played today. Multiplayer RPGs have traditionally been text-based MUDs (Multi-User Dungeons), but some of the more recent games have been graphical, such as *Ultima: Online* and *EverQuest*.

CARD GAMES

Everyone has played *Solitaire* or *FreeCell*. These card games tend to be played when the user is waiting for something to be done or is on the phone with an annoying customer. Card games can become very addictive; I know some people who wouldn't get out of bed if it weren't for *FreeCell*.

SPORTS GAMES

Another highly successful game genre is the sports genre. Here in the United Kingdom, every gamer out there has played at least one soccer game, one racing simulation, and at least one beat-em-up. Some of the first games ever created fall into this genre (*Pong* being very similar to a game of tennis without any nets).

Games such as the *FIFA* series are always bestsellers, and with good reason. They bring out the competitive instinct in the player and allow the user to kick ass without actually hurting anyone. Many a time my brother challenged me to a quick game of *Actua Soccer*, and many a time I won (and many a time he beat me up for winning).

Sports games are generally highly addictive and can lead to large tournaments among groups of friends. People like sports, and they like them even more if they don't have to get injured in the process.

WHAT MAKES A SUCCESSFUL GAME?

This is a tough question because everyone has different opinions about what makes a game good, but there are always some common factors. Successful games are always (and most important) playable. Nobody likes to play a game where you have to type for ten minutes just to get a square to move one pixel to the left.

The game also needs to have a user-friendly interface, with easy-to-navigate menus that get the player into the game as soon as it loads. Continuing from this, a good game should be very easy to learn but should take a lifetime to master. A good example of this criterion is *Street Fighter*. Anybody can play the game well, but very few are really good at it. This is because the game controls are intuitive; randomly hitting them allows even a new player to win a fight against a master. However, a master can learn the special moves and use them to their full effect.

Some games have overly complex control systems, such as *Alien versus Predator*. This game had too many controls to master before you could get into the game. This meant only a dedicated gamer could play it for more than five minutes without deleting it from the hard disk out of frustration. Having to constantly jump around the keyboard just to select a gun and fire it puts most players off for life.

Another key requirement to the success of some games (although not all) is a good plot. It's all very well to run around killing every goblin in sight, but *why* are you killing them? Did they murder your second-cousin's pet cat? Or are you just killing them because they are there to kill? Even a simple background story can contribute a huge amount to the game's success, even if the actual story has no relevance to the game itself.

Good story lines don't have to be predictable to be interesting. Take, for example, the film *From Dusk Till Dawn*. Half the film is about two criminals trying to get to Mexico, when suddenly, out of nowhere, they are attacked by a hoard of vampires. This surprising twist made the film much more interesting. Games with sudden plot twists have done very well. A good example of this is *Wing Commander III*, in which the Kil'rathi pilot who defected changes sides halfway through the story, even though he showed complete loyalty to the Terran struggle.

Sometimes, being a well-known game developer means that all your games will be a huge success, even if there is nothing special about your project. A good example of this condition is *Doom 2*, the sequel to the highly successful *Doom*. There weren't any brand-spanking new features or a supersmart AI system in this sequel to the successful *Doom* game, but people like id software, and they will buy their games. However, fame has a price. People are more than willing to jump on any bugs in a game from a successful developer, while a lesser-known developer might manage to sneak a few "inconsistencies" past the critics.

THE GAME-DEVELOPMENT PROCESS

Game development, like any form of software engineering, isn't a simple code-it-and-you're-done process. There are several stages to go through to get your game from the drawing board to being played.

THE DESIGN DOCUMENT

A good design document is probably the most helpful tool for any game developer. It helps you develop a solid idea on which you can base your game. The design document can also help you get a publisher if you choose to write a commercial game (as explained later in this chapter).

What goes into a design document? Just about everything from the story line to the 3D engine you're going to use. Some design documents are several hundred pages long and cover every single detail in the game; simpler games can use shorter design documents. Even the smallest documents should contain the following:

- **General Overview**. This section of the document covers the game story line, the main characters, a basic overview of the development timeline, and the development staff required.
- **Screen and User Interface**. This section of the document covers the in-game menus, the in-game HUD (Heads-up Display) you might use, as well as any icons used in the game.
- **Art Specification**. This section of the document lists any in-game artwork, cut-scenes, and sprites. Include any appropriate storyboards and sketches.
- **Sound and Music**. All sound effects and music must be documented in this section, as well as any voice talents the game will need.
- **Technical Specification**. This section covers how the game is going to run, including flowcharts and any benchmarking you plan to perform.
- **Legal Information**. This section includes the copyright and a disclaimer.

After you have written your design document, you should share it with everyone on the development team so that they can give you feedback on your ideas. You will probably get through several versions of the design document before you all agree on what it contains, but that isn't a bad thing. The revision process will help form new ideas from old ones and might point out some serious problems that might otherwise occur only later in the development process.

DEVELOPMENT

After your team has agreed on a design, you can actually get to work on writing the code. But where do you begin? Do you write the game engine or the menus first? And which part of the game engine? Where to start is one of the toughest choices you'll have to make when starting a new project, but fortunately, you have a design document.

One of the best places to start when writing your game is at the beginning. I don't mean that you should write the whole thing in order, from intro sequence to closing credits, I mean that you should start where the program starts: the initialization routine where you prepare any variables you may need or fire up any graphics APIs you use. Without this vital part of the program, you can't do anything.

Where you go from there is up to you, but I like to continue by developing the graphics engine. This allows me to code the core of the game next, but does make it difficult to add or modify features later in the development process.

If you are on a team that is developing a large project, you will need a way of sharing files. E-mail is a fine exchange medium if everyone is working on completely separate parts of the program and you have a clearly defined interface to work with. However, if you have problems with version concurrency, you might want to look into a CVS (Concurrency Versioning System) repository. A CVS repository allows multiple developers to work on the same problem by checking files in and out of a "repository." I'll go into further detail about CVS options in Chapter 2, "Linux Development Tools."

TESTING

One of the most important steps in the development process is testing your funky new game. If any serious bugs show up after you release the game, your reputation will be ruined. *Frontier II: First Encounters* is a good example of incomplete testing resulting in a buggy release (although I can't really place the whole blame on the developers). Because of a tight deadline, the program wasn't fully tested and several major bugs caused serious problems in the game. These bugs seriously damaged the reputation of the developer, even though it had created *Elite*, one of the most popular games ever.

There are several stages to testing your game, commonly referred to as Alpha, Beta, and Gamma testing phases. The Alpha testing stage is done by the developers, in which they fix any obvious bugs and glitches they find while writing the code. Beta testing is performed by a third party (usually a dedicated gamer) who will try to find any of the hidden bugs; finally, Gamma testing is performed by the general game playing community. When a bug is found in the game, chances are you will hear about it. When you do, you try to reproduce the problem and then generate a patch to fix the program.

When it comes to testing, one of the most useful tools you can create is a debug cheat. A cheat allows you to jump to any part of the game, gives you any extras you need (such as cash, weapons, or bonus points), and can save you hours of time. Because all cheats are removed before the game is released (honest), there are some funky tricks you can use to enable or disable them at compile time using preprocessor directives.

If your compiler allows a flag to add a symbol at compile time, you can use that flag to specify a release type, depending on whether the code you are compiling is a debug or release version of the game. For example, you can include the following code in your game program.

```
// test.c
#include <stdio.h>
main () {
#ifdef DEBUG
    puts("This is a debugging version!");
#else
    puts("This is a release version");
#endif
}
```

If you then compile the program with the following command and run the program, you should get `This is the release version.`

```
gcc -o test1 test.c
```

However, if you include the `-DDEBUG` option on the command line, as shown in the following command, the program will output the line `This is a debugging version!`

```
gcc -DDEBUG -o test2 test.c
```

This trick allows you to add cheats using `#ifdef` blocks of code. You can then turn off the cheats when you are ready to release the game, if you wish. You can also add simple debugging statements in `#ifdef` blocks to track the program flow without the use of an external debugger (as discussed in Chapter 2).

RELEASING YOUR GAME

After you have tested your game as much as is humanly possible, you can release it. You have several choices about what to do at this stage, and I will discuss three of your options here: OpenSource, commercial, and shareware.

OPENSOURCE GAMES

OpenSource is probably the simplest and quickest route to getting your games on the market. If you want people to play your game as soon as possible, you can release the game while you're still writing it. Not only does this approach let people know your game exists long before it's finished, it also lets other people work with you to help fix any problems they may find or to make suggestions for improvement.

The OpenSource route also means that you'll have a larger number of testers working for free. This approach can speed up the development process dramatically and might even mean that your game will be ported to other operating systems by third parties.

Although many people claim that it is impossible to make any money out of OpenSource software, this has been proved false too many times to count. Companies such as RedHat and SuSE have made a huge success out of distributing OpenSource software for years by offering support and printed manuals.

The first step to releasing an OpenSource project is to make it publicly available, including the source code. After you have made it possible for everyone to get your program, make an announcement on a few mailing lists and on sites such as Freshmeat (**http://freshmeat.net**).

> **NOTE**
>
> **Make sure that you don't choose a license just because everyone else is using it. Read through several licenses (printed versions of which can be found in the back of this book) and choose the one you agree with the most.**

FRESHMEAT: HTTP://FRESHMEAT.NET

After you have made your announcement, expect input from users within a very short period of time. Some may have patches, others may have criticisms, and others may need help using your game. It is good practice in the OpenSource community to reply to all e-mail messages you receive regarding the product; doing so will help you gain a name for yourself in the OpenSource community.

COMMERCIAL GAMES

Many developers have realized that Linux is a viable option for commercial software, including games. Companies such as Loki have made a name for themselves by porting successful games; other companies such as Epic (Unreal) are also starting to develop games specifically for Linux machines.

Getting a game published commercially is not the easiest thing to do, especially for the Linux platform. The process is long and complicated, involving several contracts, NDAs (Non-Disclosure Agreements), and tough milestones. However, the rewards far outweigh the costs. Cash advances, high royalties, and fame encourage many independent developers to strive for bigger, better, and faster games.

To get published, you must first approach a publisher. Look around at your local *Electronics Boutique* to see what publishers are out there. Names and sometimes addresses of games publishers appear on the packaging of the products you'll see. Be aware that many publishers such as Electronic Arts have in-house development teams and refuse unsolicited submissions. Look for companies that publish games from a wide range of developers, such as GT Interactive and ActiVision. When you have determined who you want to publish your game, request a submission pack from the publisher. This packet will contain an NDA, which protects all parties involved from any legal problems that may arise (for example, plagiarism).

When you have returned the NDA with your completed design document—and hopefully a working demo of your game—the publisher will tell you whether it is interested in your submission. If it turns you down, don't give up. Keep trying until you get a new publisher.

If the publisher approves your game, negotiations will begin. It might be a good idea to contact a lawyer because legal documents will be involved; unless you are fluent in legalese, the contracts will probably be a bit confusing.

A good guide to getting your games published has been written by Geoff Howland of Lupine Games. You can find the guide at **http://www.lupinegames.com/articles/getstart.html**.

GUIDE TO GETTING YOUR GAMES PUBLISHED:
HTTP://WWW.LUPINEGAMES.COM/ARTICLES/GETSTART.HTML

SHAREWARE GAMES

Another option when it comes to releasing your game is the shareware route. Some of the most successful games ever, such as *Doom* and *Quake*, were released initially as shareware. Releasing a game as shareware is very similar to releasing a game in the OpenSource route, except that you generally don't distribute the source code. (Note, however, that id software has now made the source code to *Quake* available, although it still requires a license for the in-game data.)

You have several options to choose from when making your game shareware. You can use an honor system and ask the user to pay you after a certain amount of time has elapsed, or you can restrict the game in some way (such as only including the first few levels) until the user has paid you for the complete version.

After you have decided how you're going to claim money from the users, you have to set a price ($20 is usually a good start) and add a message to the game letting the users know where they have to send the money. In games such as *Doom* and *Quake*, a message was displayed when you quit the game, giving the user registration details. Some games use pop-up messages during the game to get the shareware message across.

When it comes to distributing your game, you have several options. You can try and have it stuck on the cover CD of your favorite magazine, or you can upload it to the Internet and have some download sites such as Tucows (**http://www.tucows.com**), sending random surfers to get your game. The possibilities are endless.

TUCOWS: HTTP://WWW.TUCOWS.COM

CHAPTER 2

LINUX DEVELOPMENT TOOLS

Just as every plumber needs a plunger and every surgeon needs a scalpel, game developers have certain tools they need to create the next hit games. These tools range from development environments to debuggers and profilers. In this chapter, you'll learn what types of tools make up the successful game developer's toolkit.

DEVELOPMENT TOOLS

You will use several key tools when you write any software, including compilers, interpreters, debuggers, and version management tools such as make. Some tools, such as KDevelop, integrate all of these utilities into one environment.

COMPILER

The most important tool you will need is a compiler. Without one, your code is about as useful as a bikini in the Arctic Circle. Although some languages such as bash are not strictly compiled, you will still need an interpreter of some kind. Because the code in this book is written in C, I will focus on the GNU C compiler, GCC, available from **http://www.gnu.org/software/gcc/gcc.html**.

GNU C COMPILER: HTTP://WWW.GNU.ORG/SOFTWARE/GCC/GCC.HTML

Compiling with the GCC can be a problem and isn't covered by this book; if you download the source code that's available for distribution, you should read all the documentation before you begin to use the compiler. Note, however, that almost all Linux distributions include the GCC as part of the default installation, so you probably already have the compiler.

The GCC incorporates most of the tools you will ever need into one easy-to-use program. The GCC includes preprocessors, compilers, and linkers for various platforms (you can cross-compile to a Win32 executable, for example). To demonstrate GCC, copy the following example:

```
/* gcc-test.c - GCC test application */

main(int argc, char **argv) {
        printf("Line: %d - Number of arguments: %d\n", __LINE__, argc);
        printf("Line: %d - First argument: %s\n", __LINE__, argv[1]);
        printf("Compiled on %s %s\n", __DATE__, __TIME__);
        return 0;
}
```

This simple program demonstrates several features of the GCC. To compile this file, use the console command gcc. The command line to compile the program is as follows:

> **NOTE**
>
> Unless you specify -o <*filename*>, the GCC will generate a file called a.out in the current directory.

```
gcc -o gcc-test gcc-test.c
```

When you run the compiled test program, it will display a few details about itself, including the date and time at which it was compiled. This information is supplied by the __DATE__ and __TIME__ macros. Another useful macro to know is the __LINE__ macro, which contains the current line number being executed (useful for debugging).

The gcc -o gcc-test gcc-test.c command is fine for simple, single-file projects, but what if your program spans multiple files? If you include the -c option on the command line, the GCC does not generate an executable file but instead generates a linkable object file. Try the following sample program. In one file (gcc-func1.c), type the following code:

```
/* gcc-func1.c - GCC function sample */

void function() {
    printf("Hello world\n");
}
```

Before you can call this function (cleverly named function()), you must have a main() somewhere. So let's create a second file (gcc-func2.c) that contains the main() function:

```
/* gcc-func2.c - GCC function sample */

void function(void);

main() {
    function();
    return 0;
}
```

In normal situations, you'd use a makefile for multiple source files, but I'll cover that technique later in this chapter. For this example, we'll use the command line to compile this two-file program. For each file you want to *compile*, you use the -c parameter. When you want to *link* the program, you tell the compiler to use the object files for input instead of the source code, like so:

```
gcc -c -o gcc-func1.o gcc-func1.c
gcc -c -o gcc-func2.o gcc-func2.c
gcc -o gcc-func gcc-func1.o gcc-func2.o
```

Like any standard compiler, GCC supports multiple warning levels. You set the level with the `-W` command-line switch. It is generally considered good practice to enable all warnings by using the `-Wall` switch. In addition to warning levels, the GCC also has several levels of optimization. By default, GCC disables optimization for debugging purposes (`-0`); for release versions of your programs, you will probably want to enable full optimization with the `-03` switch. A word of warning, however: Full optimization may introduce stability problems to your program, so people generally use the `-02` switch instead.

If you're developing for multiple platforms, you may want to make use of the `-D` switch to define symbols such as architecture. Chapter 1 contained a simple example of the use of the `-D` switch to enable or disable debugging commands (such as cheats) at compile time. You are not limited to specifying a single symbol on the command line. In fact, you can specify as many symbols as you like. The following example demonstrates this:

```
/* gcc-define.c - GCC command line symbols */

#ifdef LINUX
#  ifdef I386
char *platform = "Linux x86\n";
#  else ifdef SPARC
char *platform = "Linux SPARC\n";
#  endif
#else
char *platform = "Unknown\n";
#endif

main() {
    printf(platform);
    return 0;
}
```

There are three possible options when compiling this program. The first is to add the `-DLINUX -DI386` switches to the command line, to add the `-DLINUX -DSPARC` switches, or to add nothing. By now, you should be able to figure out how to compile this program.

One last set of command-line switches you'll need to know about are the ones for including libraries and setting include/library paths. When you need to link another library to your program, you specify `-l<name>` on the command line; for example, `-lX11`.

NOTE

GCC automatically adds `lib` to the start of the library name, so you need to specify only the name.

If the library you want to use is not on the library search path, use the -L<*path*> switch, or set the LIBRARY_DIR environment variable to point to the directory in which the library is located. You use a similar method for includes, except that you use the -I<*path*> switch or the INCLUDE_DIR environment variable.

DEBUGGING TOOLS

How many times have you compiled a program with no compilation errors, yet found a strange bug that was nearly impossible to trace? Personally, I have lost weeks of coding time tracking down annoying bugs like this, and only found out what was going on by using my trusty debugger.

There are several debuggers available, but my personal favorite is the DDD/GDB combination. DDD is available from **http://www.gnu.org/software/ddd/**, and GDB can be downloaded from **http://www.gnu.org/software/gdb/gdb.html**. One of the main reasons I use these two debuggers is that DDD can render runtime variables into easy-to-read graphs that allow at-a-glance checking of your variables.

DDD: HTTP://WWW.GNU.ORG/SOFTWARE/DDD/
GDB: HTTP://WWW.GNU.ORG/SOFTWARE/GDB/GDB.HTML

To demonstrate the power of DDD and how to use it, let's create a short test program. The following example should display a simple table of names, except that there is a small and stupid bug that causes unexpected results.

```c
/* chapter2-1.c - A bad program */
main() {
    int I = 0, row = 1;
    /* A simple table of name */
    char *string[] = {
        "Title", "First name", "Last name",
        "Mr", "Mark", "Collins",
        "Mr", "Ernest", "Pazera",
        "Miss", "Hellen", "Russell",
        "Miss", "Joan", "O'Arc",
        0, 0, 0};

            /* Display table headings */
            while (i < 3) {
                    printf("%s\t", string[i++]);
        }

            printf("\n");
```

```
                    /* Display table data */
                    while (string[(row * 3) + i] != 0) {
                                printf("%s\t", string[i + (row * 3)]);
                                i++;
                    if (i == 3) {              /* At end of row */
                        printf("\n");
                        row++;
                        i = 0;
                }

        }


                    return 1;

}
```

When you compile and run this program, you'd expect it to display a small table of names. However, good ol' Murphy has struck again, and there is something very wrong with this simple program. Time to fire up the debugger.

Before we load DDD, we must compile the program with debugging symbols. This can be done quite easily by adding the -g option to the gcc command line, as shown here:

```
gcc -g -o chapter2-1 chapter2-1.c
```

After the program has finished compiling, load DDD and open the new executable file we just created. The main window should look something like the one shown in Figure 2.1.

Now that we can see our misbehaving program in DDD, we need to find out where the fault is. Let's try to narrow down the potential areas where the problem could occur. The program displays the table headers okay, but everything after that is just plain screwed up. If we set a breakpoint on line 20, we can interrupt the program when things start to go wrong. There are two ways of doing this. The first one is to type chapter2-1.c:22 in the textbox just above the code window, the other is to select line 22 (printf("\n");) in the code display.

Next, we also want to know what the values of our two variables (i and row) are. We can see this by right-clicking the variable names and selecting Display <variable> from the context menu. If we then click the Run button in the floating toolbox, the program will execute up to line 20. After all these manipulations, the DDD window should look like the one in Figure 2.2.

The floating toolbox contains several buttons that will be useful in our debugging efforts. The buttons we will use here are Next and Step. The differences between the two buttons are subtle, but important. When you click Step, the program runs to the next line of the program; if you click Next, the program continues to the next instruction. If you want to debug a bit of Assembler, for example, you will probably use the Next button most.

Figure 2.1

The main window of the DDD debugger.

Figure 2.2

A program running.

Keeping an eye on the values of i and row, click the Step button until the program reaches the second loop. So far, nothing has gone wrong, and everything is going as it should. Continue stepping until you get to line 29, the if statement. Now look at the value of i. What you should see is shown in Figure 2.3.

Figure 2.3

Finding the bug.

The if statement checks to see whether i is equal to 3, but the value of i is 4 when it hits line 29. How is this happening? Well, the problem is caused by using the same variable for the counter in both loops, without resetting it in-between. To fix the program, we simply add the following line before the second loop, and everything works fine:

```
i = 0;
```

If you look at the floating DDD toolbox again, you will notice that, in addition to Step and Next buttons,

> **NOTE**
> The sample program we just reviewed is a bad program, and the techniques used in it should never be used in a real-world application. Another way to prevent bugs like this one is to use one variable per loop.

there are StepI and NextI buttons. These buttons allow you to follow the program execution through the functions. This capability is very useful when tracing your program through a third-party library because it allows you to see exactly where an error occurs and then examine the possible factors.

DEVELOPMENT ENVIRONMENTS

There are several development environments under Linux, although the most popular ones are KDevelop (**http://www.kdevelop.org**) and CodeWarrior (a commercial product available from Metrowerks). I'll focus on the OpenSource environment, KDevelop, here because it is freely available to anyone who wants to use it.

KDEVELOP: HTTP://WWW.KDEVELOP.ORG

The KDevelop interface is very similar to the Microsoft Developer Studio used in Visual C++. In addition to the use of project wizards, KDevelop handles the generation of configure scripts (which in turn generate makefiles). Using KDevelop is as easy as eating pie, as I'll demonstrate now. Let's start by creating a new project. Load KDevelop and choose Project, New from the menu bar. This action displays the New Project dialog box as shown in Figure 2.4.

Figure 2.4

The KDevelop New Project dialog box.

From the list of possible projects, select Terminal - C. This option creates a simple console application. Other possible application types available from the dialog box are KDE/GNOME/Qt applications and custom projects (which allow you to import source code written by yourself or other people from other applications into a KDevelop project).

After you have selected the project type you want to make, click the Next button. KDevelop then prompts you to set the project options, such as name and location. The next screen prompts you to choose any versioning systems you want to use (such as CVS). Version management tools are very useful for larger projects that have more than one developer working on them, but for now, we can leave this option set to the default of NONE. The next two screens allow you to define the comments at the top of your source files. By default, it assumes that your project is going to be released under the GNU Public License (GPL), but you may change this if you want.

The final screen allows you to create your project based on the options you have chosen. When you click the Create button, the process window updates to tell you what part of the project it is building. When it is done, click Close and take a peek at the file located on the C/C++ Files tab (the tabs are along the top of the window). As you can see, the project wizard has created a simple Hello World application for us. The toolbar contains a button that looks like a swimming pool with a couple of arrows above it. This is the Build button. Click it to compile and link the program. The message window at the bottom of the screen keeps you updated on what is happening. If there are no errors (there shouldn't be), the message window displays *** `success` *** when it has finished building the project. When the project is successfully built, click the button that looks like a gear to run the program.

Voilá! You have just successfully created your first KDevelop application. Feels good, doesn't it? Play around with the environment for a bit and read the documentation (located on the DOC tab on the right of the screen).

LIBRARIES

In addition to the various development tools I have already described in this chapter, you will also need some libraries to help you write the next *Quake*. These libraries help save you time by giving you access to functions that people have written before which you may require in your application. There are literally hundreds of libraries out there, but I will focus on the more commonly used ones here.

SIMPLE DIRECTMEDIA LAYER

SDL (Simple DirectMedia Layer) is probably the most used gaming API under Linux (see Figure 2.5). It is used in several commercial games by Loki, such as *Civilization II: Call To Power*, as well as hundreds of OpenSource games.

Figure 2.5

Civilization II: Call To Power.

You can download the SDL from **http://www.libsdl.org**. Features in the SDL include video, sound, threads, and event management, as well as CD-Audio. These features are accessible through a DirectX-like API, making it a very simple library to use if you are an experienced Windows programmer. KDevelop documentation for the SDL can also be found at **http://www.libsdl.org**, which will prove invaluable if you choose to develop your games under it.

SDL LIBRARY: HTTP://WWW.LIBSDL.ORG

OpenGL

OpenGL is the most used 3D graphics API on any platform, originally created by SGI. Because it is available for the Windows, Linux, and MacOS platforms, using OpenGL in your games will make porting them to another platform a walk in the park.

An OpenGL implementation for Linux, called MesaGL, can be downloaded from **http://mesa3d.sourceforge.net**. MesaGL supports a growing number of 3D accelerators as well as software rendering (for those of us without high-end video cards). The list of supported hardware is constantly growing, and with hardware developers such as nVidia now taking an interest in Linux, more stable drivers are also coming on the market.

MesaGL: HTTP://MESA3D.SOURCEFORGE.NET

LibX11

If you are not averse to a bit of masochism now and then, you might want to try to program your games using the libX11 library. If you want to skip the wrapper functionality that higher-level APIs provide, the libX11 library makes you handle every aspect of the code yourself, from displaying the window to writing event managers.

However, the library does allow you to do some things that other APIs don't, such as changing the screen resolution (you now can change color depth with XFree86 4, which also incorporates GLX). Also, if you plan on working with OpenGL, using libX11 may be a more suitable choice than any of the other libraries because OpenGL requires you to provide some details about the window that other APIs don't supply.

Other Libraries

There are more libraries out there, such as Crystal Space and ClanLib, as well as the traditional game library SVGAlib. Although these aren't used as much as the SDL, OpenGL, and libX11 libraries just described, some OpenSource developers will try to convince you to use them. Some of these libraries act as wrappers to lower-level libraries, while others interface with the hardware directly.

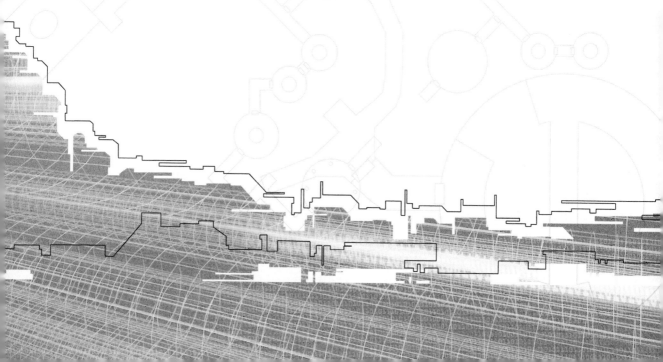

CHAPTER 3

THE STRUCTURE
OF A GAME

N ow that you know *what* you need to create a game, you need to know *how* to make a game. In other words, you can have all the monkey wrenches in the world, but that still doesn't mean you're a mechanic. This chapter starts your training as a game programmer by outlining the basic structure of a typical game.

THE PARTS OF A GAME

Every game has several parts, the most important of which is the game loop. After you have initialized all the required hardware and loaded any data you need, the game enters a loop during which the actual play occurs. But before it gets to the loop, the game must do several other things to make it playable.

The first thing a game must do is start. This sounds pretty obvious, but I've seen people try to write the main loop before anything else and then wonder why the game won't work. When I say "start," I mean that the game must open any windows you need, activate sound drivers, and load any graphics required for the basic operation of the game.

After the initialization process is completed, most games usually enter a "message loop" in which a check is performed to see whether anything must be done regarding user input and then process that input. The message loop works by first checking to see whether any events are waiting and processing them. If there are no messages waiting, an idle function is called which processes any information that isn't dependent on user input, such as setting up the enemy AI or updating the screen.

The final part of the game is where you close everything down. Although some people believe that this step isn't necessary, not doing it results in wasted memory and hardware being locked up, which in turn prevents other applications from using these system resources.

A GAME FRAMEWORK

When it comes to programming, one of the most useful things you can have is a simple framework on which you can build more complex projects. Included in this framework is a makefile that you can use regardless of which editor you are using to code the program, be it KDevelop or vi.

Here is the first file in our little framework; it handles the startup and shutdown of the program, and also handles events.

```c
/* main.c - Game startup */

#include <stdio.h>
#include "game.h"

char *title_string = "Game framework version 1.0";

char IsMessage(void) {
    char message_waiting = 0;
    /* Code to check for messages goes here */

    if (message_waiting) {
        return 1;
    } else {
        return 0;
    }
}

void *GetMessage(void) {
    void *message;
        /* Code to retrieve message from queue goes here */

    return message;
}

void ProcessMessage(void *message) {
    /* Process the message here */
}

int main(int argc, char **argv) {
    void *message;

    /* Display game title message */
    fprintf(stderr, title_string);

    /* Startup code goes here */

    /* Enter main game loop */
    while (1) {
        /* Check the message queue */
        if (IsMessage()) {
```

```
                    /* There is a message, so process it */
                    message = GetMessage();
                    ProcessMessage(message);
            } else {
                    /* No message, so perform standard stuff */
                    gameloop();
            }
    }

    /* Shutdown code goes here */

    return 1;
}
```

Note the use of the void * type for the messages. The void * type allows the code to work with any message API transparently. Instead of passing structures, you pass pointers to the structures so that you can implement different libraries at the same time without having to rewrite large chunks of code.

The next file in the framework is the game loop itself. This function handles stuff that doesn't require input from the user, such as running an intro sequence or displaying a funky menu animation.

This has two states, INIT and SHUTDOWN, that can be used for processing data while doing other tasks, such as updating a progress bar on the screen when loading a number of files.

```
/* game.c - Main game loop */

#include <stdio.h>
#include "game.h"

char game_state = INIT;

void gameloop(void) {
    switch(game_state) {
    case INIT:
        /* Game initialization code goes here */
        break;
    case INTRO:
        /* Game intro sequence code goes here */
        break;
    case MENU:
        /* Game menu goes here */
        break;
```

```c
        case GAME:
            /* Main game code goes here */
            break;
        case SHUTDOWN:
            /* Game shutdown code goes here */
            break;
        default:
            fprintf(stderr, "Bad game state");
            break;
    }
}
```

In addition to the game.c file, we need a game.h file, which contains function definitions as well as several symbols used in the various files.

```c
/* game.h - Game loop definitions and prototypes */
#ifndef __GAME_H__
#define __GAME_H__

void gameloop(void);

#define INIT            0
#define INTRO           1
#define MENU            2
#define GAME            3
#define SHUTDOWN        4
#endif
```

Finally, our game framework needs a makefile. This file is generated automatically if you are using KDevelop; if you prefer to code using a text editor instead of a full IDE, you'll have to hand-code the makefile as shown here.

```makefile
# Makefile for game framework
CFLAGS=-Wall
CC=gcc

LIBS=

C_FILES=game.c main.c
OBJ_FILES=game.o main.o
OUT_FILE=framework
```

```
all: framework

framework: $(OBJ_FILES)
                $(CC) $(CFLAGS) -o $(OUT_FILE) $(OBJ_FILES)

main.o: main.c
                $(CC) $(CFLAGS) -c -o $@ $^

game.o: game.c
                $(CC) $(CFLAGS) -c -o $@ $^
```

Now, to compile the framework, either type make at the console or click the Build icon in KDevelop.

If you run the program we've set up in this framework, not much will happen because this is only a simple framework. But we will add further functionality in the next chapter.

NOTE

If you are using KDevelop, compare the makefile just shown to the one that KDevelop generates for you. You will notice a lot of extra features in the KDevelop makefile, such as install sections used for automated installs of the program.

CHAPTER 4

2D Graphics Under Linux

N ow that we have the tools we need and a framework for the game, we can actually start making a game. The most important aspect of a game is probably the ability to interact with the user. This requires some form of output. I'll start with the most useful of all outputs, the screen.

THE SDL API

Every saga has a beginning, and here is ours. Before we dive into the vast realms of 3D graphics, you'll need an understanding of how simple 2D graphics work.

SDL (Simple DirectMedia Layer) is a powerful cross-platform multimedia API used in several commercial games released for Linux (such as *Civilization II: Call To Power*). It offers a DirectX-like API, which allows an experienced Windows coder to learn it quite quickly.

STARTING UP SDL

Before we can draw anything to the screen, we need to initialize SDL. You can do this with the command SDL_Init(). The function prototype is shown here:

```
extern DECLSPEC int SDL_Init(Uint32 flags);
```

SDL_Init() takes one argument that specifies what parts of SDL you want to use in your program. There are several possible flags, shown in Table 4.1. For now, we are interested only in video, so the SDL_INIT_VIDEO flag is all we need to use at this point.

In the event of an error, SDL_Init() returns NULL; otherwise, it returns 1. In the event of an error, you can use the SDL_GetError() function to retrieve an error message to pass back to the user.

> **NOTE**
> The SDL_Init() values can be combined by using the bitwise OR operator.

Assuming that the call to SDL_Init() was successful, we can now call atexit() to make sure that everything SDL instantiates is cleaned up when the program exits by calling the SQL_Quit() function, whose prototype is shown here:

```
extern DECLSPEC void SDL_Quit(void);
```

The atexit() function should be called whenever the program exits, and for whatever reason the program exits. Using atexit() is the best way to guarantee that SQL_Quit() is called.

Now that we know which functions we need to call, let's add them to our game framework. Where the source code has a comment saying "Startup code goes here" in main.c, add the following code:

Table 4.1 SDL_Init() Parameters

Name	Value	Description
SDL_INIT_TIMER	0x00000001	Activates the timer subsystem
SDL_INIT_AUDIO	0x00000010	Activates the audio subsystem
SDL_INIT_VIDEO	0x00000020	Activates the video subsystem
SDL_INIT_CDROM	0x00000100	Enables support for CD audio
SDL_INIT_JOYSTICK	0x00000200	Activates joystick support
SDL_INIT_NOPARACHUTE	0x00100000	Does not catch fatal errors
SDL_INIT_EVENTTHREAD	0x01000000	Activates event and thread support
SDL_INIT_EVERYTHING	0x0000FFFF	Activates everything

```
/* Initialize SDL */
if (!SDL_Init(SDL_VIDEO | SDL_AUDIO)) {
    fprintf(stderr, "SDL error: %s\n", SDL_GetError());
    return 0;
}
atexit(SDL_Quit);
```

Before the program will compile, we must tell the compiler to link in the SDL libraries and to include the header files. Add the following line to the start of game.h to tell it to include the function prototypes for SDL:

```
#include <SDL.h>
```

The next step is to modify the makefile (or the project settings in KDevelop) so that the compiler knows where the include files are located. Because the location of these files can vary, you may want to familiarize yourself with a useful tool called sdl-config, which helps set up these parameters. On the C_FLAGS line in the makefile, add the following code:

NOTE

In the C_FLAGS line just shown, those characters are backticks, not apostrophes. The character is located on the key to the left of the 1 on the keyboard.

```
C_FLAGS=-Wall `sdl-config --libs --cflags`
```

If you are using KDevelop, you must add the command `sdl-config --cflags` to the compiler options (these options can be accessed by pressing F7) and add `sdl-config --libs` to the linker options.

CREATING A WINDOW

Now that we have initialized SDL, we can create a window. This process is nowhere near as complicated or longwinded as it is under Win32—or libX11 for that matter. A single function call handles the creation of the window; that function is SDL_SetVideoMode(), whose prototype is shown here:

```
extern DECLSPEC SDL_Surface *SDL_SetVideoMode (int width, int height, int bpp,
Uint32 flags);
```

The width, height, and bpp arguments set the width, height, and color depth of the window. The fourth argument sets any special flags for the window, such as double buffering. There are more flags for this argument than there are fish in the sea (at least I've been told there are many fish in the sea, but I can't seem to find them). Table 4.2 lists the options for the flags argument.

NOTE

In addition to working with the SDL_SetVideoMode() function, these flags also work with the SDL_CreateRGBSurface() function, which I'll cover later in the chapter.

Table 4.2 Surface Flags

Name	Value	Description
SDL_SWSURFACE	0x00000000	Surface is in system memory
SDL_HWSURFACE	0x00000001	Surface is in video memory
SDL_ASYNCBLIT	0x00000004	Use asynchronous blits if possible
SDL_ANYFORMAT	0x10000000	Allow any color depth/pixel format
SDL_HWPALETTE	0x20000000	Surface has exclusive palette
SDL_DOUBLEBUF	0x40000000	Set up double-buffered video mode
SDL_FULLSCREEN	0x80000000	Surface is a full-screen display
SDL_OPENGL	0x00000002	Create an OpenGL rendering context
SDL_RESIZEABLE	0x00000010	The surface may be resized

For most applications, we'll only need to use the SDL_HWSURFACE and SDL_DOUBLEBUF flags, although the SDL_HWPALETTE flag may be required if you are working with a color depth of 8 bits, which requires a palette.

If the call to SDL_SetVideoMode() is successful, it returns a pointer to a surface; otherwise, it returns NULL. The surface contains important information about what we have to do to draw things to the screen, including details about the pixel format.

After you have created the window, you can set a caption for the window using the SDL_WM_SetCaption() function call. SDL_WM_SetCaption() takes two arguments: the caption and a pointer to an icon. The caption is a simple character string, while the icon is a pointer to a surface (as explained in the next section, "Creating a Surface").

Add the following code to main.c after the SDL initialization code and compile the program.

```
screen = SDL_SetVideoMode(
    320, 200,            /* width and height of window */
    8,                   /* 8 bit color depth (256 colors) */
    SDL_HWSURFACE | SDL_DOUBLEBUF     /* video flags */
);

if (screen == NULL) {
    fprintf(stderr, "Video error: %s\n", SDL_GetError());
    exit(1);
}

SDL_WM_SetCaption(title_string, NULL);
```

When you run the program, a window should appear with the dimensions specified by SDL_SetVideoMode().

CREATING A SURFACE

Now that we have our window, let's draw something to it. There are two ways to do this. The first is to draw directly to the video, which can be slightly faster; the second is to draw the entire scene to an off-screen surface and then copy, or "flip," the surfaces to the window, which will eliminate any flicker. The second option is known as *double buffering*.

To create a new surface, we use the SDL_CreateRGBSurface() and SDL_CreateRGBSurfaceFrom() functions. The prototypes for these two functions follow, as does the prototype for SDL_FreeSurface(), which must be called when the surface is no longer needed.

```
extern DECLSPEC SDL_Surface *SDL_CreateRGBSurface  (Uint32 flags, int width, int
height, int depth, Uint32 Rmask, Uint32 Gmask, Uint32 Bmask, Uint32 Amask);

extern DECLSPEC SDL_Surface *SDL_CreateRGBSurfaceFrom(void *pixels, int width,
int height, int depth, int pitch,  Uint32 Rmask, Uint32 Gmask, Uint32 Bmask,
Uint32 Amask);

extern DECLSPEC void SDL_FreeSurface(SDL_Surface *surface);
```

Let's first look at SDL_CreateRGBSurface(). The flags parameter takes the same values used by the SDL_SetVideoMode() function (refer back to Table 4.2). The options you'll use most often for the flags parameter are SDL_SWSURFACE, SDL_HWSURFACE, and SDL_ASYNCBIT. The width, height, and depth values are also the same as their SDL_SetVideoMode() counterparts. The next four values are slightly more complicated. If you are creating an 8-bit surface, you don't need to bother with them. However, if you want to use a higher color depth, you must set them up correctly. Fortunately, the values are specified in the structure returned from SDL_SetVideoMode().

Every surface has a pixel format description of type SDL_PixelFormat, which is kept in the SDL_Surface-> format. The definition for SDL_PixelFormat is shown here:

```
typedef struct SDL_PixelFormat {
    SDL_Palette *palette;
    Uint8  BitsPerPixel;
    Uint8  BytesPerPixel;
    Uint8  Rloss;
    Uint8  Gloss;
    Uint8  Bloss;
    Uint8  Aloss;
    Uint8  Rshift;
    Uint8  Gshift;
    Uint8  Bshift;
    Uint8  Ashift;
    Uint32 Rmask;
    Uint32 Gmask;
    Uint32 Bmask;
    Uint32 Amask;

    /* RGB color key information */
    Uint32 colorkey;
    /* Alpha value information (per-surface alpha) */
    Uint8  alpha;
} SDL_PixelFormat;
```

As you can see, this structure contains the Rmask, Gmask, Bmask, and Amask values (Red, Green, Blue, and Alpha masks) that are required by SDL_CreateRGBSurface().

The SDL_CreateRGBSurfaceFrom() function is almost identical to the SDL_CreateRGBSurface() function except that it allows you to specify several extra parameters to give the surface an image. The pixels argument points to the raw image data (uncompressed), and the pitch argument is the number of bytes between pixels (1 for 8-bit color, 2 for 16-bit color, and so on).

The final function we'll look at in this section is the SDL_FreeSurface() function. You must call this function when your program is finished with the surface to release any memory that may have been allocated for it, or when you no longer need to surface. If you do not call this function, your program may develop memory leaks that can result in a loss of performance and stability.

DRAWING A BITMAP IMAGE

As soon as we have created a surface, we can load and render a bitmap image onto it. Before we look at drawing the bitmap, however, let's look at the different ways you can load the image. The simplest way is to use the SDL_LoadBMP() function, which takes one argument: a pointer to a character array containing the location of the bitmap. On success, it returns a pointer to a surface; on failure, it returns NULL. Of course, if you want to load an image in a format other than Windows bitmap (BMP), you'll have to write the parser yourself. The Web site **www.wotsit.org** has a comprehensive list of graphics file formats. At the end of this chapter is a section on loading a PCX file, which can be used here as well.

LIST OF GRAPHICS FILE FORMATS: WWW.WOTSIT.ORG

After you have loaded the bitmap, you must draw it to the screen. To do this, you use the SDL_BlitSurface() function, shown here:

```
extern int SDL BlitSurface(SDL_Surface *src, SDL_Rect *srcrect,
SDL_Surface *dst, SDL_Rect *dstrect);
```

The src and dst arguments are pointers to surfaces. Generally, dst is the pointer to your screen surface and src is the pointer to the bitmap/image you want to display. However, you can use SDL_BlitSurface() to build an image before you actually display it on the screen. For example, if you want to generate a string from a bitmapped font, you could use a temporary surface as the destination.

The other two arguments, srcrect and dstrect, point to structures of type SDL_Rect that contain information about what parts of the surfaces to draw. If srcrect is NULL, the entire surface is drawn. The dstrect argument contains the area to draw the bitmap on the destination surface.

The SDL_Rect structure has the following format:

```
typedef struct {
    Sint16 x, y;              // x and y coordinates of the rectangle
    Uint16 w, h;              // width and height of the rectangle (in pixels)
} SDL_Rect;
```

The SDL_Rect structure is almost identical to the RECT structure in Win32. Although the structures have different names, the concepts behind the use of the structures are exactly the same.

After you have drawn the BMP image to the screen, you may have to "flip" the surfaces if you have enabled double buffering. You flip the surfaces by using the SDL_Flip() function call. This takes one parameter: the surface you want to flip.

DRAWING DIRECTLY TO THE SCREEN

This is where things get interesting. Drawing to the screen can be stupidly easy or stupidly complicated, depending on what color depth you have set up. If you are working in 8-bit mode, it's quite simple to draw to the screen. If you're working in 16-bit or 32-bit color, it's slightly more difficult to draw directly to the screen. The *really* fun part comes when you are working in a 24-bit color depth.

PIXEL FORMATS

Different color depths use different pixel formats. The simplest color depth is 8-bit color, which uses a single byte of memory to specify the color of each pixel in the image. The value of the byte points to a color index. The exact color you get on the screen depends on your *palette*, which is discussed later in this chapter.

The next color depth, 16-bit color, is much more complicated. The red and blue components each use five bits, while the green component uses six bits. Take, for example, the binary block of memory 1111100000011111. The first five bits signify the red component of the pixel; the next six bits specify the green component of the pixel; the last five bits specify the blue component. The color specified by this particular value would produce magenta on the screen (full red, full blue, and no green).

The function SDL_MapRGB() calculates exactly what format the pixel has to be. The function takes four parameters: the surface, and the red, green, and blue components of the pixel. You can use this function if you are not 100% sure of the pixel format of the surface you are using or if you are using an 8-bit display with a color palette. The function prototype is shown here:

```
extern Uint32 SDL_MapRGB(SDL_PixelFormat *fmt, Uint8 r, Uint8 g, Uint8 b);
```

The next highest color depth supported by SDL is 24-bit color. This color depth is slightly more complicated to use than 16-bit color. You cannot use the SDL_MapRGB() function to calculate the exact value for the pixel, so you must do it yourself. You must place each color component in the right place for the pixel to appear correctly.

Because the bit masks for each surface may be slightly different, you must figure out how to display something before you go into your code to display it. If you look at the structure definition for SDL_PixelFormat, you'll notice several masks and shifts that tell you how to set up your memory.

A very simple function for plotting a pixel in 24-bit mode follows.

```
void Plot24(SDL_Surface *surface, int x, int y,  Uint32 pixel) {
    Uint8 *bits;
    Uint8 r, g, b;

    // Prepare the components
    r = (pixel>>screen->format->Rshift) & 0xFF;
    g = (pixel>>screen->format->Gshift) & 0xFF;
    b = (pixel>>screen->format->Bshift) & 0xFF;

    // Lock the surface and work out where to plot the pixels
    SDL_Lock(surface);
    bits = ((Uint8 *)surface->pixels)+y * surface->pitch + x * surface->format-
>BytesPerPixel;

    // Plot the pixels
    *((bits) + screen->format->Rshift/8) = r;
    *((bits) + screen->format->Gshift/8) = g;
    *((bits) + screen->format->Bshift/8) = b;

    // Unlock the surface
    SDL_Unlock(surface);
}
```

Although SDL_MapRGB() does not work with 24-bit color, 32-bit color depths support the use of SDL_MapRGB(), so this is a very simple color depth to use. The 32-bit color depth has an extra byte of memory per pixel for alpha. This is useful if you want to have a transparent surface.

If you are using alpha, the SDL_MapRGB() function won't cut it. You will need to calculate the pixel yourself, using a method very similar to that for calculating the pixels for 24-bit colors. The Plot32() function shown here demonstrates how to calculate the pixel.

```
void Plot32(SDL_Surface *surface, int x, int y, Uint32 pixel) {
    Uint8 *bits;
    Uint8 r, g, b, a;
```

```
// Prepare the components
r = (pixel>>screen->format->Rshift) & 0xFFr;
g = (pixel>>screen->format->Gshift) & 0xFF;
b = (pixel>>screen->format->Bshift) & 0xFF;
a = (pixel>>screen->format->Ashift) & 0xFF;

// Lock the surface and work out where to plot the pixels
SDL_Lock(surface);
bits = ((Uint8 *)surface->pixels)+y * surface->pitch + x *
    surface->format->BytesPerPixel;

// Plot the pixels
*((bits) + screen->format->Rshift/8) = r;
*((bits) + screen->format->Gshift/8) = g;
*((bits) + screen->format->Bshift/8) = b;
*((bits) + screen->format->Ashift/8) = a;

// Unlock the surface
SDL_Unlock(surface);
}
```

PLOTTING PIXELS

After you have worked out the format for your pixel, you can plot it to the screen. Before you do this, however, you'll have to lock the surface to prevent other parts of the program from accessing it. This is an issue only if your program is multithreaded, but SDL requires you to lock the surface whether or not your program uses threads.

SDL_Lock() takes only one parameter: the address of the surface to lock. On success, it returns 0; otherwise, you should use SDL_GetError() to see what went wrong.

When you have locked your surface, you must then calculate the address to draw to. This isn't necessarily the easiest of things to do if your math isn't up to scratch. The SDL_Surface structure has a member called pixels that contains the actual image of the surface.

To work out the exact location of the pixels you want to plot, you need to know how many bytes of memory are between each horizontal line. You can calculate this value by using the color depth and the pitch member of the surface definition. The exact formula for working out the location of the pixel follows (it may be worth making a little macro for this):

```
offset = Y * pitch + X * bitdepth
```

Here is the same formula in a more useful form:

```
address = ((Uint8 *)surface->pixels) + Y * surface->pitch + X
    * surface->format->BytesPerPixel;
```

When you have calculated the address of the pixel you want to plot, you can then set its value in memory to the color you desire with the following command.

```
(*address) = color;
```

After you have plotted the pixel, you must unlock the surface with SDL_Unlock(). As does SDL_Lock(), SDL_Unlock() takes a single parameter: the address of the (locked) surface to unlock. If you are plotting more than one pixel, you may want to wait until you have finished drawing your scene before you unlock the surface.

Using Palettes

If you are unfortunate enough to be working in 8-bit color, you might need to create a color palette for your game. Luckily, this is a simple task. The 8-bit video modes support up to 256 colors.

The function SDL_SetColors() is used to set the color palette. It takes several parameters: a surface, a pointer to the color palette, the starting color index, and the number of colors. Here is the prototype for the function:

```
extern int SDL_SetColors(SDL_Surface *surface, SDL_Color *colors,
int firstcolor, int ncolors);
```

The colors argument simply points to an array of type SDL_Color that contains the palette information. SDL_Color has four members: r, g, b (red, green, and blue, respectively), and unused. The unused member is reserved for future expansion, so we'll ignore that.

The recommended way of using SDL_Color is to allocate (sizeof(SDL_Color) * ncolors) bytes of memory for the array. After you have allocated enough memory, you set the values for the palette. Each component can have a value up to 255 (0xFF). The following sample code demonstrates how to allocate a grayscale palette.

```
SDL_Color   *colors;
SDL_Surface *screen;
int i;

// Allocate the memory
colors = (SDL_Color*)malloc(screen->format->palette->ncolors *
    sizeof(SDL_Color));
```

```
// Set up the palette
for (i = 0; i < screen->format->palette->ncolors; i++) {    colors[I]->.r = i;
colors[I]->g = i;
 colors[I]->b = i;
 }

// Set the palette
SDL_SetColors(screen, colors, 0, screen->format->palette->ncolors);
```

If you look at the preceding example, you will notice the use of screen->format->palette. This is a pointer to the current palette for the surface (in this case, the screen). Every surface has such a palette, and these palettes prove useful for several things. The most useful is to find out how many colors are available for a surface; the second is to get the current palette.

SDL_Palette (which the SDL_Surface->format->palette pointer refers to) contains two members. The first is the number of entries in the palette, the second is a pointer to an array of type SDL_Color. The SDL_Color array contains the specifics of the current palette.

CLEANING UP

When it comes time to quit your program, you must make sure that every single byte of memory allocated is freed. This can be a pain if you are taking over someone else's project (I'm sure you'd never introduce a memory leak into your own code). Fortunately, SDL handles all the cleanup for us.

Earlier in this chapter, I mentioned the SDL_Quit() function and noted that you should always call it when your program exits. This function cleans up any memory allocated by SDL when the program exits. It is also called on the event of a signal (such as a segmentation fault or a user interrupt).

However, it is good practice to free any memory you've allocated yourself, instead of leaving the cleanup process to the API. There are several functions for this, such as free() (for memory you've allocated yourself) and SDL_FreeSurface() (for surfaces).

THE XLIB API

If you want to do raw X programming, you need to see a psychiatrist or you want to write a simple X application that doesn't require all of the functionality and overhead of a larger API such as SDL. If you're going to program in X, you'll want to understand the basics of X graphics (a full discussion of X graphics is way out of the scope of this book). The next few sections cover the basics of coding for X.

I covered SDL before I covered Xlib because Xlib is more complicated than SDL. In my opinion, you can use SDL to do just about everything you could ever want to do in X—except for a few things such as changing the resolution.

CREATING A WINDOW

The first thing you must do when opening a window under X is to tell it where the screen is. The X Windowing System uses a client/server architecture, and one machine (the client) sends the window to a different machine (the server). Although there are several ways of telling the client where the server is, the most foolproof way is to use the DISPLAY environment variable.

The DISPLAY variable takes the form <address>:<desktop>, where <address> is the name or IP address of the X server, and <desktop> is the server to use. (Note that a single machine can run X multiple times.)

The function XOpenDisplay() makes the connection to the X server. It takes one argument: a string using the display format described above, or NULL to use the default. It returns a pointer to the display (of type Display) on success, or NULL on error.

When you have a pointer to your display, you need a screen. You can find your screen using the DefaultScreenOfDisplay() function. This function takes one parameter: the pointer to the display we found using the XOpenDisplay() function. DefaultScreenOfDisplay() returns a pointer of type Screen on success, or NULL on error. You also must find the screen you will be using with the DefaultScreen() function. DefaultScreen() is almost identical to DefaultScreenOfDisplay() except that it returns an integer.

Now that we have a display, a screen, and a screen (Xlib coding is quite pointless at times), we can actually create the window. You create the window using the XCreateSimpleWindow() function. (Although you can use XCreateWindow(), doing so is infinitely more complicated.) The prototype for XCreateSimpleWindow() is shown here:

```
Window XCreateSimpleWindow(Display *display, Window *parent, int x, int y,
unsigned int width, unsigned int height, unsigned int border_width,,
unsigned long border, unsigned long background);
```

The first argument, display, is the pointer to the display we got using the XOpenDisplay() function. The next argument, parent, is a pointer to the window that is opening the new one. If this is the first window the program is opening, you must use the RootWindowOfScreen() function. This function takes one argument: the pointer to the screen we got using DefaultScreenOfDisplay().

The next four arguments are the location and size of the window. The border_width argument specifies the width of the window border in pixels. The next argument, border, is the color of the border. The last parameter, background, is simply the background color of the window.

The next step is to clear the window using the XClearWindow() function. This function takes two arguments: the display and the window to clear (in that order). Finally, you must raise the window using the XMapRaised() function, which uses the same two arguments as XClearWindow().

The following sample code demonstrates how to open a window in X:

```c
// Xsample1.c
#include <X11/Xlib.h>

int main() {
    Display *display;
    Window window;
    Screen *screen;
    int myscreen;
    char *display_str = (char *)getenv("DISPLAY");

    // Open the display using the environment variable
    display = XOpenDisplay(display_str);
    screen = DefaultScreenOfDisplay(display);
    myscreen = DefaultScreen(display);

    // Open the window
    window = XCreateSimpleWindow(
        display, RootWindowOfScreen(screen),
        0, 0,
        320, 200,
        1, BlackPixel(display, DefaultScreen(display)),    // Black border
        WhitePixel(display, DefaultScreen(display)));      // White background

    XClearWindow(display, window);
    XMapRaised(display,window);

    // do something

    // Cleanup
    XCloseDisplay(display);
    return 1;
}
```

> **NOTE**
>
> The getenv() function in this example returns NULL in the event that the environment variable is not found. The XOpenDisplay() function uses the default display (usually 0:0, meaning the first X server of the local machine).

To compile this program, use the following command line:

```
gcc -lX11 -L/usr/X11R6/lib -I/usr/X11R6/include -o Xsample1 Xsample1.c
```

Drawing to the Screen

The Xlib routines for drawing graphics are relatively (!) straightforward. Depending on what you want to do, you have a range of functions from which to choose. I'll start with the simpler ones, such as drawing text to the screen.

Plotting a Pixel

The easiest thing to do when doing any graphics is usually plotting a pixel. This rule also applies to programming in X, but because it is X, plotting a pixel still isn't the easiest thing in the world to do. Before you can draw anything, you must initialize several items, including "drawables" and graphics contexts.

I'll start by describing the Graphics Contexts (GCs for short). These are like the surface definitions used in SDL and are even more similar to Device Contexts used in Windows programming. The function to create a GC is XCreateGC(); its prototype is shown here:

```
extern GC XCreateGC(Display *display, Drawable d,
unsigned long valuemask, XGCValues* gcv);
```

As is true for most Xlib functions, XCreateGC() needs to know about the machine running the X server. This information is passed using the display argument. The next argument, the drawable, is the "surface" you want to draw on (in this example, it's the window, but it could be a pixmap or any other drawable object). The next parameter is a mask of which values are used in the description; the description itself is the final argument.

The available masks for XCreateGC() as well as the XGCValue member they refer to are shown in Table 4.3.

The only mask value we need to plot a pixel is GCForeground; the other masks are covered later in this chapter. To set a color, use the [Color]Pixel() functions, such as BlackPixel() or WhitePixel(), as demonstrated in the Xsample1.c code, earlier in this chapter.

After you have set up your GC descriptor, call XCreateGC() to create a new Graphics Context. Now you can draw pixels to the screen (or use any other graphics operation that requires a GC). You can use the function XDrawPoint() to plot single pixels. XDrawPoint() takes five parameters: a display, a drawable, a GC, and the window coordinates, as shown in the following function prototype:

```
extern int XDrawPoint(Display* display, Drawable d, GC gc,  int x, int y, );
```

Now it's time to put the theory into practice. Take the sample program Xsample1.c and add the following lines just before we initialize X to enable us to draw something on the screen:

```
GC gc;
XGCValues gcv;
int x, y;
```

Table 4.3 Graphics Context Value Masks

Mask Name	XGCValue Member	Description
GCFunction	function	Logical operation
GCPlaneMask	plane_mask	Plane mask
GCForeground	foreground	Foreground color
GCBackground	background	Background color
GCLinewidth	line_width	Width of line
GCLineStyle	line_style	Style of line (LineSolid, LineOnOffDash, LineDoubleDash)
GCCapSize	cap_size	End style (CapNotLast, CapButt, CapRound, CapProjecting)
GCJoinStyle	join_style	JoinMiter, JoinBevel, or JoinRound
GCFillStyle	fill_style	FillSolid, FillTiled, FillStippled, or FillOpaqueStippled
GCFillRule	fill_rule	EvenOddRule, WindingRule
GCTile	tile	A pixmap for tiled fills
GCStipple	stipple	1bpppixmap for stippled fills
GCTileStipXOrigin	ts_x_origin	Offset for tile stipple operations
GCTileStipYOrigin	ts_y_origin	Offset for tile stipple operations
GCFont	font	Default font for text operations
GCSubwindowMode	subwindow_mode	ClipByChildren or IncludeInferiors
GCGraphicsExposures	graphics_exposures	Boolean, should exposures be generated
GCClipXOrigin	clip_x_origin	Offset for clipping region
GCClipYOrigin	clip_y_origin	Offset for clipping region
GCClipMask	clip_mask	Bitmap clipping (pixmap)
GCDashOffset	dash_offset	Patterned/dashed line information
GCDashList	dashes	Data for dash list

In addition, where the original file has the comment saying "do something", insert the following code:

```
 // Describe the context we want
gcv.foreground = BlackPixel(display, myscreen);

// Create the context
gc = XCreateGC(display, window,
    GCForeground,
    &gcv);

while (1) {
        x = rand() % 320;
        y = rand() % 200;

        // Draw the pixel
        XDrawPoint(display, window, gc, x, y);
}

// Free memory
XFreeGC(display, gc);
```

The above code simply fills the screen using random black pixels.

DRAWING IMAGES

Now that we can plot single pixels in X, it's time to do something a little more exciting. Although Xlib isn't really suited for programming ultra-high-performance games on its own, simple sprite-based games work quite well in X. Several popular games have been written along these lines, such as *Xbill*.

For simple images, the X Windowing System uses a format called .XPM (X PixMap). The .XPM files are quite simple and resemble standard C header files (they can, in fact, be used as header files). The function XReadBitmapFile() loads an .XPM file and creates a standard pixmap that you can use on your display. The function prototype is as follows:

```
extern int XReadBitmapFile(Display* display, Drawable d,
_Xconst char* filename, unsigned int* width_return,
unsigned int* height_return, Pixmap*  bitmap_return, int* x_hot_return,
int* y_hot_return);
```

The first two arguments are the display and the object you plan to draw the image on. The next argument is the path and filename of the pixmap you want to draw. The other arguments are pointers to where information about the image is going to be stored.

After you have loaded the pixmap, you can draw it using the XCopyPlane() function, whose prototype is shown here:

```
extern int XCopyPlane(Display* display, Drawable src, Drawable dest, GC gc,
int src_x, int src_y, unsigned int width, unsigned int height,  int dest_x,
int dest_y, int depth);
```

Using XCopyPlane() is pretty straightforward. As with other X functions, you must pass the pointer to the display. You also must specify two drawable objects (the source and the destination). The next parameter is a standard GC, which you can create by calling XCreateGC(display, window, 0, NIL). The next four arguments describe the dimensions of the source image, and are followed by the destination coordinates. The final argument is the color depth of the source image.

The following sample code demonstrates the use of XCopyPlane(). Add the following code to the definitions section at the beginning of the original Xsample1.c sample, shown earlier in this chapter.

```
    Pixmap pic;
    GC gc;
    XGCValues gcv;
    int x, y;
    int width, height, hotx, hoty;
    int err;
char *FILE = "/usr/share/pixmap/clock.xpm";
```

Now, in the original Xsample1.c code, replace the "do something" comments with this last bit of code. Compile the file as you have done before and run it.

```
    // Prepare the context
    gcv.foreground = BlackPixel(display, myscreen);
    gcv.graphics_exposures = 0;

    gc = XCreateGC(display, window, GCForeground, &gcv);

    // Load the bitmap
    if ((err = XReadBitmapFile(display, window,
        FILE,
        &width, &height, &pic,
        &hotx, &hoty))) {
        XCloseDisplay(display);
        fprintf(stderr, "Can't load image: %d", err);
    }
```

```
while (1) {
        x = rand() % 320;
        y = rand() % 200;

        XCopyPlane(
            display, pic,          // Source image
            window, gc,            // Destination details
            0, 0,                  // Source origin
            width, height,         // Dimension of image
            x, y, 1);              // Destination coordinates
}
// Free the memory
XFreeGC(display, gc);
XFreePixmap(display, pixmap);
```

DOUBLE BUFFERING

Drawing directly to the window has several drawbacks, including having to redraw the screen manually when it needs to be done and putting up with flickering sprites. A common tactic in avoiding screen flicker is to use double buffering. This process involves drawing everything to an off-screen object and then copying that object to the window when everything is drawn.

Copying objects in X is stupidly simple. First you create an exact copy of the window using XCreatePixmap(), and then you copy the newly created image to the window whenever you need to. To achieve the second part of this process, use XCopyArea(). The function prototypes for these functions are shown here:

```
extern Pixmap XCreatePixmap(Display* display, Drawable d, unsigned int width,
unsigned int height, unsigned int depth);
extern int XCopyArea(Display* display, Drawable src, Drawable dest, GC gc,
int src_x, int src_y, unsigned int width, unsigned int height,  int dest_x,
int dest_y);
```

XCopyArea() is almost identical in functionality to XCopyPlane() (described in the preceding section), except that it has no depth argument. Because you do not specify the color depth of the area, you must be sure that both drawable objects have the same color depth, or a BadMatch error will occur and your program will terminate.

XCreatePixmap() is a relatively simple function to use. The following example demonstrates its use for creating an off-screen window.

```
// Create the double buffer
Pixmap dbl_buf = XCreatePixmap(display, window,
window_width, window_height,          // Dimensions of window
DefaultDepth(display, myscreen));     // Color depth
```

After you have created the double buffer, you use that object as the drawable surface instead of the window. When it comes time to display what you have drawn, you copy the buffer to the window. The code for doing this is presented here.

```
GC gc = XCreateGC(display, window, 0, NIL);
XCopyArea(display, dbl_buf, window, gc, 0, 0,
    window_width, window_height, 0, 0);
```

INSTALLING COLOR MAPS

If you are working in an 8-bit color depth, you might want to set up your own color map. You need a color map only if you are using 8-bit color because any other color depth uses RGB indexing. To detect the color depth being used, you can use the DisplayDepth() function, which takes the display and the screen number (myscreen in the samples) as arguments.

If the color depth being used is 8-bit color, you may have to install a color map. You can create your own color map using XCreateColormap(). An example of this function is shown here:

```
Colormap c_map = XCreateColormap(display, window,
DefaultVisual(display, myscreen), AllocNone);
```

After you have created your color map, you need to assign the colors. The first step is to create a color definition of type XColor. This data type is similar to the SDL_Color data type discussed earlier; it contains members that describe each component of the color (red, green, and blue), as well as a member called pixel that is the color index.

When you have defined the color, you call XAllocColor() to include it in your color map. The first argument for this function is the now more-than-familiar display pointer. The next argument is the ID of the color map you created using XCreateColormap(). The final argument is a pointer to the color definition.

```
extern Status XAllocColor(Display* display, Colormap colormap,
XColor* screen_in_out);
```

Now that you have created a color map (in theory), you need to install it with the function XSetWindowColormap(). This function takes three arguments, the first being the usual display pointer. The second argument is the ID of the window in which you want to install the color map, and the final parameter is the ID of the color map itself.

The following sample code demonstrates the installation of a color map:

```
// Create the color map
Colormap c_map = XCreateColormap(display, window,
    DefaultVisual(display, myscreen),
    AllocNone);

// Install an entry
XColor red;
red.pixel = 1;
red.red = 0xFF;
red.green = 0;
red.blue = 0;
XAllocColor(display, c_map, &red);

// Set the color map
XsetWindowColormap(display, window, c_map);
```

Now that we have our brand-spanking-new color map installed, we might as well use it. To use the color map, call the XSetForeground(), which specifies the color of pixels, and XSetBackground() functions. Each of these functions takes three parameters: a pointer to the display, the GC to change, and the color index.

Cleaning Up

When it comes time to exit your superb new X Windows game, you'll have to clean up a few things. Every object you create must be destroyed using the Xlib API. You should destroy any windows you created with XFreeWindow(), destroy any GCs with XFreeGC(), and so on. If there isn't a specific function for the object you created, you can destroy it using the general-purpose XFree() function.

When you have freed the memory used by the various objects in your program, you must then close the connection to the server. To do this, use the XCloseDisplay() function, which takes the more-than-familiar display pointer as its single argument.

The SVGAlib API

A long time ago, SVGAlib was just about the only way to write fast-paced games under Linux. Since its reign of suid-terror, other APIs have been introduced, such as SDL. These newer APIs make X a viable platform for games, but some users

CAUTION

SVGAlib programs must be run as root, or suid to root, because they require direct access to the hardware. This can mean people may be able to exploit bugs in your software to compromise system security.

choose not to run X. Some of those users still like to play games, but their systems may not be capable of running X Windows.

SWITCHING TO A GRAPHICS MODE

The first thing any SVGAlib program should do is set an appropriate graphics mode. The first step down this path is to initialize the SVGAlib by calling `vga_init()`, defined in the header file `vga.h`. This function starts up the SVGAlib subsystem and then surrenders root privileges.

If the function call is successful, `vga_init()` returns 0. Assuming that `vga_init()` was called with no problems, you can then switch to a graphics mode. Personally, I like to check whether a mode is available before I try to switch to it by calling `vga_hasmode()`. This function takes a single parameter: the symbol for the video mode you want to take. Table 4.4 shows the different video modes available. If the mode is available, a non-zero value is returned; otherwise, the function returns 0.

As soon as you know that your chosen video mode is available, you can call `vga_setmode()` to change resolutions. The `vga_setmode()` function takes one parameter: the resolution (specified in Table 4.4). On success, it returns 0; on failure, it returns -1.

Table 4.4 VGA Modes

Name	Resolution
TEXT	Standard text mode (original console mode)
G320x200x16	320x200 16-color
G640x200x16	640x200 16-color
G640x350x16	640x350 16-color
G640x480x16	640x480 16-color
G320x200x256	320x200 256-color
G320x240x256	320x240 256-color (mode X)
G320x400x256	320x400 256-color (mode X)
G320x480x256	320x480 256-color
G640x480x2	640x480 monochrome

When your program quits, it is a good idea to call vga_setmode(TEXT) in case vga_init() wasn't able to assign its own console device for output and is using one of the standard console devices.

Drawing to the Screen

After you have set up your video mode, you will probably want to draw something on it. And I don't blame you. Fortunately, drawing directly to the screen using SVGAlib is as easy as pie (even with the recommended double buffering).

There are two ways to draw directly to the screen with SVGAlib, and they both equate to the same thing. The first is to call vga_getgraphmem() to find the start location of the video memory, and the second is to use the graph_mem pointer, which already points to the start of the video memory.

Drawing pixels to memory is very similar to direct access under SDL, except that we can ignore the pitch variable. The simple macro shown here demonstrates how to draw a pixel to memory:

```
#define PLOT(x, y, c)        *(graph_mem + (y * WIDTH + x)) = c
```

The following sample code demonstrates how to change the resolution and draw a pretty pattern to the screen:

```c
// VGAsample1.c
#include <vga.h>

#define WIDTH      320
#define PLOT(x,y,c)      *(graph_mem + (y * WIDTH + x)) = c

main() {
    // Initialize SVGAlib
    if (vga_init()) {
        puts("vga_init() error");
        return 1;
    }

    // Check if mode is available
    if (!vga_hasmode(G320x200x256)) {
        puts("Mode not available");
        return 1;
    }

    // Change the mode
    if (vga_setmode(G320x200x256) == -1) {
        puts("Can't change mode.");
        return 1;
    }
```

```
    // Draw some pattern
    for (x = 0; x < 320; x++)
        for (y = 0; y < 200; y++)
            PLOT(x,y,x ^ y);

    return 0;
}
```

To compile this sample program, use the following command:

```
gcc -lvga -o VGAsample1 VGAsample1.c
```

When the program has compiled, either run `"chown root VGAsample1"` followed by `"chmod 4755 VGAsample1"` while logged in as root, which enables any user to run the program by setting the suid bit of the application, or run the program from a root shell.

DISPLAYING IMAGES

SVGAlib doesn't have built-in support for image files, so you'll need to implement your own little function library to load and display images. In these examples, I'll demonstrate how to load (and display) a PCX file, but if you want to use another image file format, you can easily modify the functions to load a different file format.

UNDERSTANDING THE PCX FORMAT

PCX files use a simple compression method known as RLE (Run-Length Encoding). This system represents long runs of pixels of the same color in 3-byte blocks (instead of however many bytes it would take to normally represent that string of individual pixels). This makes the PCX format suitable for images with large blocks of the same color (such as logos and simple sprites) but unsuitable for complex images such as photos.

As with most graphics formats (apart from raw data), PCX files start off with a simple header. This header can be represented using a simple structure that contains the different header fields, as shown here:

```
typedef struct PCXHeader{
    char    manufacturer;        // Always 10 (ZSoft .pcx)
    char    version;             // Version number
    char    encoding;            // Encoding method (1=RLE)
    char    bitsperpixel;        // Number of bits per pixel
    short   xmin;                // X Origin of image
    short   ymin;                // Y origin of image
    short   xmax;                // Width of image
```

```
short    ymax;                       // Height of image
short    hdpi;                       // Horizontal resolution
short    vdpi;                       // Vertical resolution
char     colormap[48];               // Palette information
char     reserved1;                  // Reserved
char     nplanes;                    // Number of planes
short    bytesperline;               // Number of bytes in a line
short    paletteinfo;                // Palette interpretation info
short    hscreensize;                // Horizontal screen size (v 4+)
short    vscreensize;                // Vertical screen size (v4+)
char     filler[54];                 // Unused data
};
```

After the header, the actual image data is stored. The dimensions of the image when it is decompressed are equal to (xmax – xmin + 1) and (ymax – ymin + 1). The total amount of storage is the area of the image (xsize * ysize) multiplied by the number of bytes per pixel (1 for 256 color images).

Decoding the data is quite simple. Each byte of the image data represents a pixel. If the top two bits of the pixel are 1 (that is, the value of the byte is greater than or equal to 192), then it is an encoded pixel. The remaining six bits of the pixel indicate the length of the run, and the following byte is the value of the pixel. The following sample code demonstrates how to decode the pixel.

```
int i = 0;
int tot_bytes = ((xmax - xmin + 1) * (ymax - ymin + 1)), curr_byte  = 0;

while (curr_byte < tot_bytes) {
    ch = (*image_data + i);
    if (ch & 0xC0) {                      // Encoded bit
        num_bytes = ch - 192;            // Length of run
        i++;
        ch = *(image_data + i);          // Color of pixel
        for (n = 0; n < num_bytes; n++) {
            curr_byte++;
            *(image + curr_byte) = ch;
        }
    } else {                              // Standard pixel
        curr_byte++;
        *(image + curr_byte) = ch;
    }
    I++;
}
```

After you have successfully decoded the data, you nearly have a complete image. However, 739 bytes before the end of the file is where the palette data may begin. If the first byte of the supposed palette data is 12, then the remaining data is the information for the image palette. Each entry for the palette is 3 bytes, one byte for each component (red, green, and blue, in that order).

The complete code for loading the image is as follows:

```
// Palette information
typedef struct {
    char r, g, b;
} RGBval;

// PCX image
typedef struct {
    PCXHeader       header;         // header information
    char            *image;         // Decompresses image
    RGBval          palette[256];   // Palette data
} PCXImage;

PCXImage pcx_load(char *filename) {
    FILE *fp;
    PCXHeader head;
    PCXImage image;
    int xsize;
    int ysize;
    int I, curr_byte, num_bytes;

    // Open the file
    if (!fp = fopen(filename, "r")) {
        fprintf(stderr, "pcx_load(): Error opening file for reading");
        return NULL;
    }

    fread(image.header, sizeof(image.header), 1, fp);

    if (image.header.manufacturer != 10) {
        fprintf(stderr, "pcx_load(): Invalid file format");
        return NULL;
    }
```

```
    // Work out image size
    xsize = (image.header.xmax - image.header.xmin + 1);
    ysize = (image.header.ymax - image.header.ymin + 1);


    // Allocate enough memory for the image
    image.image = (char *)malloc(xsize * ysize);

    while (curr_byte < (xsize * ysize) {
        ch = fgetc(fp);
        if (ch & 0xC0) {                // Encoded data
            num_bytes = ch - 192;
            ch = fgetc(fp);
            for (i = 0; i < num_bytes; i++) {
                *(image.image + curr_byte) = ch;
                curr_byte++;
            }
        } else {                        // Unencoded data
            *(image.image + curr_byte) = ch;
            curr_byte++;
        }
    }


    // Read the palette
    fseek(fp, SEEK_END, 769);

    if (fgetc(fp) == 12) fread(image.palette, sizeof(image.palette), 1, fp);

    fclose(fp);

    return image;
}
```

DISPLAYING THE IMAGE

Now that you have loaded the image into memory, it's time to draw it. There are two ways to do this. The first is to copy each pixel to the screen, one at a time. Although this approach is slower than the alternative, it does allow you to use a transparent color in the image. The second way to draw the image is to copy each row of the image to the screen. This approach is faster than the first, but requires a bit more work. I'll demonstrate both methods here.

The pcx_show_trans() function shown here takes an argument that represents the transparent color. Each time the function goes to draw a pixel, it checks to see whether the current pixel is transparent. If the pixel is transparent, the function ignores it.

```
void pcx_show_trans(PCXImage image, int dx, int dy, char key) {
    int x, y;
    int xsize = ((image.header.xmax - image.header.xmin + 1);
    int ysize = ((image.header.ymax - image.header.ymin + 1);

    for (x = 0; x < xsize; x++) {
        for (y = 0; y < ysize; y++) {
            pixel = *(image.image + (y * ysize + x);
            if (pixel != key) {
                *(graph_mem + ((y + dy) * WIDTH + (x + dx))) = pixel;
            }
        }
    }
}
```

The second approach to drawing the image uses memcpy() to copy each scanline to the screen. This method is slightly faster than pcx_show_trans(), hence the name pcx_show_fast(). This function copies each line of the image to the appropriate place on the screen.

```
void pcx_show_fast(PCXImage image, int dx, int dy) {
    int x, y;
    int xsize = ((image.header.xmax - image.header.xmin + 1);
    int ysize = ((image.header.ymax - image.header.ymin + 1);

    for (y = 0; y < ysize; y++) {
        memcpy((graph_mem + ((y + dy) *  WIDTH + x)), (image + (y * xsize)),
xsize);
    }
}
```

USING COLOR PALETTES

Some of you may have read the section explaining the PCX image format and wondered how the hell you can set up a color palette for your images. Good question. And a very simple question at that. The function vga_setpalette() handles palette creation for us. The function prototype for vga_setpalette() is shown here:

```
void vga_setpalette(int index, int r, int g, int b);
```

As you can see, this function takes four arguments: a color index and the three values for that color. The following sample code demonstrates how to use the information obtained by loading the PCX file to change the color palette.

```
void pcx_set_palette(PCXImage pcx) {
    int n;

    for (n = 0; n < 256; n++) {
        vga_setpalette(n,
          pcx.palette[n].r,          // Red
          pcx.palette[n].g,          // Green
          pcx.palette[n].b);         // Blue
    }
}
```

Isn't it easy when you know how?   :-)

CLEANING UP

When it comes time to exit your console game, you'll have to do some cleaning up. Freeing any memory you have allocated in the program (such as the PCXImage.image data) is essential because you may get some very large memory leaks if you use large images.

You should also make sure that you return to the default console resolution to allow the user to return to whatever he was doing (and log out of root before some script-kiddie comes along and finds a nice root shell).

A MINI-PROJECT

To help you learn the things discussed in this chapter, I'm going to give you some homework. To test your newly acquired knowledge of Linux graphics, see whether you can build a simple wrapper library for all the principles mentioned in this chapter (setting up the display, drawing pixels and images, managing palettes, and cleaning up the code).

When you have completed the library, incorporate it into the game framework we created in Chapter 3.

CHAPTER 5

INPUT WITH SDL

A game is all about control. Whether you are racing around the track at Daytona or piloting your damaged fighter in the most important battle in the galaxy's history, you are in control. As a game designer and programmer, it is your job to make your game's control system as simple and as intuitive as possible. But the player should never remember how good your control system was; it should be so intuitive that the player will forget it's even there. Of course, this isn't always possible: The best control system for a submarine simulator would require an entire bridge crew, a periscope hanging from your roof, and a red lightbulb (for effect). We are restricted to a small set of general-purpose input devices: keyboards, mice, and joysticks. Successfully forging these simple devices into the controls of starships, the hands of warriors, and even the minds of gods is what turns a game into an experience.

UNDERSTANDING INPUT DEVICES

If you have browsed through a computer games magazine or strolled through your local computer store, you may have noticed the vast array of game controllers available. You have your bread and butter: the keyboard and mouse. You also have your age-old classic, the joystick, in many different shapes and sizes: analog, digital, gamepads, flight controllers, arcade-style, and whatever else. There are even some more specialized devices, the steering wheels, the light-guns, and even (my personal favorite) the mind-control devices (what ever did happen to those?). Luckily for us, the designers and manufacturers of these devices realize that they are going to be used and bought only if they are supported by the games people want to play, and the best way to make sure that this happens is to use a standard interface, like that of a keyboard, mouse, or joystick. So that's what they do: They make a steering wheel that usually just plugs into a joystick port and acts like a joystick, and they make a light gun that acts just like a mouse. This is great! We don't have to worry about anything but three simple, established, and well-supported devices.

KEYBOARD

For the uninitiated, a *keyboard* is an array of largely alphanumeric switches. It has been the standard input device for computers for many years. Keyboards usually consist of just over one hundred keys which are divided into three logical sets: alphanumeric keys, function keys, and modifier keys. The alphanumeric keys consist of letters, digits, and punctuation characters. The function keys are made up of general-purpose keys, often named F1 through F12, and several special-purpose keys such as Esc, Home, and End. Finally, the modifier keys are used to "modify" the meaning of the other two sets of keys (for example, the Shift key capitalizes letters).

A modern keyboard communicates with a computer by sending 8-bit data sequences to a peripheral processor. These data sequences are called *scancodes*, and each key on a keyboard is assigned a scancode based on a certain standard. The modern IBM PC-compatible keyboard is based on the AT scancode set. For example, according to the AT standard, when the A key is pressed, a scancode of value 0x1C is sent to the computer. Also, when a key is released, a break code is sent, which in the case of an AT keyboard is 0xF0; the break code is then followed by the scancode of the key that was pressed. It is up to the Linux keyboard driver—or sometimes the application—to convert these scancodes into useable character data of control codes.

Mouse

The *mouse* was first developed by a team led by Doug Engelbart at the Stanford Research Institute in the late 1960s. The mouse is the most commonly used 2D pointing device for computer software. The basic roller-ball mouse contains a ball that is in contact with a desk surface and two internal rollers at right angles to each other. Sensors (usually photo-diodes) on the rollers detect movement along the two axes; the movement is transmitted to the computer and is usually converted by the mouse driver to the movement of a pointer on the screen. A mouse usually has several buttons used for clicking and selecting items onscreen.

The really wonderful thing about a mouse is that it provides smooth and fluid movement; because it plays such an important role in most modern computer software, it's a device that can quickly gain a natural feel. Over the past few years, mice have become very popular in the First Person Shooter genre, a type of shoot-em-up, where they are used to control the head movements of the player's character.

Joystick

Traditionally, a *joystick* is a vertical stick that pivots around its base and reports the angle to the computer. A joystick may also have buttons positioned on the base or on the stick itself. The traditional joystick has been transformed over the years into the *gamepad*, which is similar to the joystick in function, but the stick is replaced by a four-way pad, similar to the cursor keys on a keyboard. Other controls have also been added to joysticks to complement the basic buttons. *Hats* are four-way mini-joysticks placed at the top of the stick. Hats were originally used in flight simulators to allow the player to easily glance in the four directions. Throttle levers have also been added, originally to enhance flight simulators; the throttle is usually treated as a third or fourth axis. One recent and very rare feature is a trackball mounted on the joystick's base, which provides all the functions a mouse in conjunction with a joystick.

Trackballs are another form of pointing device similar to mice. The device remains stationary while the user moves the pointer by rotating a ball mounted on the top of the device.

The Linux joystick driver sees a joystick as a collection of axes and switches. The stick, throttles, hats, and balls are all mapped to axes—which can make things confusing when you're trying to determine what is what. It is, however, safe to assume that the X axis of the joystick (its left-to-right motion) is mapped to the first axis and the Y axis of the joystick (its up-and-down motion) is mapped to the second axis. An axis has an integer range from –32767 to 32767; –32767 on the X axis is far left and 32767 on the Y axis is far down.

HANDLING METHODS

After you have decided which devices you will be supporting in your game, you must decide how you will actually read from the devices and use the data in your game. Reading from a device is often a complex task, requiring hardware knowledge and precise timing techniques.

Thankfully, APIs such as SDL are designed to do the grunt work for you. SDL gathers input information from the devices it implicitly opens (the mouse and keyboard) and from devices you explicitly tell it to open (joysticks). Internally, SDL keeps track of the state of all opened input devices and provides you with two interfaces through which you can read these states, event queues and polling.

EVENT QUEUES

A *queue* is a common data structure in computer science. It is much like a queue in real life: The person at the head of the queue is the next person to be served, and someone who wants to be served gets in line at the end of the queue. A queue in computer science contains data; data at the head of the queue is processed first. When that data is processed, it is then removed from the queue. Data that needs to be processed is added to the end of the queue and is eventually processed when all the data ahead of it has been processed.

NOTE

A queue is more traditionally known as a FIFO (First In, First Out) array, where the data that goes into the array first is accessed first.

Queues have many applications and can be very useful for handling input. When an input "event" takes place—such as a joystick button being pressed—information about that event is added to the end of a particular queue called the *event queue*. With an API such as SDL, the event queue is internal, and input events are added to the queue as they are detected.

POLLING

When you *poll* a device, you are asking it what its current state is. Note that you are not asking it what has happened since the last time you polled it, you just want to know what is happening right now.

Polling was popular in the earlier days of computers, when reading from a device was not handled by the operating system and required direct access to the hardware. With the advent of modern operating systems such as Linux, polling has become a less common way to receive input data from devices and has been superseded by event queues.

Using the SDL Event Queue

The SDL event queue is one of SDL's most powerful features. It does much more than simply relaying keyboard, mouse, and joystick events; it also relays important window manager events and can be used as a simple messaging system.

The SDL_Event Union

The SDL_Event union is the key to all event handling in SDL. It can contain the information of any event SDL supports. The SDL event queue is composed entirely of SDL_Event unions; when an event occurs, an SDL_Event union is filled with the required data and placed on the end of the event queue. The functions used to read events from the head of the event queue use SDL_Event unions to return their data.

> A *union* in C/C++ is like a C structure (struct) in that it can contain members of different types and sizes. Unlike structures, however, all the members of a union are overlaid in the same storage space, and the compiler allocates enough space for only the largest member.

In SDL, each event type has a structure associated with it: A mouse button event has an SDL_MouseButtonEvent structure, and a mouse motion event has an SDL_MouseMotionEvent structure. The event structures all have two things in common: Their first member is a Uint8 called type, and they are all contained within the SDL_Event union.

Layout

Following is the prototype for the SDL_Event union. This is returned by the event functions, and it should contain the various details about the event that has occurred. The details of the events are explained later in this section.

```
typedef union{
    Uint8 type;
    SDL_ActiveEvent active;
    SDL_KeyboardEvent key;
```

```
      SDL_MouseMotionEvent motion;
      SDL_MouseButtonEvent button;
      SDL_JoyAxisEvent jaxis;
      SDL_JoyBallEvent jball;
      SDL_JoyHatEvent jhat;
      SDL_JoyButtonEvent jbutton;
      SDL_ResizeEvent resize;
      SDL_QuitEvent quit;
      SDL_UserEvent user;
      SDL_SysWMEvent syswm;
} SDL_Event;
```

This definition should clarify things a bit. The SDL_Event union can store all the information you'll need for any possible SDL event.

INTERPRETING EVENT TYPES

All SDL event types are enumerated and given a symbolic name; this value is stored in the type member of the SDL_Event union. The value in the type member allows you to determine the event type and hence from which member of the SDL_Event union you are to read the event information. Table 5.1 lists the possible event types.

READING FROM THE EVENT QUEUE

SDL provides two simple functions for reading from the event queue: SDL_PollEvent() and SDL_WaitEvent(). Following are the function prototypes:

```
    int SDL_PollEvent(SDL_Event *event);

    int SDL_WaitEvent(SDL_Event *event);
```

These functions are quite similar; they both examine the event queue and place the event at the head of the queue into the structure pointed to by the event parameter. The event is then removed from the queue, and the function returns a value of 1. The two functions differ in how they behave if there is no event to be removed from the queue. SDL_PollEvent() simply returns a value of 0; however, SDL_WaitEvent() waits until there is an event on the queue and then removes it and copies it into the event structure as usual. The only time SDL_WaitEvent() returns 0 is when an internal error has occurred, which is rare.

Table 5.1 SDL Event Types

Event Type	Event Structure	SDL_Event Member
SDL_ACTIVEEVENT	SDL_ActiveEvent	active
SDL_KEYDOWN/UP	SDL_KeyboardEvent	key
SDL_MOUSEMOTION	SDL_MouseMotionEvent	motion
SDL_MOUSEBUTTONDOWN/UP	SDL_MouseButtonEvent	button
SDL_JOYAXISMOTION	SDL_JoyAxisEvent	jaxis
SDL_JOYBALLMOTION	SDL_JoyBallEvent	jball
SDL_JOYHATMOTION	SDL_JoyHatEvent	jhat
SDL_JOYBUTTONDOWN/UP	SDL_JoyButtonEvent	jbutton
SDL_QUIT	SDL_QuitEvent	quit
SDL_SYSWMEVENT	SDL_SysWMEvent	syswm
SDL_VIDEORESIZE	SDL_ResizeEvent	resize
SDL_USEREVENT	SDL_UserEvent	user

The following listing is a simple example of the use of SDL_WaitEvent(). The program simply waits for a user to press a key and then exits. Although this program is basic, it does demonstrate how to pull events from the event queue and how to act on the event type.

```
/* Include required SDL header files */
#include "SDL.h"

/* Wait for a keypress then exit */
int main(){
    /* SDL_Event union to store events taken from */
    /* the event queue */
    SDL_Event event;
```

```
    /* Quit flag */
    int quit=0;

    /* Initialize SDL */
    SDL_Init(SDL_INIT_VIDEO);

    /* An application must have a window or a video */
    /* instance before it can be used for event handling */
    SDL_SetVideoMode(320, 200, 0, 0);

    /* Loop until the quit flag is set */
    while(!quit){
        /* Wait for an event */
        if(SDL_WaitEvent(&event)){
            /* When an event is received, check if it's a */
            /* SDL_KEYDOWN event, if so then set the quit flag */
            if(event.type==SDL_KEYDOWN) quit=1;
        }
    }

    /* Exit cleanly */
    SDL_Quit();
}
```

The SDL_WaitEvent() function is suitable for basic tasks like the one in the preceding listing. However, when you are handling input in a game, you can't wait around for events to arrive; you must actively go looking for those events. So you must use SDL_PollEvent(). The most efficient and versatile way to use SDL_PollEvent() is in conjunction with a while loop and a switch statement. This approach allows you to handle all events from a central location and to handle all events based on their type. The following listing is a skeleton for this type of system.

```
/* Function to gather and handle events */
void HandleEvents(){
    SDL_Event event;

    /* Loop until all events have been removed from the queue */
    while(SDL_PollEvent(&event)){
```

```c
        /* Jump to an appropriate handler */
        /* depending on the event type    */
        switch(event.type){

            /* Keyboard Events */
            case SDL_KEYDOWN:
            case SDL_KEYUP:
                HandleKeyboardEvent(&event);
                break;

            /* Mouse Events */
            case SDL_MOUSEMOTION:
            case SDL_MOUSEBUTTONDOWN:
            case SDL_MOUSEBUTTONUP:
                HandleMouseEvent(&event);
                break;

            /* Joystick Events */
            case SDL_JOYAXISMOTION:
            case SDL_JOYHATMOTION:
            case SDL_JOYBALLMOTION:
            case SDL_JOYBUTTONDOWN:
            case SDL_JOYBUTTONUP:
                HandleJoystickEvent(&event);
                break;

            /* Miscellaneous Events */
            default:
                HandleMiscEvent(&event);
                break;
        }
    }
}
```

The HandleEvents() function forms the basis for all your input handling when you use an event queue. This function simply and efficiently dispatches events to the required handler for each event type. I will expand on this idea further when I explain in detail how to integrate input handling into your game design, but first you need to understand how to interpret the different event types.

KEYBOARD EVENTS

A keyboard is a relatively simple device. It is, after all, just a lot of switches that are either on (pressed) or off (released). On one hand, handling keyboard input with SDL is also simple. There are two keyboard event types, SDL_KEYUP and SDL_KEYDOWN, that refer to a key press and a key release. Looking at the list of event types in Table 5.1, we can determine that information for an SDL_KEYUP or SDL_KEYDOWN event is stored in an SDL_KeyboardEvent structure. Here is the prototype for that structure:

```
typedef struct{
    Uint8 type;
    Uint8 state;
    SDL_keysym keysym;
} SDL_KeyboardEvent;
```

As you can see, the SDL_KeyboardEvent structure contains an SDL_keysym structure—and here, I fear, is where matters become complicated.

```
typedef struct{
    Uint8 scancode;
    SDLKey sym;
    SDLMod mod;
    Uint16 unicode;
} SDL_keysym;
```

If you didn't read the explanation of keyboards at the beginning of the chapter, shame on you! Go back and read it. As was explained, when a key is pressed or released, the device generates a scancode. On its own, a scancode is not very useful; it is just a number representing a key on the keyboard and is often associated with the position of the key and not the key's alphanumeric or symbolic value. The SDL_keysym structure, however, contains everything we need to know about a key press or a key release. The scancode field contains our beloved keyboard scancode, with which we are now comfortable and familiar. The sym and mod fields are what we are really interested in, however. The sym field contains one of the key symbol values listed in Table 5.2. For example, if the left cursor key is pressed, the sym field contains the value SDLK_LEFT. The mod field contains information about any modifier keys (such as Ctrl, Alt, Shift, and so on) that were active when this key was pressed or released. The mod field is an ORed combination of the modifier symbols in Table 5.3. For example, if both the Shift and Ctrl keys were pressed, the mod field would be equal to KMOD_CTRL|KMOD_SHIFT.

Table 5.2 SDL Key Symbols

SDL Key Symbol	ASCII Value	Common Name
SDLK_BACKSPACE	'\b'	backspace
SDLK_TAB	'\t'	tab
SDLK_CLEAR		clear
SDLK_RETURN	'\r'	return
SDLK_PAUSE		pause
SDLK_ESCAPE	'^['	escape
SDLK_SPACE	' '	space
SDLK_EXCLAIM	'!'	exclaim
SDLK_QUOTEDBL	'"'	quotedbl
SDLK_HASH	'#'	hash
SDLK_DOLLAR	'$'	dollar
SDLK_AMPERSAND	'&'	ampersand
SDLK_QUOTE	'''	quote
SDLK_LEFTPAREN	'('	left parenthesis
SDLK_RIGHTPAREN	')'	right parenthesis
SDLK_ASTERISK	'*'	asterisk
SDLK_PLUS	'+'	plus sign
SDLK_COMMA	','	comma
SDLK_MINUS	'_'	minus sign
SDLK_PERIOD	'.'	period
SDLK_SLASH	'/'	forward slash
SDLK_0	'0'	0
SDLK_1	'1'	1
SDLK_2	'2'	2

(continues)

Table 5.2 SDL Key Symbols (continued)

SDL Key Symbol	ASCII Value	Common Name
SDLK_3	'3'	3
SDLK_4	'4'	4
SDLK_5	'5'	5
SDLK_6	'6'	6
SDLK_7	'7'	7
SDLK_8	'8'	8
SDLK_9	'9'	9
SDLK_COLON	':'	colon
SDLK_SEMICOLON	';'	semicolon
SDLK_LESS	'<'	less-than sign
SDLK_EQUALS	'='	equals sign
SDLK_GREATER	'>'	greater-than sign
SDLK_QUESTION	'?'	question mark
SDLK_AT	'@'	at
SDLK_LEFTBRACKET	'['	left bracket
SDLK_BACKSLASH	'\'	backslash
SDLK_RIGHTBRACKET	']'	right bracket
SDLK_CARET	'^'	caret
SDLK_UNDERSCORE	'_'	underscore
SDLK_BACKQUOTE	'`'	accent grave
SDLK_a	'a'	a
SDLK_b	'b'	b
SDLK_c	'c'	c
SDLK_d	'd'	d
SDLK_e	'e'	e

SDL Key Symbol	ASCII Value	Common Name
SDLK_f	'f'	f
SDLK_g	'g'	g
SDLK_h	'h'	h
SDLK_i	'i'	i
SDLK_j	'j'	j
SDLK_k	'k'	k
SDLK_l	'l'	l
SDLK_m	'm'	m
SDLK_n	'n'	n
SDLK_o	'o'	o
SDLK_p	'p'	p
SDLK_q	'q'	q
SDLK_r	'r'	r
SDLK_s	's'	s
SDLK_t	't'	t
SDLK_u	'u'	u
SDLK_v	'v'	v
SDLK_w	'w'	w
SDLK_x	'x'	x
SDLK_y	'y'	y
SDLK_z	'z'	z
SDLK_DELETE	'^?'	delete
SDLK_KP0		keypad 0
SDLK_KP1		keypad 1
SDLK_KP2		keypad 2
SDLK_KP3		keypad 3

(continues)

Table 5.2 SDL Key Symbols (continued)

SDL Key Symbol	ASCII Value	Common Name
SDLK_KP4		keypad 4
SDLK_KP5		keypad 5
SDLK_KP6		keypad 6
SDLK_KP7		keypad 7
SDLK_KP8		keypad 8
SDLK_KP9		keypad 9
SDLK_KP_PERIOD	'.'	keypad period
SDLK_KP_DIVIDE	'/'	keypad divide
SDLK_KP_MULTIPLY	'*'	keypad multiply
SDLK_KP_MINUS	'-'	keypad minus
SDLK_KP_PLUS	'+'	keypad plus
SDLK_KP_ENTER	'\r'	keypad enter
SDLK_KP_EQUALS	'='	keypad equals
SDLK_UP		up arrow
SDLK_DOWN		down arrow
SDLK_RIGHT		right arrow
SDLK_LEFT		left arrow
SDLK_INSERT		insert
SDLK_HOME		home
SDLK_END		end
SDLK_PAGEUP		page up
SDLK_PAGEDOWN		page down
SDLK_F1		F1
SDLK_F2		F2
SDLK_F3		F3

SDL Key Symbol	ASCII Value	Common Name
SDLK_F4		F4
SDLK_F5		F5
SDLK_F6		F6
SDLK_F7		F7
SDLK_F8		F8
SDLK_F9		F9
SDLK_F10		F10
SDLK_F11		F11
SDLK_F12		F12
SDLK_F13		F13
SDLK_F14		F14
SDLK_F15		F15
SDLK_NUMLOCK		numlock
SDLK_CAPSLOCK		capslock
SDLK_SCROLLLOCK		scroll lock
SDLK_RSHIFT		right shift
SDLK_LSHIFT		left shift
SDLK_RCTRL		right ctrl
SDLK_LCTRL		left ctrl
SDLK_RALT		right alt
SDLK_LALT		left alt
SDLK_RMETA		right meta
SDLK_LMETA		left meta
SDLK_LSUPER		left Windows key
SDLK_RSUPER		right Windows key
SDLK_MODE		mode shift

(continues)

Table 5.2 SDL Key Symbols (continued)

SDL Key Symbol	ASCII Value	Common Name
SDLK_HELP		help
SDLK_PRINT		print-screen
SDLK_SYSREQ		SysRq
SDLK_BREAK		break
SDLK_MENU		menu
SDLK_POWER		power
SDLK_EURO		euro

Table 5.3 SDL Modifier Symbols

Modifier	Meaning
KMOD_NONE	No modifiers applicable
KMOD_NUM	Num Lock is down
KMOD_CAPS	Caps Lock is down
KMOD_LCTRL	Left Control is down
KMOD_RCTRL	Right Control is down
KMOD_RSHIFT	Right Shift is down
KMOD_LSHIFT	Left Shift is down
KMOD_RALT	Right Alt is down
KMOD_LALT	Left Alt is down
KMOD_CTRL	A Control key is down
KMOD_SHIFT	A Shift key is down
KMOD_ALT	An Alt key is down

The unicode field is a special case. It is disabled by default and is only enabled by the following call:

```
SDL_EnableUNICODE(1);
```

The Unicode standard was devised by the Unicode Consortium to replace the ASCII encoding standard. It uses a 16-bit value instead of an 8-bit value to represent a character. (You can read more about the Unicode standard at **http://www.unicode.org**.) Unicode values of less than 128 map directly to the equivalent ASCII characters; all other values are unprintable with a standard ASCII character set. By using the unicode field, we can easily read text input from the keyboard, as shown in the following listing.

THE UNICODE STANDARD: HTTP://WWW.UNICODE.ORG

```c
/* Handle all keyboard events */
void HandleKeyboardEvent(SDL_Event *event){
    /* Get a convenience pointer to the structure we will use */
    SDL_KeyboardEvent *key=event->key;

    /* Switch based on the key symbol */
    switch(key->keysym.sym){
        case SDLK_LEFT:
            printf("Left key ");
            break;
        case SDLK_RIGHT:
            printf("Right key ");
            break;
        case SDLK_UP:
            printf("Up key ");
            break;
        case SDLK_DOWN:
            printf("Down key ");
            break;
        default:
            printf("Other key ");
            break;
    }

    /* Switch based on the type */
    /* Released or Pressed */
    switch(key->type){
        case SDL_KEYUP:
            printf("released.\n");
            break;
```

```
        case SDL_KEYDOWN:
            printf("pressed.\n");
        default:
            break;
    }
}
```

MOUSE EVENTS

While the keyboard has two separate event types associated with it, the mouse has three event types and two different event structures.

Events of type `SDL_MOUSEMOTION` refer to mouse movement; information about that event is stored in an `SDL_MouseMotionEvent` structure. Here is its prototype.

```
typedef struct{
    Uint8 type;
    Uint8 state;
    Uint16 x, y;
    Sint16 xrel, yrel;
} SDL_MouseMotionEvent;
```

The `SDL_MouseMotionEvent` structure contains three separate groups of data. The `state` field contains the current state of the mouse buttons, which are either pressed or released. The data is stored in the bits of the 8-bit byte. The LSB bit refers to button 1 (the left button), the second LSB refers to button 2 (the right button, or sometimes the middle button). The best way to read this data is to use the `SDL_BUTTON(X)` macro provided by SDL, where *X* can be one of the following values: `SDL_BUTTON_LEFT`, `SDL_BUTTON_MIDDLE`, or `SDL_BUTTON_RIGHT`. If `(state & SDL_BUTTON(X))` is `true`, then button *X* is pressed.

The `x` and `y` fields in the `SDL_MouseMotionEvent` structure store the screen coordinates to which the mouse was moved. These values are bound by the width and height of the screen, respectively. Finally, the `xrel` and `yrel` fields store the relative motion of the mouse, that is, the distance the mouse has moved since the previous `SDL_MOUSEMOTION` event.

Although the `SDL_MOUSEMOTION` event provides us with all possible information related to the mouse, it only allows us to act on mouse motion and not on mouse button presses (and releases). Therefore, we also have the `SDL_MOUSEBUTTONUP` and `SDL_MOUSEBUTTONDOWN` events, which are associated with the `SDL_MouseButtonEvent` structure, shown here.

```
typedef struct{
    Uint8 type;
    Uint8 button;
    Uint8 state;
    Uint16 x, y;
} SDL_MouseButtonEvent;
```

At first glance, the SDL_MouseButtonEvent structure seems to convey the same information as the SDL_MouseMotionEvent structure. Every time a mouse button is pressed or released, an event of this type is added to the event queue. The button field tells us which mouse button has been pressed or released; it can contain one of the following values: SDL_BUTTON_LEFT, SDL_BUTTON_MIDDLE, or SDL_BUTTON_RIGHT. The SDL_BUTTON(X) macro is not used with this structure, so don't get confused with that.

The state field is redundant; it simply tells us whether the button has been pressed or released, but we have already determined this from the event type. Ignore the state field because it only adds confusion. Finally, the x and y fields are the same as those in the SDL_MouseMotionEvent structure: they are simply the position of the mouse when the button was pressed or released.

At this stage, you have probably realized that the key to understanding events is understanding all the different structures that make up the SDL_Event union. Don't rush through these explanations; make sure that you understand the purpose of each structure and the information it conveys. When you are confident that you know what's going on, take a look at the HandleMouseEvent() function in the following listing.

```
/* Handle all mouse events */
void HandleMouseEvent(SDL_Event *event){

    /* Useful pointers to the required event structures */
    SDL_MouseMotionEvent *motion=event->motion;
    SDL_MouseButtonEvent *button=event->button;

    /* Switch based on the event type */
    switch(event->type){
        /* handle motion events */
        case SDL_MOUSEMOTIONEVENT:
            /* Print mouse position */
            printf("Mouse moved to: (%d, %d)\n",
                    motion->x, motion->y);
```

```
                    /* Print relative motion */
                    printf("Relative motion: (%d, %d)\n",
                            motion->xrel, motion->yrel);
                    break;

                /* Handle button presses */
                case SDL_MOUSEBUTTONDOWN:
                    printf("Mouse button %d pressed at (%d, %d)\n",
                            button->button, button->x, button->y);
                    break;

                /* Handle button releases */
                case SDL_MOUSEBUTTONUP:
                    printf("Mouse button %d released at (%d, %d)\n",
                            button->button, button->x, button->y);
                    break;

                /* This should never be reached */
                default:
                    break;
            }
    }
```

JOYSTICK EVENTS

If you thought the two keyboard structures and the two mouse structures were hard work, then you'll love working with joystick events. There are a total of four joystick event structures—but don't worry, they are all very similar. When you understand their similarities, understanding their differences is easy. However, before we explore the joystick event structures, we must understand the one thing that makes joysticks different from keyboards and mice. A joystick is not considered to be a compulsory device. The SDL_INIT_JOYSTICK flag must be passed to SDL_Init to instruct SDL to enable its joystick subsystem. SDL assumes that there is only one keyboard and only one mouse connected to the system, but it understands that there may be, and often is, more than one joystick connected to a system. Because of this possibility, you must specify which joysticks are to be used; of course, SDL provides functions to allow you to do this.

```
int SDL_NumJoysticks(void);
```

The SDL_NumJoysticks() function should always be the first step you take when working with joysticks. It simply returns the number of joysticks connected to the system. If it returns 0, there's no point trying to open any joysticks because there are none there.

```
SDL_Joystick *SDL_JoystickOpen(int index);
```

The `SDL_JoystickOpen()` function opens a joystick and returns a pointer to a structure that stores information about the joystick. You should save the returned structure pointer because you'll need it when closing the joystick. The joystick you want to open is specified with the `index` parameter (0 being the first joystick, 1 being the second, and so on). The `index` is a very important value because it is used by the joystick event structures to indicate which joystick generated the event. When you are finished using a joystick, it's good practice to close it by passing the `SDL_Joystick` structure returned by `SDL_JoystickOpen()` into `SDL_JoystickClose()`.

Having an open joystick isn't much good if you don't know anything about it, is it? SDL provides several functions for getting the name of a joystick, as well as getting the number of axes, buttons, hats, and balls available. These functions are the following:

```
const char *SDL_JoystickName(int index)

int SDL_JoystickNumAxes(SDL_Joystick *joystick)

int SDL_JoystickNumButtons(SDL_Joystick *joystick)

int SDL_JoystickNumHats(SDL_Joystick *joystick)

int SDL_JoystickNumBalls(SDL_Joystick *joystick)
```

The function of these five functions is simple and is clearly explained in the SDL documentation. We will use these functions in some later sample listings.

By default, the SDL event queue does not gather events from opened joysticks, so you must explicitly instruct the queue to do so with the call `SDL_JoystickEventState(SDL_ENABLE)`. Without this call, you can only poll the joysticks for input.

The four joystick event structures all have a similar layout, as you can see in these structure prototypes:

```
typedef struct{
    Uint8 type;
    Uint8 which;
    Uint8 axis;
    Sint16 value;
} SDL_JoyAxisEvent;

typedef struct{
    Uint8 type;
    Uint8 which;
    Uint8 button;
    Uint8 state;
} SDL_JoyButtonEvent;
```

```
typedef struct{
    Uint8 type;
    Uint8 which;
    Uint8 hat;
    Uint8 value;
} SDL_JoyHatEvent;

typedef struct{
    Uint8 type;
    Uint8 which;
    Uint8 ball;
    Sint16 xrel, yrel;
} SDL_JoyBallEvent;
```

The first two fields in all four structures have identical meanings. The type field has the same meaning as the type field in all other event structures; the which field indicates which joystick the event refers to. It has the same value as the index parameter passed to SDL_JoystickOpen(). The third field in each event structure indicates which axis, button, hat, or ball the event refers to. For this third field, a value of 0 indicates the first axis, button, hat, or ball; a value of 1 indicates the second; and so on. Note that the field is named differently in each structure: In SDL_JoyAxisEvent, the field is axis; in SDL_JoyBallEvent, the field is ball; and so on.

The type of input data contained in each structure varies. SDL_JoyAxisEvent contains the new axis position in the value field, which is a signed 16-bit integer value as explained at the beginning of this chapter. Because hats only have nine possible positions, the value field of the SDL_JoyHatEvent structure contains one of the following defined values:

- SDL_HAT_CENTERED
- SDL_HAT_UP
- SDL_HAT_RIGHTUP
- SDL_HAT_RIGHT
- SDL_HAT_RIGHTDOWN
- SDL_HAT_DOWN
- SDL_HAT_LEFTDOWN
- SDL_HAT_LEFT
- SDL_HAT_LEFTUP

Unlike the other joystick controls, balls do not have a position; they only report movement relative to the previous reading. This movement data is stored in the xrel and yrel fields of the SDL_JoyBallEvent structure.

Joysticks are not terribly complex devices, but you must take care when writing code to handle them. You must make sure that your code is capable of handling the many different types of joystick configurations by handling the which and control number fields correctly. The following example listing demonstrates the basics of interpreting joystick events correctly.

```
/* Handle all joystick events */
void HandleJoystickEvent(SDL_Event *event){
    /* Useful pointers to event structures */
    SDL_JoyAxisEvent *axis=event->jaxis;
    SDL_JoyButtonEvent *button=event->jbutton;
    SDL_JoyBallEvent *ball=event->jball;
    SDL_JoyHatEvent *hat=event->jhat;

    /* Switch on the type */
    switch(event->type){
        /* Axis motions */
        case SDL_JOYAXISMOTION:
            printf("Joystick %d, Axis %d position: %d\n", axis->which,
                                                          axis->axis,
                                                          axis->value);

            break;

        /* Button presses */
        case SDL_JOYBUTTONUP:
            printf("Joystick %d, Button %d released\n", button->which,
                                                        button->button);
            break;

        /* Button releases */
        case SDL_JOYBUTTONDOWN:
            printf("Joystick %d, Button %d pressed\n", button->which,
                                                       button->button);
            break;

        /* Ball movement */
        case SDL_JOYBALLMOTION:
            printf("Joystick %d, Ball %d motion %d, %d\n", ball->which,
                                                           ball->ball,
                                                           ball->xrel,
                                                           ball->yrel);
            break;
```

```c
                    /* Hat movement */
                    case SDL_JOYHATMOTION:
                        printf("Joystick %d, Hat %d moved to: ", hat->which, hat->hat);
                        /* Print a nice bit of text for each position */
                        switch(hat->value){
                            case SDL_HAT_CENTERED:
                                printf("Center\n");
                                break;
                            case SDL_HAT_UP:
                                printf("Up\n");
                                break;
                            case SDL_HAT_RIGHTUP:
                                printf("Up-right\n");
                                break;
                            case SDL_HAT_RIGHT:
                                printf("Right\n");
                                break;
                            case SDL_HAT_RIGHTDOWN:
                                printf("Down-right\n");
                                break;
                            case SDL_HAT_DOWN:
                                printf("Down\n");
                                break;
                            case SDL_HAT_LEFTDOWN:
                                printf("Down-left\n");
                                break;
                            case SDL_HAT_LEFT:
                                printf("Left\n");
                                break;
                            case SDL_HAT_LEFTUP:
                                printf("Up-left\n");
                                break;
                            default:
                                break;
                        }
                        break;

                    /* This should never happen */
                    default:
                        break;
                }
            }
```

Polling with SDL

SDL provides a set of functions that you can use to bypass the normal event queue methods and get immediate information about current device states. It should be noted that these functions don't query the hardware directly; instead, they use the internal information that SDL maintains about devices. This internal information may not always be up-to-date, especially if you are not actively using the event queue. To update these internal states, you can call SDL_PumpEvents(), which forces SDL to gather information from the input devices.

Polling the Keyboard

The simplest way to get the state of the keyboard is to poll it. This can be achieved using the following two functions.

```
Uint8 *SDL_GetKeyState();

SDLMod SDL_GetModState(void);
```

Internally, SDL keeps track of the state of all the keys on the keyboard, which ones are currently pressed and which ones are not. The SDL_GetKeyState() function returns a pointer to this internal array. The array contains an entry for each SDL key symbol; if the entry is 1, the key is pressed; otherwise, it is not. So, if you want to check whether or not the Enter key is pressed, you could use the following code:

```
Uint8 *key_table;

SDL_PumpEvents();
key_table=SDL_GetKeyState();
if(key_table[SDLK_ENTER])
    printf("Enter key is pressed\n");
```

SDL_GetModState() returns a value that is a bitwise ORed combination of modifier symbols. The return value indicates which modifier keys (such as Shift, Caps Lock, Ctrl, and so on) are currently pressed. You can check for a specific modifier by bitwise ANDing the value returned from SDL_GetModState() with the required modifier symbol. The following example checks to determine whether the Shift key is pressed:

```
SDL_PumpEvents();
if(SDL_GetModState() & KMOD_SHIFT)
    printf("Shift key is pressed\n");
```

Both the SDL_GetModState() and SDL_GetKeyState() functions can be very useful if used correctly. They allow you to get the current state of the keyboard at any time without your having to maintain it yourself.

POLLING THE MOUSE

Like keyboard polling, you can also poll the mouse in a very similar method using the following functions.

```
Uint8 SDL_GetMouseState(int *x, int *y);

Uint8 SDL_GetRelativeMouseState(int *x, int *y);
```

Retrieving information about the current mouse position and button states is a simple task. The SDL_GetMouseState() function copies the current mouse position in the x and y pointers passed to it and returns the button states in the same format as the button data stored in the SDL_MouseMotionEvent structure. The SDL_GetRelativeMouseState() function returns the same button data; however, the position data is relative to the previous mouse position, not to the screen origin.

CONFIGURING THE CONTROL SYSTEM

A control system that can be completely configured by the user offers complete and total freedom. However, such a system can also overwhelm users by offering them too many choices and options before they have even started playing the game. Note that you should always allow several features to be configurable by the user. For instance, users should be able to remap keyboard keys and buttons to their liking. Mouse and joystick sensitivity should also be adjustable. It is worth noting that the buttons of some joysticks may actually be axes, as the joystick hardware sees it, so you should be careful not to restrict joystick actions to buttons only, such as an obscure throttle control or view-hat.

> Do not make assumptions based on your own personal preferences. Remember, you will not be the only person playing your game. If possible, get friends and colleagues to experiment with your control methods and your configuration options.

A simple and effective way to do this is to use a structure containing the key presses as well as a function pointer specifying the function to call when the appropriate input is activated. The following sample code demonstrates this.

```
#define KEY_UP      0
#define KEY_DOWN    1
#define KEY_LEFT    3
#define KEY_RIGHT   4
#define KEY_FIRE    5
```

```
typedef struct {
    unsigned int key;
    void (*func_ptr)(void);
} KeyMap;

// Define the default keyboard map
KeyMap DefaultMap[] = {
    {SDL_KEYUP, UpButton},
    {SDL_KEYDOWN, DownButton},
    {SDL_KEYRIGHT, RightButton},
    {SDL_KEYLEFT, LeftButton},
    {SDL_SPACE, FireButton}
    {0, NULL}
};
```

When the time comes to change the mapping for the inputs, it's simply a case of changing the associated key press for the event, contained in the key member of the KeyMap function for the appropriate event. When you check the inputs, refer to the map structure and call the function that is appropriate.

CHAPTER 6

3D Graphics for Linux Games

For several years now, 3D has been taking more of an emphasis in gaming, with titles such as *Quake III* and *Half-Life* showing developers what they should be doing. To make life easy for us, several companies have developed 3D APIs to handle the more complex aspects of 3D programming.

SOME HISTORY: MESA AND OPENGL

Currently, only two 3D graphics interfaces are in common use for computer games: Direct3D and OpenGL. Direct3D is available only under Microsoft Windows, but OpenGL is implemented on just about every kind of computer with power to run 3D graphics—including Windows machines. So, when fast 3D graphics hardware came to the PC, it was inevitable that some sort of OpenGL implementation would be needed for Linux.

Brian Paul had been experimenting with a graphics library he'd written for the Commodore Amiga and ported that code to Linux. Daryll Strauss and David Bucciarelli adapted Mesa to drive 3DFX Voodoo graphics cards. Mesa has subsequently been adapted to drive many other graphics cards. In addition to supporting more card types, Mesa has grown into an almost perfect implementation of the OpenGL API (although, for legal reasons, it's not allowed to be called OpenGL). Nonetheless, if you have a program that's written using OpenGL, it's pretty much a sure bet that it'll work when compiled and linked against Mesa.

> **NOTE**
>
> In 2001, 3DFX was bought by its competition, nVidia. While support for the older chipsets is going to continue, no more Voodoo-based cards are going to be manufactured.

Additionally, there are now several true OpenGL implementations for Linux, including those from XiG, Metro-Link, and nVidia. Therefore, for the remainder of this chapter and the next, I'll talk about the "OpenGL" graphics interface, even though the chances are that you'll be pronouncing it "Mesa."

In this chapter, I'll introduce you to enough OpenGL to get you writing games. Because it's a deep subject worthy of several volumes, much of it is out of the scope of this book, but for more information on this extensive topic, pick up a copy of *OpenGL Game Programming* (Prima Publishing).

WHAT IS OPENGL?

OpenGL is an extremely powerful graphics API. One of its nicest features is that all implementations have to provide all of the core functionality required by the specification of the API. That means that programs should run correctly whether you have an aging Voodoo-1 card or an up-to-date GeForce-2

ULTRA. If your hardware does not implement a feature, then the OpenGL driver emulates that feature in software—and your program will not be aware of any problem except that it may run rather slowly. In addition to the core functionality, OpenGL implementations are allowed to extend the API to take advantage of the special features of some cards that lie outside the core functions.

This flexibility is something of a double-edged sword. Although any program written using OpenGL should work correctly on any implementation, if you want the program to run quickly, you'll have to pay careful attention to which particular OpenGL calls are likely to be fast on most 3D hardware. We'll discuss these particulars in more detail later.

So what can OpenGL do? Essentially, most 3D applications describe the game's "world" and everything in it in terms of triangles, lines, and points—each of which can be colored, illuminated by some light sources, fogged by the simulated atmosphere, and "textured" by wall-papering it with a picture of some kind. This may sound rather limiting, but keep in mind that even graphically sophisticated games such as *Quake* are written in OpenGL using just those basic primitives. Even multimillion-dollar flight simulator graphics systems are most often written using OpenGL.

Some things that OpenGL doesn't do are also significant: It doesn't deal with opening a window to draw the graphics into, and it doesn't include routines for keyboard, mouse, joysticks, text output, or GUI elements such as menus, buttons, or sliders. Consequently, you always have to include some other library to handle those things. Many simple OpenGL games use Mark Kilgard's GL Utility Toolkit (GLUT) library or its OpenSource clone, freeglut. GLUT is also used for examples in most OpenGL manuals, but there are plenty of alternatives to this library. Nearly all Linux GUI toolkits provide a way to create a window into which OpenGL can render; you can use SDL, GTK+, FLTK, TCL/Tk, Lesstif, or even raw X Windows calls.

In addition, you'll probably want to pull in some add-on libraries to render text, to load images, and perhaps to handle some of the low-level drawing for you. A good place to look for these things is the official OpenGL Web site, located at **http://www.opengl.org**.

OFFICIAL OPENGL WEB SITE: **HTTP://WWW.OPENGL.ORG**

Early versions of Mesa had support for software-only rendering under SVGAlib, but as I write this, that version is not actively maintained. All modern implementations of OpenGL for Linux work within the XFree86 windowing system. If you are a console programming enthusiast, you'll either have to get into X or forget about doing hardware-accelerated 3D graphics.

WHERE CAN 1 GET OPENGL?

Unless your Linux distribution is hopelessly outdated, you'll probably find that Mesa is already installed. However, it's possible that you'll need to hunt down a vendor-specific version to take advantage of your hardware. The site at **http://www.mesa3d.org** is a good place to start that search. However, if you have nVidia 3D hardware, for example, you'll do better to visit the Web site of the company that makes your graphics hardware and look for a section containing appropriate Linux drivers.

Mesa/OpenGL: HTTP://WWW.MESA3D.ORG

For the purposes of this chapter, however, you can get by with whatever came with your Linux distribution. Although it'll be slower than hardware-accelerated OpenGL, it should work perfectly.

Buffers, Hidden Surface Elimination, and Animation

To make images that appear to move smoothly, it's necessary to redraw the complete image at a rate of around 20 to 60 times per second. Unlike some 2D animation techniques, it's absolutely necessary to redraw the entire 3D picture at that speed because even the smallest movement of the eye point causes the entire scene to change. Consequently, the graphics have to be drawn behind the scenes in a "back buffer" so that you can't see the image in the process of being drawn. After the new scene is computed, you can swap the front and back buffers so that the new image is displayed on the screen and the old one can be recycled. This double-buffer technique is pretty much universally used in OpenGL games, and is what I'll describe in the remainder of this chapter.

In addition to the two image buffers, OpenGL makes use of a depth buffer (also known as a Z-buffer). The depth buffer is a part of a common technique to deal with the problem of "hidden surface removal," that is, of making sure that the things that are far off in the distance of your 3D scene are correctly hidden behind the things that are closer to the camera. For every pixel on the screen, there is also a depth buffer pixel that can store distances from the camera (or more often, the reciprocal of that distance).

When OpenGL draws a pixel, it also calculates the depth of the pixel. If the value of that pixel's depth is larger than the value currently stored in the depth buffer, that pixel won't be drawn. If the

> **NOTE**
>
> The reciprocal is stored instead of the real distance because the exact distance is not actually required, just the order objects appear in. Finding the square root can be a very expensive task.

value is closer, the pixel will be drawn—and the new "closest" value will overwrite whatever was in the depth buffer before. By setting the depth buffer to the largest possible depth at the start of each screen redraw, OpenGL resolves the problem of hidden surface elimination with virtually no impact on the application.

GETTING STARTED

For the sake of getting us started, let's look at a simple OpenGL program that uses the GLUT library to handle all the windowing issues. We'll romp through enough of the OpenGL API to get something going onscreen, and then backtrack and fill in some details.

First, we need to include some definitions:

```
#include <math.h>        /* The Standard C math library */
#include <GL/gl.h>       /* Include definitions of the OpenGL API */
#include <GL/glu.h>      /* Include definitions of the OpenGLUtilities API */
#include <GL/glut.h>     /* Include definitions of the GLUT API */
```

All these GL header files are, by default, supposed to be in /usr/include/GL, but some Linux distributions place them (incorrectly) in /usr/X11/include/GL. Adding the direction -I/usr/X11/include to your compilation line will ensure that these files are found no matter where they are installed.

The main() function for a GLUT-based OpenGL program generally looks something like this:

```
extern void redisplay( void );
extern void initCamera( void );
int main( int argc, char **argv )
{
    glutInit( &argc, argv );
    glutInitDisplayMode( GLUT_RGB | GLUT_DOUBLE | GLUT_DEPTH );
    glutInitWindowSize( 640, 480 );
    glutCreateWindow( "My First OpenGL Program"    );
    glutDisplayFunc( redisplay );

    initCamera();

    glutMainLoop();
    return0;
}

void initCamera( void )
{
    glMatrixMode( GL_PROJECTION );
    glLoadIdentity();
    glOrtho(-1,1,-1,1,-1,1);
    glMatrixMode( GL_MODELVIEW );
}
```

The glutInit() call initializes GLUT and should always be the first GLUT or OpenGL function in the program. C++ programmers beware: Don't put OpenGL calls in global constructor functions!

The glutInitDisplayMode() call tells GLUT that you want an RGB window that is double-buffered and that there should be a depth buffer. Virtually all 3D games need these three things, so we won't waste space discussing the alternatives.

Next, the glutInitWindowSize() call tells GLUT about the initial size of the window we want; the next call to glutCreateWindow() creates that window with a title. Then glutDisplayFunc() tells GLUT which function to call when the window needs to be redrawn. You can also select callback functions for keyboard or mouse input, window resize, expose and iconify events, timers, and so on.

The initCamera() function is something we'll come back to later; for now, I'll just say that it initializes the "virtual" camera through which we view the virtual world. It's not legal to make OpenGL calls until the rendering context (a window) is set up, so initCamera() has to be called sometime *after* the glutCreateWindow() call.

Finally, main() hands control over to GLUT by calling glutMainLoop(), which never returns. Some people find it uncomfortable to hand control over to GLUT, but you can't get around that with GLUT. However, the freeglut library from OpenSource has a way to get around that by letting the application call glutMainLoopUpdate() inside a loop of its own.

Now all that's left to do in this simple example is to draw something:

```
void redisplay( void )
{
    glEnable( GL_DEPTH_TEST );
    glClearColor( 0.0f, 0.5f, 0.0f, 1.0f );     /* Dark Green */
    glClear( GL_COLOR_BUFFER_BIT | GL_DEPTH_BUFFER_BIT );

    /* DRAW SOMETHING! */

    glutSwapBuffers();
    glutPostRedisplay();
}
```

The glEnable() function is used to turn on various optional OpenGL features (the glDisable() function turns them off again). In this example, the function is being used to turn on depth testing. Most 3D rendering requires depth testing, so it's prudent to start your drawing routines with this feature enabled.

The glClearColor() call tells OpenGL what color to clear the screen to. The first three parameters are the values for the red, green, and blue components of the color; the last parameter is Alpha, which isn't important in this context. Because colors run from 0 to 1, the color I've specified in this example is a tasteful shade of dark green (my favorite color). The `glClear()` call tells OpenGL to clear the screen; in this case, we've told it to clear the color *and* to set the depth buffer to its maximum value.

In a real application, we'd draw some polygons, lines, and points next. Because this is the simplest of OpenGL programs, we'll just tell GLUT to swap the double-buffer(so that you can see the dark-green window) and then to post a request to redisplay the window. That last call to `glutPostRedisplay()` ensures that the redisplay function will be called repeatedly as fast as possible—which is probably what most games need. GLUT also provides a way to redisplay the window at fixed time intervals, but I won't go into that here.

You can find this program under the name `ex1.c` on the CD-ROM that accompanies this book.

COMPILING AND LINKING WITH OPENGL

Now that you have coded a simple OpenGL program, you'll want to compile that program. Compiling with OpenGL generally requires you to pull in several other libraries. A suitable set of compile commands for a program called `my_program.c` is shown here:

```
cc -c -I/usr/X11/include my_program.c
cc -o my_program my_program.o -L/usr/X11/lib -lglut -lGLU -lGL -lX11-lXext -lm
```

But to compile the examples for this chapter, you can use the makefile that you'll find in the directory corresponding to this chapter on the CD-ROM that accompanies this book. Just copy all the files onto your hard disk and type `make`.

In the default Linux installation, the OpenGL libraries are supposed to be in `/usr/lib/libGL.so` and `/usr/lib/libGLU.so` (with GLUT in `/usr/lib/libglut.so` or more often `/usr/lib/libglut.a`). Note that some Linux distributions (incorrectly) place these libraries in `/usr/X11/lib`. Picking up the wrong OpenGL libraries for the hardware you have is probably the most common problem for users of OpenGL under Linux; sometimes your Linux distribution will install the libraries in one place and the version you download for your specific graphics card may install somewhere else. Then it ends up being a bit of a lottery as to which library will be linked to your program. I advise you to use the find program to track down errant copies of your OpenGL libraries before you install any new drivers.

When you run this example, you should have a green window that takes up perhaps a quarter of the screen (depending on your display resolution). Nothing very exciting, but a significant step forward nonetheless.

LET'S DRAW SOMETHING!

Okay, so we have the basic structure of an OpenGL/GLUT program in place. Let's add some interesting drawing commands. There are really three aspects to drawing anything in OpenGL that we have to consider, and I'll introduce them one by one:

- Drawing polygons, lines, and points
- Drawing in 3D: perspective and movement
- Texturing and other "state" elements

DRAWING POLYGONS, LINES, AND POINTS

OpenGL can draw a wide range of basic shapes: points, lines, polygons, triangles, and quadrilaterals.

When you tell OpenGL to draw one of those basic primitives, you only have to tell it where the corners—the *vertices*, to use the correct term—of triangles are in 3D space. OpenGL does all the rest. You don't generally have to worry about the order in which you draw things, and you don't have to write code to draw every individual pixel. Because all the apparatus needed to draw a complete triangle is typically provided in your 3D graphics card, this operation can happen very quickly—perhaps in less than a millionth of a second for a small triangle! On a modern graphics adapter, your biggest worry is often how to arrange the triangle vertex data in memory so that you can send it to the graphics card fast enough to keep it busy; only rarely will you have to wait for the hardware!

Those basic shapes (point, line, polygon, triangle, and quadrilateral) are all pretty obvious. OpenGL also offers line-strips, line-loops, quad-strips, triangle-strips, and triangle-fans. These strips, loops, and fans are there to allow you to draw collections of connected shapes without having to send the vertices that they share more than once. Using these shapes can save you typing and will also make your program run faster because those shared vertices don't have to be processed more than once.

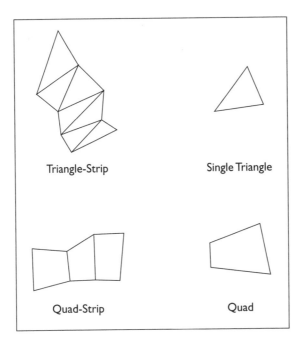

Triangle-Strip

Single Triangle

Quad-Strip

Quad

Figure 6.1

OpenGL surfaces.

Suppose that you wanted to draw the simplest possible solid object: a three-sided pyramid, also called a *tetrahedron*. How would you tell OpenGL to do that? If you start with the GLUT program from earlier in this chapter, you can simply replace the DRAW SOMETHING! comment with some actual code.

First, you tell OpenGL what kind of primitive to draw (for the tetrahedron, you want triangles) and then give it a list of vertex coordinates in 3D space. When you have finished describing the shape, you tell OpenGL that you are done, and the drawing will commence while your program gets on with something else.

Just for fun, let's also color each triangle with a different color so that we can see which triangle is which. Here's the code to accomplish these lofty goals:

```
glBegin( GL_TRIANGLES );    /* Start describing triangles */

glColor3f(    1.0f,    0.0f,    0.0f );    /* Red */
glVertex3f(   0.0f,    0.0f,    0.0f );    /* First triangle */
glVertex3f(  -1.0f,   -1.0f,   -1.0f );
glVertex3f(   1.0f,   -1.0f,   -1.0f );

glColor3f(    0.0f,    1.0f,    0.0f );    /* Green */
glVertex3f(   0.0f,    0.0f,    0.0f );    /* Second triangle */
glVertex3f(   1.0f,   -1.0f,   -1.0f );
glVertex3f(   0.0f,    1.0f,   -1.0f );

glColor3f(    0.0f,    0.0f,    1.0f );    /* Blue */
glVertex3f(   0.0f,    0.0f,    0.0f );    /* Third triangle */
glVertex3f(   0.0f,    1.0f,   -1.0f );
glVertex3f(  -1.0f,   -1.0f,   -1.0f );

glColor3f(    1.0f,    1.0f,    0.0f );    /* Yellow */
glVertex3f(  -1.0f,   -1.0f,   -1.0f );    /* Fourth triangle */
glVertex3f(   0.0f,    1.0f,   -1.0f );
glVertex3f(   1.0f,   -1.0f,   -1.0f );

glEnd();    /* All done - let the drawing commence. */
```

You may be wondering why these commands end in 3f. There are many versions of the glColor() and glVertex() commands, some taking more or fewer arguments—glVertex2f() is for 2D drawing, for example. The number sets the number of arguments and the letter f tells the system that we are passing C float arguments (usually preferred for best performance). (You can also pass bytes, shorts, ints, and doubles.) You can also pass an array containing the coordinates by adding a v to the end of the function name, as in this example:

```
float vertex [ 3 ] = { 1.0, 2.0, 3.0 };

glVertex3fv( vertex );
```

The `glColor3f()` call sets OpenGL's current drawing color; the `glVertex3f()` call sends vertex coordinate data off to OpenGL. If you put a `glColor3f()` call in front of each `glVertex()` call, you'll see that OpenGL will blend the colors across each triangle.

OpenGL uses a default 3D coordinate system in which X and Y are in the plane of the screen with the origin in the middle (just like a 2D coordinate system); Z decreases (becomes increasingly negative) as things move farther "into" the screen (that's why some vertices have negative Z values). So (if you are good at visualizing things in three dimensions), you'll see that this is a tetrahedron that's in the middle of the screen with its point facing us.

Another important thing to know is that OpenGL is very picky about what commands it allows you to use between the `glBegin()` and `glEnd()` calls. Only the following commands (and a handful of other obscure calls) are allowed:

- `glVertex()`
- `glColor()`
- `glNormal()`
- `glTexCoord()`
- `glMaterial()`

If you compile and run this code (it's called `ex2.c` on the CD-ROM that accompanies this book), you'll see red, green, and blue triangles—the yellow one is hidden behind the others (depth buffering, remember!).

Now let's get this object to move.

DRAWING IN 3D: PERSPECTIVE AND MOVEMENT

Making things move in OpenGL is just a matter of drawing them in a slightly different position in each frame—just as you do in 2D graphics—but recomputing all those `glVertex()` values each time would be tedious. Fortunately, OpenGL can do this computing for you; on modern graphics cards, it might be done for you on lightning fast hardware.

Moving objects in 3D is tricky, especially if your vector and matrix math isn't strong. All rotations, translations, scaling, shearing, mirroring, and other "linear" transformations can be described by 16 numbers arranged in a 4×4 matrix. This compact representation is at the heart of most 3D algorithms. If you are going to become an effective 3D programmer, you'll have to come to grips with 4×4 matrices.

A 4×4 matrix can combine any number of transformations applied in any order. OpenGL represents matrices as a single-dimension 16-element array—which is a little curious since they are universally written down as a 4×4 two-dimensional array of numbers. The order of the matrix elements in an OpenGL matrix array is shown here:

```
0    4    8    12
1    5    9    13
2    6    10   14
3    7    11   15
```

OpenGL uses the idea of a "current" matrix (well, actually *three* current matrices), which is automatically applied to every glVertex() call before it's used to draw something. This means that once you've set up those 16 numbers, everything you draw from that point on can be transformed for no extra cost.

Better still, each of the current matrices is actually just the top element of a stack of matrices that you can push or pop. OpenGL has commands to multiply matrices together—which has the effect of combining their effects. You can also use handy utility routines to create matrices that rotate, translate, or scale; each of these routines operates on the matrix at the top of the stack. Here are the utility routines with which you'll want to make friends:

```
glPushMatrix();
glPopMatrix();
glLoadMatrixf( float matrix [ 16 ] );
glLoadIdentity();
glMultMatrixf( float matrix [ 16 ] );
glTranslatef( float x, float y, float z );
glRotatef( float angle, float x, float y, float z );
glScalef( float x, float y, float z );
```

Most of these routines are named to make their functionality fairly obvious: The glRotate() command creates a matrix that rotates around a line from the origin to the point (specified by x, y, and z), through the specified angle and multiplies it into the current matrix (the one on top of the stack). The glTranslatef() and glScalef() commands are similar.

glLoadMatrixf() and glLoadIdentity() replace the matrix on the top of the stack with the matrix you specify or a "do nothing" matrix, respectively. The identity matrix is a "do nothing" operation; therefore, glLoadIdentity() is a handy way to reset the current matrix.

Be careful with the matrix push and pop commands; the OpenGL matrix stacks are often quite small (16 is a common maximum number).

If you add the following lines to our rapidly growing sample program, the tetrahedron will rotate by one degree every time it's redrawn. (This version of the program is ex3.c on the CD-ROM that accompanies this book.)

```
#define ROTATION_SPEED    1.0f

static float a = 0;

a += ROTATION_SPEED;
glLoadIdentity();
glRotatef( a, 0.0f, 0.0f, 1.0f );
```

> **NOTE**
>
> **Whereas the code read** glRotatef(), **it will be referred to as** glRotate() **in the text because there are several functions that rotate an object, such as** glRotatefv() **and** glRotatei().

If you change the numbers in the glRotate() command, the tetrahedron will rotate in different directions. Notice that we load the current matrix with the identity matrix every time around to reset it. The glRotate() command multiplies the matrix on the top of the stack; as a result, the rotation we apply gets a little larger in each frame and the object spins.

It's tempting to simplify this code to the following two lines; the current rotation would still be increased by one degree per redraw:

```
#define ROTATION_SPEED    1.0f
glRotatef( ROTATION_SPEED, 0.0f, 0.0f, 1.0f );
```

However, you shouldn't simplify the code to this degree; the roundoff errors within OpenGL will gradually build up, and the simple rotation will gradually deteriorate and produce very bad effects if you don't reset the matrix from time to time.

Another thing to notice is that the actual rotation speed of the tetrahedron depends on the speed of your computer, the speed of your graphics card, and the amount of other stuff you have running at the time. It's a good idea (in most cases) to measure the amount of time that has elapsed between the last frame and this one and use that value to adjust the amount of movement to make the speed of the game action appear constant no matter what.

PERSPECTIVE AND THE PROJECTION MATRIX

Earlier I mentioned that there are three OpenGL matrix stacks and three current matrices. The one we've been messing with so far is the ModelView matrix. It controls how objects (models) are positioned relative to the viewer.

The second matrix is the Projection matrix; it determines how the 3D coordinates in the model are squished down into two dimensions so that polygons can be drawn on the screen.

We won't concern ourselves with the third Texture matrix at this stage.

So, what's the Projection matrix for? You may have realized that the OpenGL viewing "volume" has coordinates that run from –1.0 to +1.0 in the X and Y directions; you can see that from the way the tetrahedron in `ex1.c` exactly fits the window. The viewing volume also runs from 0.0 to –1.0 in the Z direction (the positive Z region would be "behind your head," so you can't see it).

That space is rather restrictive and doesn't allow for the effects of perspective. The Projection matrix takes care of all of these things and is capable of doing some *very* strange things to your images. However, for most practical games purposes, you only want a simple 3D projection that achieves perspective.

Setting the Projection matrix to produce the exact effect you need would be hard. Fortunately, there is an OpenGL utility command to do all the messy math for you:

```
gluPerspective( double fovY, double aspect,
                       double zNear, double zFar );
```

The `fovY` parameter sets the field of view in the Y (vertical) direction. This is the angle (measured at the eye) between the highest thing you can fit onto the screen and the lowest. In practice, it's generally set to somewhere between 40 and 80 degrees. Smaller numbers generate telephoto views, as if you were looking through a telescope. Larger numbers produce wide-angle views and in the extreme can produce "fish-eye" distortions.

The `aspect` parameter is the aspect ratio of your window. For a 640×480 window, this parameter should be 640/480 (about 1.3). Getting this number wrong tends to produce distortions as things

> **NOTE**
>
> Notice that some OpenGL commands start with `glu` rather than `gl`. This difference indicates that they come from the optional libGLU library rather than from the core libGL set. Although GLU functions can always be rewritten in terms of core OpenGL functions, the GLU functions are generally a worthwhile convenience. Plan to use libGLU in most of your programs.

rotate. If you watch our spinning tetrahedron, you'll notice that the red triangle is initially the same width as the screen; after 90 degrees of rotation, however, it's the same height as the screen, which is quite a bit smaller! Setting the Projection matrix appropriately for the window size will fix that problem.

If you played with the `glRotate()` command in the preceding example, you may have managed to spin the tetrahedron so that parts of it seemed to be cut off—even though they lie within the window. That happens when parts of the object come too close and "poke through the screen" or get too far away and fall beyond the far edge of OpenGL's little world. These two places are called `zNear` and `zFar`, and you can position them with `gluPerspective()`.

Most beginners instantly try to set these numbers out so far that objects can never possibly be clipped, but that's a bad mistake. The depth buffer we discussed earlier has only limited precision; if you put `zNear` too close to the eye, you'll create problems with depth precision. The `zFar` value is less critical, and you can safely set it to a large number.

People debate long and hard about what value to use for zNear, but it really depends on the general scale of your models. If you are building a human-scale game, perhaps 0.1 meter is a good value. If your game is "The Attack of the Mutant Bacterium," you'll probably want a much smaller value for zNear.

To cut a long story short, we'll want something like this:

```
gluPerspective( 40.0, 1.333, 0.1, 100000.0 );
```

There isn't a float version of gluPerspective(); its arguments are always doubles. In addition, this command is like glRotate(): It multiplies the current matrix rather than replacing it. Finally, all OpenGL matrix operations affect only one of the matrix stacks at a time; you decide which stack that is by using the glMatrixMode() command. Considering all that, the sequence of statements to set the Projection matrix to a "reasonable" value looks like this:

```
/* Select the Projection matrix */
glMatrixMode    ( GL_PROJECTION );

glLoadIdentity();
gluPerspective( 40.0, 1.333, 0.1, 100000.0 );

/* Go back to the ModelView matrix */
glMatrixMode    ( GL_MODELVIEW );
```

It's usual to leave the matrix mode set to GL_MODELVIEW when you've finished messing with the GL_PROJECTION or GL_TEXTURE matrix because the ModelView stack is by far the most active in most applications.

DRAWING IN ORTHOGRAPHIC OR PERSPECTIVE MODE

You may have noticed that this code is quite similar to the initCamera() function we used earlier in the chapter. That's no accident: The previous examples used glOrtho() rather than gluPerspective() to produce a Projection matrix that simulated orthographic drawings. (An *orthographic* drawing is one in which things stay the same size no matter how far from the eye they are.) For some occasions, you want to use orthographic rendering in a game—perhaps for a board game or for a game in which the action happens from a God's eye view. Some games are just better suited to orthographic rendering: *SimCity* would be hard to play in perspective, for example.

You'll probably want to switch your game into orthographic mode for drawing overlay information such as scores, damage indicators, and such. Games that attempt realism usually use perspective for most of the rendering, though.

Now you can place those lines of code at the end of the last section into the evolving sample program in place of the old initCamera() call. Alternatively, you can call these lines of code in every frame if you think you'll want to be able to change the field of view or the clip planes during the game.

If you just replace initCamera() in this way, you'll notice that the sides of the tetrahedron have vanished, and all you can see is a huge spinning yellow triangle. That's because the tetrahedron's apex is at (0,0,0), which is where the camera is. "Losing the model" is a frequent problem when you first write 3D programs; the usual treatment for this condition is to change your program so that the camera moves backward until things come into view and you can see what's going on.

Confusingly, OpenGL doesn't allow you to "move the camera"; it's always at the origin facing along the Z axis. The way to give the impression that you are moving through the virtual world is to transform the world in the opposite direction to the way we want the camera to move. That is, rather than the camera advancing through the static world, the world moves past the static camera.

Now we have to add a glTranslatef() call to the ModelView matrix setup in the redisplay function, as shown here:

```
glLoadIdentity();
glTranslatef( 0.0f, 0.0f, -10.0f );
glRotatef( a, 0.0f, 0.0f, 1.0f );
```

The order of matrix operations is generally rather important because matrix multiplication is not commutative as are simple numbers (in other words, A×B doesn't always equal B×A if A and B are matrices).

We can make the camera appear to move backward (by ten units in this example) by moving the model forward ten units. Because "forward" means along the negative Z axis in OpenGL, we must apply a Z translation of –10 to give the impression that the camera moved back ten units. The resulting code is in ex4.c on the CD-ROM.

CODE THAT MOVES THE OBJECT

To wrap up this discussion on moving an object in perspective, it's generally a good idea to structure the drawing part of your code like the following pseudo-code:

```
glMatrixMode( GL_PROJECTION );
glLoadIdentity();
gluPerspective( {camera parameters} );
glMatrixMode( GL_MODELVIEW );
glLoadIdentity();

{apply the inverse camera rotation to the modelview matrix}
{apply the inverse camera translation to the modelview matrix}
```

```
for( each object in the scene )
{
    glPushMatrix();

    {apply the translation for the N'th object}
    {apply the rotation for the N'th object}
    {draw the N'th object}

    glPopMatrix();
}
```

Look carefully at the order of the operations. Notice that the camera is first rotated and *then* translated. Objects are generally rotated *after* they are translated.

Notice that we push and pop the ModelView matrix stack as we draw each object so that we can restore the initial camera positioning matrix before each frame.

If you want to play some more with this example (and you are sick of that multicolored tetrahedron), you can use some convenient GLUT routines that draw spheres, cubes, dodecahedrons, and even a teapot!

Try adding these lines of code just after the glEnd() function call in our last example:

```
glColor3f(0.5f,0.3f,0.0f);    /* Chocolate */
glutSolidTorus(1,2,30,30);    /* Donut      */
```

Mmmmm! Donuts!

TEXTURING AND OTHER "STATE" ELEMENTS

OpenGL is an API that has many hidden "states"; we've already seen the current color and the current ModelView and Projection matrices, and just about every other aspect of rendering is handled in a similar manner.

OpenGL has a current set of enabled options. You turn these on and off with the glEnable() and glDisable() functions. In the sample program from the first part of this chapter, the GL_DEPTH_TEST option was set using glEnable(). The following sections discuss some of the options you can enable; there are many others, these are just the highlights.

> **NOTE**
>
> You can find out about the other options in the mountains of documentation at **http://www.opengl.org**.

Table 6.1 GLUT Pre-defined Objects

Function	Description
glutWireTetrahedron(void);	Draws a wireframe tetrahedron
glutWireOctahedron(void);	Draws a wireframe octahedron
glutWireCube(double size);	Draws a wireframe cube
glutWireDodecahedron(void);	Draws a wireframe dodecahedron
glutWireIcosahedron(void);	Draws a wireframe icosahedron
glutWireSphere(double radius, int slices, int stacks);	Draws a wireframe sphere
glutWireTorus(double innerRadius, double outerRadius, int sides, int rings);	Draws a wireframe torus
glutWireCone(double base, double height, int slices, int stacks);	Draws a wireframe cone
glutWireTeapot(double size);	Draws a wireframe teapot
glutSolidTetrahedron(void);	Draws a solid tetrahedron
glutSolidOctahedron(void);	Draws a solid octahedron
glutSolidCube(double size);	Draws a solid cube
glutSolidDodecahedron(void);	Draws a solid dodecahedron
glutSolidIcosahedron(void);	Draws a solid icosahedron
glutSolidSphere(double radius, int slices, int stacks);	Draws a solid sphere
glutSolidTorus(double innerRadius, double outerRadius, int sides, int rings);	Draws a solid torus
glutSolidCone(double base, double height, int slices, int stacks);	Draws a solid cone
glutSolidTeapot(double size);	Draws a solid teapot

THE GL_CULL_FACE OPTION

Polygons in OpenGL look like they were cut out of paper—they are infinitely thin—and have two sides. In the real world, the surfaces of solid objects can't usually be seen from the inside. This is a useful property. If you could somehow mark the inside of an object, you wouldn't have to draw those polygons when the OpenGL camera is on the outside of the object. In the case of the tetrahedron in the sample program, you can't see the yellow face until the tetrahedron starts rotating, so there is really no need to draw it. Drawing fewer polygons saves processor time, so you can see that culling the back-facing polygons is a good thing.

OpenGL uses the convention that the order of the vertices of the polygon determines which side is the visible side. Therefore, if you make a call to glEnable(GL_CULL_FACE), a polygon is drawn only if its vertices appear in counterclockwise order. Consider the red triangle in the tetrahedron example:

```
glColor3f(    1.0f,    0.0f,    0.0f );    /* Red */
glVertex3f(    0.0f,    0.0f,    0.0f );    /* First triangle */
glVertex3f( -1.0f, -1.0f, -1.0f );
glVertex3f(    1.0f, -1.0f, -1.0f );
```

If you plot out the X,Y coordinates on graph paper, you'll see that this is a counterclockwise ordering; when it's displayed without any rotation, the tetrahedron will be drawn. However, if you rotate the polygon (for example, if you took the graph paper, held it up to the light, and flipped it over so that you were seeing the back side of the paper), magically, those vertices would be in clockwise order—and OpenGL won't draw the polygon under those conditions when the GL_CULL_FACE option is turned on.

So, most of the time, you'll want back-face culling enabled. Keep in mind, however, that there may be times when it's inconvenient.

THE GL_LIGHTING OPTION

In the examples so far in this chapter, we have seen OpenGL draw our tetrahedron in the exact colors we asked it to use. However, in the real world, objects have their colors modified by the lights shining on them. If you take a red cube and a blue cube and view them under red light, the blue cube will appear black because it only reflects blue light—and there isn't any.

Also, objects are brighter on the side nearest to the light source and shiny objects have a highlight on them that moves around depending on the geometrical relationship between the shape and the position of the object, the position of the light source, and the position from which the object is being viewed.

All of these lighting influences are included in OpenGL's lighting scheme (a subject we'll return to later). Suffice to say at this point that disabling or enabling the GL_LIGHTING option switches between a scheme in which all things are colored exactly as you specify with glColor() and a scheme in which light sources and material properties are used to perform subtle lighting effects. All of the examples in this chapter so far have had GL_LIGHTING disabled, which is the OpenGL default.

THE GL_TEXTURE_2D OPTION

As I explained earlier in the chapter, polygons (and lines and points as well) can be "wallpapered" with texture patterns. We'll cover texturing later in this chapter, but for now let's say that the GL_TEXTURE_2D option turns texturing on and off.

THE GL_COLOR_MATERIAL OPTION

This option is related to the GL_LIGHTING flag; it allows you to continue to use glColor() commands to set some aspects of the color of objects even when GL_LIGHTING is turned on. More about this later in this chapter.

THE GL_BLEND OPTION

There is a version of the glColor() command called glColor4f() that adds a fourth component to the three standard color components of red, green, and blue. This fourth component, the Alpha component, is a measure of the opacity of objects. If Alpha is 1.0, the object is utterly opaque (which is the default in glColor3f() calls); if Alpha is 0.0, the object is utterly transparent. Values between 0.0 and 1.0 are used to define varying degrees of transparency between those extremes.

However, for transparency to work correctly, you need to tell OpenGL to blend the color of the polygon into the background. That's what enabling GL_BLEND does. Transparency is a subject we'll come back to later.

THE GL_ALPHA_TEST OPTION

Once you start rendering with the Alpha component (to permit transparency), you'll often want to avoid drawing completely transparent pixels—or perhaps even pixels that are *almost* completely transparent. We'll talk more about this flag in the "Transparency and the Alpha Component" section, later in this chapter.

THE GL_DEPTH_TEST OPTION

This option is one we've already seen; it allows you to turn depth testing on and off. Generally, you'll want it enabled all the time, although you might want to turn it off when you're rendering scores, power-ups, and so on that you want to appear onscreen in front of everything else.

LIGHTING

Having lights shining on your models makes them look much more realistic. As you might imagine, the subject of doing great lighting could fill a book all by itself.

When you place a call to glEnable(GL_LIGHTING), OpenGL uses a set of light sources and a set of material properties to figure out how things should be illuminated. The representation of light that OpenGL uses contains four components: ambient, diffuse, specular, and emission.

Ambient light comes from all directions and scatters in all directions. In general scenes, you need quite a lot of ambient light to make things look reasonable in daylight scenes. A deep-space game needs much less ambient light if you are trying to create the harsh shadows you'd see in the absence of a bright sky.

Diffuse light comes from one specific direction—but after it hits a surface, it scatters off in all directions. Diffuse lighting gives your brain most of the information it needs to deduce the three-dimensional shape of smoothly shaped objects.

Specular light also comes from one specific direction, but it's reflected from the surface in a tight beam. This kind of light is used to produce the shiny spots on objects.

Emissive light is the light that is emitted in all directions from the objects themselves. Anything that has to glow in the dark needs emissive light.

SPECIFYING THE LIGHTING QUALITIES OF THE OBJECT

You can set how reflective the object you're drawing is in each of those four kinds of light by using the glMaterial() function:

```
float white[ 4 ] = { 1.0f, 1.0f, 1.0f, 1.0f };
float red[ 4 ] = { 1.0f, 0.0f, 0.0f, 1.0f };
float yellow[ 4 ] = { 1.0f, 1.0f, 0.0f, 1.0f };
float black[ 4 ] = { 0.0f, 0.0f, 0.0f, 1.0f };

glMaterialfv( GL_FRONT_AND_BACK, GL_AMBIENT, yellow );
glMaterialfv( GL_FRONT_AND_BACK, GL_DIFFUSE, yellow );
glMaterialfv( GL_FRONT_AND_BACK, GL_EMISSION, black );
glMaterialfv( GL_FRONT_AND_BACK, GL_SPECULAR, white );

glMaterialf( GL_FRONT_AND_BACK, GL_SHININESS, 5.0f );
```

This code defines a material that's quite shiny and reflects all light colors (that's why GL_SPECULAR is set to white and GL_EMISSION is set to black so that the material does not emit any light). Apart from that, this material reflects only the yellow component of ordinary, ambient light. In fact, it's so common to set the ambient and diffuse lighting options with the same reflectances that there is a special token for that:

```
glMaterialfv( GL_FRONT_AND_BACK, GL_AMBIENT_AND_DIFFUSE, yellow);
```

The first parameter of the glMaterial() call tells OpenGL which side of the polygon is to have these properties. You can (in principle) have different material properties on the front and back sides of each polygon, but in practice, that arrangement is pretty slow under most OpenGL implementations. It's also not very useful. Therefore, we've set the parameter to GL_FRONT_AND_BACK, which applies the effect to both sides. The second parameter indicates which property of the material we are applying, and the third property is an array containing red, green, blue, and alpha values for each component. Including the alpha value in the color array seems rather strange because, in fact, the alpha values are ignored for all except the GL_DIFFUSE component. In the case of GL_SHININESS, the third parameter sets how large or small the highlight will be on the object (in the range 0.0 to 128.0).

Generally, it's rather inconvenient (and slow) to have to use glMaterial() to set the color of every vertex, so there is a trick you can use:

```
glEnable( GL_COLOR_MATERIAL );
glColorMaterial( GL_FRONT_AND_BACK, GL_AMBIENT_AND_DIFFUSE );
```

What these statements do is tell OpenGL that subsequent changes in glColor() will also set glMaterial() with GL_FRONT_AND_BACK and GL_AMBIENT_AND_DIFFUSE to that color. Because most real-world materials have no emission and reflect specular light without changing their own colors, it's usually good to set up your object like this:

```
float white [ 4 ] = { 1.0f, 1.0f, 1.0f, 1.0f };
float black [ 4 ] = { 0.0f, 0.0f, 0.0f, 1.0f };
glEnable( GL_LIGHTING );
glMaterialfv( GL_FRONT_AND_BACK, GL_EMISSION, black );
glMaterialfv( GL_FRONT_AND_BACK, GL_SPECULAR, white );
glMaterialf( GL_FRONT_AND_BACK, GL_SHININESS, 5.0f );
glEnable( GL_COLOR_MATERIAL );
glColorMaterial( GL_FRONT_AND_BACK, GL_AMBIENT_AND_DIFFUSE );
```

ESTABLISHING THE LIGHT SOURCE

The next thing you have to do is set up one or more light sources. OpenGL allows you to set a maximum of eight sources. Note that using more light sources than you strictly need can be slow, so use only what you need.

The following code demonstrates how to set up a light source.

```
float pos[ 3 ] = { 1000.0f, 5000.0f, 0.0f };
float white[ 3 ] = { 1.0f, 1.0f, 1.0f };
float dim_white[ 3 ] = { 0.3f, 0.3f, 0.3f };

glLightfv( GL_LIGHT0, GL_POSITION, pos );
glLightfv( GL_LIGHT0, GL_AMBIENT , dim_white );
glLightfv( GL_LIGHT0, GL_DIFFUSE , white );
glLightfv( GL_LIGHT0, GL_SPECULAR, white );
glEnable( GL_LIGHT0 );
```

The first parameter of glLightfv() selects which light is being set up. This parameter can be GL_LIGHT0, GL_LIGHT1, and so on up to GL_LIGHT7. Alternatively, you can index the light sources using references such as GL_LIGHT0+1, GL_LIGHT0+2, and so on. The second parameter specifies which attribute of the light source is being set up. Setting the ambient, diffuse, and specular colors is easy; in the real world, these are usually identical colors, with the ambient color being about 30 percent of the brightness of the other components. The glEnable() call turns the light source on; glDisable() turns it off. This is quite convenient: You can preset all your lights and switch them on and off at will with a single call.

Setting up the position of the light is a little trickier because the GL_POSITION parameter is transformed by the ModelView matrix—in the same way as a vertex of your model. Establishing the position of the light source can become confusing. If you set up the light position before setting up the camera's position, it'll look like the light source is moving around with the camera. If you want the light source to stay fixed with respect to your world, you'll have to set up the position of the light source after you set up the camera matrix. If you want the light to move around like a car headlight, you'll have to transform the position of the light source using the same matrix as the car.

SETTING UP SURFACE NORMALS

The final part of getting lighting to work is to set up the surface normals for each of the surfaces. To compute the amount of diffuse and specular light reflected into the camera from the light source, OpenGL needs to know the angle of the polygon to the light and to your eye. You might think it could compute that from the vertex information you've already given it, but doing so produces very facetted-looking models. When you build a sphere, for example, you'd be approximating the angles of reflection with triangles that are dead flat. A sphere made from flat surfaces doesn't look very smooth.

The solution for that is to provide OpenGL with the orientation of the true surface (the sphere in this case) at every vertex. OpenGL then computes the amount of light falling at each vertex, does the lighting math, and then blends the light over the polygon. If we set up the right orientations, the sphere will look perfectly smooth.

The representation OpenGL uses for the orientation of the surface is a surface normal. This is a vector that is 1 unit long at right angles to the surface.

Even though we want our tetrahedron to look facetted, we still have to calculate the surface normals. Here is a function that can compute the normal of a triangle using its three vertices as input:

```
void makeNormal(float *dst, float *a, float *b, float *c )
{
    float ab[3], ac[3], len;
    ab[0] = b[0] - a[0]; ab[1] = b[1] - a[1]; ab[2] = b[2] - a[2];
    ac[0] = c[0] - a[0]; ac[1] = c[1] - a[1]; ac[2] = c[2] - a[2];

    dst[0] = ab[1] * ac[2] - ab[2] * ac[1];
    dst[1] = ab[2] * ac[0] - ab[0] * ac[2];
    dst[2] = ab[0] * ac[1] - ab[1] * ac[0];

    len =(float) sqrt((double)( dst[0]*dst[0] +
                                dst[1]*dst[1] +
                                dst[2]*dst[2] ) );

    dst[0] /= len;
    dst[1] /= len;
    dst[2] /= len;
}
```

If you need the surface normal of a quadrilateral or a general polygon, you can pick any three of its vertices as long as they don't all lie in a straight line.

Generally, you should precompute the surface normals during program initialization (or load them with your model from disk). However, there will be times when you have to compute them on-the-fly.

Running the makeNormal() function on the four triangles in our sample program yields four surface normals. We can pass these values on to OpenGL using the glNormal3f() function. With the addition of these commands, we now have the following code to set up the surfaces of the tetrahedron:

```
        glBegin( GL_TRIANGLES );       /* Start describing triangles */

        glNormal3f( 0.000000,-0.707107, 0.707107);
        glColor3f( 1.0f, 0.0f, 0.0f );      /* Red */
        glVertex3f( 0.0f, 0.0f, 0.0f );     /* First triangle */
        glVertex3f( -1.0f, -1.0f, -1.0f );
        glVertex3f( 1.0f, -1.0f, -1.0f );
```

```
glNormal3f( 0.816497, 0.408248, 0.408248);
glColor3f( 0.0f, 1.0f, 0.0f );    /* Green */
glVertex3f( 0.0f, 0.0f, 0.0f );   /* Second triangle */
glVertex3f( 1.0f, -1.0f, -1.0f );
glVertex3f( 0.0f, 1.0f, -1.0f );

glNormal3f( -0.816497, 0.408248, 0.408248);
glColor3f( 0.0f, 0.0f, 1.0f );    /* Blue */
glVertex3f( 0.0f, 0.0f, 0.0f );   /* Third triangle */
glVertex3f( 0.0f, 1.0f, -1.0f );
glVertex3f( -1.0f, -1.0f, -1.0f );

glNormal3f( 0.000000, 0.000000, -1.000000);
glColor3f ( 1.0f, 1.0f, 0.0f );   /* Yellow */
glVertex3f( -1.0f, -1.0f, -1.0f );   /* Fourth triangle */
glVertex3f( 0.0f, 1.0f, -1.0f );
glVertex3f( 1.0f, -1.0f, -1.0f );

glEnd();                /* All done - let the drawing commence. */
```

All of this is rolled into the file `ex5.c` on the CD-ROM that accompanies this book. Notice now that the tetrahedron changes color as it spins and presents different faces to the incoming sunlight. You can experiment with changing the colors of the light—moving it around, adding more lights, and so on. If you move the light source positioning command down below the object's `glRotate()` command, you'll see that the light source seems to move around with the model so that the tetrahedron no longer changes color as it rotates.

TEXTURING THE MODEL

The ability to apply textures to an OpenGL model is a tremendously powerful feature. You can use this ability to make surfaces more interesting by putting brick textures on walls, grass textures on hills, and so on. But texture can do much more than this simple patterning; you can turn a simple cube into a visually complex building simply by texturing photographs of a real building onto polygons.

The images you use for texturing are commonly called *texture maps*, or just *maps* for short.

Here are the steps involved in applying a texture to a polygon:

1. Load an image.
2. MIP map it and set texture parameters.
3. Apply the texture.
4. Select the texture coordinates for each vertex.

Each texture has a unique handle number that you use to refer to the texture you want to load next or to apply to a polygon. OpenGL allows you to choose your own texture handles; any non-zero 32-bit number is legal. However, it's more friendly to generate texture handle numbers using OpenGL's `glGenTextures()` function. That way, if you are using third-party library software or writing software in a large team, you can be assured that your texture handles are unique across the entire program.

> **NOTE**
>
> MIP mapping is a technique where you use different resolution images for the texture depending on how far away it is from the camera.

```
unsigned int handle;

glGenTextures( 1, &handle );
```

When you have a handle number, you can bind that number (that is, make it refer to) the current texture at any time with the following call:

```
glBindTexture( GL_TEXTURE_2D, handle );
```

After you have bound the texture to a handle, you can load an image into the texture or use it to texture a polygon. To unbind a texture from its handle, just bind the texture to the special handle 0:

```
glBindTexture( GL_TEXTURE_2D, 0 );
```

When you are finished with a texture, you can delete it again:

```
glDeleteTextures( 1, &handle );
```

LOADING THE TEXTURE IMAGE

When you have generated a handle number and bound it to a texture, you can load images into that texture using any of the standard Linux image libraries (libpng is especially suitable, but libjpg and others also work). The format of the image on disk is of no concern to OpenGL (although you are well-advised to pick a format that supports full 24-bit RGB and preferably an alpha plane so that you can have texture maps with transparent parts). In the interests of making a simple example program, I'll define a simple 2×2 pixel texture in memory as a constant array so that we won't have to get into file I/O at this stage:

```
unsigned char texture [ 16 ] =
{
    0xFF, 0x00, 0x00, 0xFF,    0xFF, 0xFF, 0xFF, 0xFF,
    0xFF, 0xFF, 0xFF, 0xFF,    0xFF, 0x00, 0x00, 0xFF
};
```

I've set up this texture map with four bytes for each pixel and have packed in the colors as red/green/blue/alpha at one byte each. This array defines a simple red-and-white checkerboard with all the alpha components set to 0xFF, which means that the colors are opaque.

Most practical texture maps are much larger—256×256 is a commonly used size, and some cards allow 2K×2K maps! It becomes quite confusing to talk about pixels on the screen and pixels in the textures, so 3D graphics programmers generally refer to texture pixels as *texels*.

There are some restrictions on the size and shape of texture maps in OpenGL: They have to be square or rectangular, with both dimensions being exact powers of 2 (1, 2, 4, 8, 16, and so on). On PC-based hardware, you can be confident that map sizes up to 256×256 will be supported, but some early hardware can't cope with maps larger than that. Assuming that the texture is loaded into main memory, we next have to perform a process known as *MIP mapping*.

MIP Mapping the Image

If you simply wallpapered a texture onto a polygon, when that polygon moved off into the distance, it would eventually get so small that the wallpaper map would also have shrunk to appear at the correct size. If OpenGL shrunk the map by simply dropping out texels, the textured image would look terrible. What's really needed is to average the texels that contribute color to each screen pixel. However, that can get computationally expensive if, for example, a complete 2K×2K map had to fit into a single screen pixel—the machine would have to add up four million numbers just to draw that single pixel!

To avoid that, OpenGL uses a clever technique called *MIP mapping*. MIP is an acronym for the Latin phrase *multim in parvo*, which can be paraphrased as "a lot in a little space." The idea is to pre-compute not just the original texture map but also maps that are half sized, quarter sized, and so on, all the way down to a 1×1 map. This pre-calculation means that whenever the hardware needs a map that's a lot smaller than the one it is currently using, it has one nearby that's roughly the right size.

It's perfectly possibly to compute or load your own MIP maps, but generally, it's handy to use the function gluBuild2DMIPMaps() to do the work:

```
gluBuild2DMIPMaps(GL_TEXTURE_2D,GL_RGBA,width,height,
                               GL_RGBA,GL_UNSIGNED_BYTE,texture);
```

Finally, you need to tell OpenGL what options you want to set for the rendering of the texture when it's magnified or shrunk ("minified" in OpenGL parlance):

```
glTexParameteri( GL_TEXTURE_2D, GL_TEXTURE_MIN_FILTER,
                            GL_LINEAR_MIPMAP_LINEAR );
```

To magnify the texture map, you have two choices:

```
glTexParameteri( GL_TEXTURE_2D, GL_TEXTURE_MAG_FILTER, GL_LINEAR );
glTexParameteri( GL_TEXTURE_2D, GL_TEXTURE_MAG_FILTER, GL_NEAREST );
```

The first of these commands causes OpenGL to blend for a smooth transition. It's great for natural objects and produces a generally nicer image quality when the texture isn't magnified to a huge degree. However, when you want to see the texels as hard-edged squares, that's what the GL_NEAREST version produces.

You can loop through this process to load and install your textures, each with its own handle, during program startup. Then you're ready to apply texture to your models.

> **NOTE**
>
> There are other options you can use with the glTexParameteri() function that might be appropriate for older graphics cards if you want to trade quality for speed. For more details, check the OpenGL FAQ at **http://www.opengl.org**.

APPLYING THE TEXTURE

One issue with applying the defined texture to your objects is that the glBindTexture() call cannot be made between calls to glBegin() and glEnd(). This rule means that all the things you draw between those two commands must use the same texture map.

Another issue is to decide how the texture should be oriented on each face of your object. OpenGL provides another of those per-vertex calls—similar to glNormal() and glColor()—that sets the current texture coordinate. After a texture map has been loaded, OpenGL considers it to have coordinates that run from 0 to 1, with the origin in the bottom-left corner. Because we are already using the letters X and Y to refer to the vertex coordinates, OpenGL uses S and T to refer to the horizontal and vertical axis names for the texture map. Some graphics programmers use U and V for the same reason (something to be aware of when discussing this topic on mailing lists and such).

Each vertex of a polygon can have a separate texture coordinate, and OpenGL interpolates between those coordinates to find the texture coordinate of each screen pixel—and therefore which texel is drawn at that pixel. This arrangement gives you a lot of power: You can stretch, squash, shear, rotate, or translate the texture in any combination before gluing it onto the model. Even more powerful than that, you do not have to restrict yourself to texture coordinates in the range 0..1. If you use coordinates outside that range, OpenGL can do one of two things: It can clamp the coordinate to the range 0..1, or it can wrap the coordinate (by taking it modulo 1.0). In the first case, the map's edge texels are repeated if you map areas outside 0..1 onto the polygon. In the second case, the map repeats itself as often as necessary to cover the polygon. You can even make the map repeat in one direction and clamp in the other.

For the S direction, you can set the treatment of the texture map to either clamp or repeat with a call to one of the following functions:

```
glTexParameteri( GL_TEXTURE_2D, GL_TEXTURE_WRAP_S, GL_CLAMP );
glTexParameteri( GL_TEXTURE_2D, GL_TEXTURE_WRAP_S, GL_REPEAT);
```

For the T direction, use the GL_TEXTURE_WRAP_T option to repeat or clamp the texture map.

When rendering textured polygons, you have to remember to turn on the texturing feature for the object:

```
glEnable( GL_TEXTURE_2D );
```

Don't forget to turn off the texturing for the object before drawing untextured polygons!

Now that the texture has been assigned to the surface, we need to specify the coordinates of the texture relative to each point on the surface. Texture coordinates are set for each vertex using:

```
glTexCoord2f( S_coord, T_coord );
```

Let's add our texturing knowledge to our evolving tetrahedron program. Take a look at the ex6.c file on the CD-ROM at the back of this book. When you run this program, you'll notice that the colors in the texture are not directly presented because they are modified by the color of the underlying polygons. Therefore, texture maps are generally applied to white polygons. To fix that little blip in the sample program, delete all the glColor() commands and add a single new one at any point before the polygon vertices are applied:

```
glColor3f( 1.0f, 1.0f, 1.0f );
```

TRANSPARENCY AND THE ALPHA COMPONENT

We have been talking about alpha components in glColor() and glMaterial() and inside texture maps, but by default, the alpha component doesn't do anything. Transparency, like most OpenGL effects, is disabled by default. To enable the alpha channel and permit transparencies to invade your images, make calls to the following functions:

> **NOTE**
>
> You may be wondering why many of these texture functions use GL_TEXTURE_2D as a parameter. This is because OpenGL can also apply 1D textures (a single row of texels that repeat indefinitely to either side) and 3D textures (in which a 3D volume of texels is stored and a polygon is rendered as a slice through that volume). Although 3D textures are wonderful, many OpenGL cards do not support 3D textures in hardware. And because 3D textures consume the limited texture memory at a voracious rate, they are not yet generally used.

```
glEnable( GL_BLEND );
glBlendFunc( GL_SRC_ALPHA, GL_ONE_MINUS_SRC_ALPHA );
```

When you add these statements to the sample program and then change one of the texels in the texture map to have an alpha value of 0, you'll see that small square holes have been punched through the polygons. This is great because you can use alpha-textures to make complicated irregular shapes like trees without having to draw thousands of polygons. All you need to do is take a photograph of a tree and, using a program like The GIMP, remove the parts of the photo that are not a part of the tree.

Now, with a single textured polygon, you have a complete tree. If you let the texture map repeat, you'd have a whole row of trees. Of course, if the camera is allowed to see them edge-on, you'll see that they are just cardboard cut-out trees, but there are situations in which that isn't a problem.

You can also change one or more of the `glColor3f()` commands into a `glColor4f()` command and add a fourth alpha component. Notice that you can set the alpha of just one corner of a triangle to 0 to make the triangle gradually fade out to nothing.

SOLVING TRANSPARENCY PROBLEMS

Transparency using alpha has one truly major problem, though. The standard depth buffer hidden surface algorithm fails to work as you'd hope for transparent surfaces. The problem is that even if a pixel is rendered with an alpha of 0, it still sets the Z value for that pixel. That means that even though the pixel is transparent, it prevents you from seeing things behind it, unless those objects were drawn beforehand.

This leads to one partial solution to the problem. If you always draw translucent polygons *after* the opaque ones, the transparent top polygons won't incorrectly occlude the solid "background" images. However, you can still run into problems if translucent polygons are drawn behind one another. Ultimately, the only solution is to sort your translucent polygons as a function of range from the eye and render them in order from farthest to nearest. This is quite hard to do, and for many 3D games it isn't necessary because there are very few partially transparent polygons (or texels). The best solution is a trick that solves the problem for utterly transparent parts of polygons (such as our cardboard cutout trees):

```
glEnable( GL_ALPHA_TEST );
glAlphaFunc( GL_GREATER, 0.01f );
```

These statements tell OpenGL to render only those pixels whose alpha component is greater than 0.01. (We don't choose 0.0 because roundoff error can creep into the calculations inside OpenGL.) These commands prevent utterly transparent pixels from writing to the depth buffer, which solves a *lot* of problems.

The alpha test code is incorporated into the `ex7.c` file on the CD-ROM at the back of this book.

FOGGING

OpenGL incorporates a very simple model to account for the scattering and absorption of light by our atmosphere. You can use it to produce the effect of a dense fog or some more subtle haze. By using a colored fog, you can create effects such as the change in color of far-distant mountains compared to nearby grassy slopes.

Adding fog to a program is fairly simple, although you'll need to tweak the color and density of the fog to achieve the effect you need. Choosing a fogging value is rarely a cut-and-dried computation; it's hardly ever possible to be sure of a good number to type in.

```
glEnable( GL_FOG );
glFogf( GL_FOG_DENSITY, 0.2f );
glFogfv( GL_FOG_COLOR, white );
```

This code can go anywhere at the start of the redisplay routine or even somewhere in the initialization code if you don't plan to change the amount of fog as the game progresses.

As you can see, there is a call to set the density of the fog and another to set the color (white in this case). However, if you do nothing else to this code when you add it to the sample program, it won't look right. The problem is that OpenGL doesn't apply fogging to the clear-screen color. If you add this code as-is, you'll have a foggy model shown starkly against a dark-green screen. The fix for that is to change the clear-screen color to equal the fog color.

With this fix, we've arrived at the final example for this chapter: file ex8.c on the CD-ROM. This version of the tetrahedron program shows off the fogging effect.

I've added a glTranslate() command to move the model toward the eye so that it appears to be moving toward you, gradually out of the mist.

By default, fog is computed as an exponential function (which happens to be mathematically how fog works in the real world). However, there are times when you want the fog to become opaque more or less rapidly as a function of range to the object. For those situations, OpenGL supports these three options:

```
glFogi( GL_FOG_MODE, GL_LINEAR );
glFogi( GL_FOG_MODE, GL_EXP );
glFogi( GL_FOG_MODE, GL_EXP2 );
```

Experiment with these functions as well as with the basic glFogf(GL_FOG_DENSITY, 0.2f) call; it's largely a matter of taste which one you use.

You can have fun with colored fog for underwater effects and to blend objects into the sky as a function of range if you don't want to spend the time drawing objects all the way out to the horizon.

CHAPTER 7

USING OPENGL IN GAMES

In the preceding chapter, we covered the basic set of OpenGL features that every 3D game will use. In this chapter, we'll dip into a group of topics that build on that basic knowledge and hopefully get you to the point where you'll be able to start writing your masterwork.

UNDERSTANDING DISPLAY LISTS

OpenGL provides a feature that lets you record long sequences of commands into an object called a *display list*. A display list has a handle (rather like a texture handle, described in Chapter 6); you can replay the commands in a list with a single function call.

First, create a handle for your display list using the following command:

```
unsigned int handle ; handle = glGenLists ( 1 ) ;
```

The parameter to glGenLists() is the number of consecutive handle numbers you want to generate.

Now, you can record something into the list by using the following sequence:

```
glNewList ( handle, GL_COMPILE ) ;
   /* Some sequence of OpenGL commands */
glEndList () ;
```

Whatever OpenGL commands are issued between glNewList() and glEndList() are recorded into the specified display list instead of being executed. You can then replay those commands at any time in the future by "calling" the display list:

```
glCallList ( handle ) ;
```

Most graphics cards can execute commands from a display list faster than if you issued them normally. That's because the OpenGL driver can do some calculations associated with the command at the time when the display list is created and thus save time when the list is eventually called.

Think of display lists as being a little like subroutines in a programming language with the exception that display lists can be changed and re-created on-the-fly. You can even call one display list from within another list simply by issuing the glCallList () command while you're recording another list.

You can change the contents of a list by simply recording over the top of it again. You can delete the list to free up memory using this command:

```
glDeleteLists(handle, n)
```

In this syntax, n is the number of consecutive handle numbers you want to delete (typically, this value is 1).

UNDERSTANDING VERTEX ARRAYS

In Chapter 6, we talked about drawing lists of vertices (along with their color, normal, and texture coordinate data) using glBegin() and glEnd() sequences. This is the classical way to send vertex data to OpenGL, but more recent versions of the API (such as those available under Linux) have vertex arrays that allow you to place all your vertex information into one or more arrays and render them all with one convenient call. If you examine the code for ex1.c on the CD-ROM that accompanies this book, you'll notice that it contains five pre-initialized arrays:

```
#define NUM_VERTS (3*4) /* Four triangles - three vertices each */
float normals [ 3 * NUM_VERTS ] ;
float colors [ 3 * NUM_VERTS ] ;
float texcoords [ 2 * NUM_VERTS ] ;
float vertices [ 3 * NUM_VERTS ] ;
unsigned short indices [ NUM_VERTS ] ;
```

The first four arrays contain the raw data for colors, normals, texture coordinates, and 3D coordinates. The last array (in this example) just contains the numbers 0 through 11 in order.

Next, it's necessary to tell OpenGL that the various data items used for drawing are driven by vertex arrays. Generally, programs set up this feature just once during initialization:

```
glEnableClientState ( GL_NORMAL_ARRAY ) ;
glEnableClientState ( GL_COLOR_ARRAY ) ;
glEnableClientState ( GL_TEXTURE_COORD_ARRAY ) ;
glEnableClientState ( GL_VERTEX_ARRAY ) ;
```

The next step is to tell OpenGL where to find these arrays:

```
glColorPointer ( 3, GL_FLOAT, 0, colors ) ;
glTexCoordPointer ( 2, GL_FLOAT, 0, texcoords ) ;
glNormalPointer ( GL_FLOAT, 0, normals ) ;
glVertexPointer ( 3, GL_FLOAT, 0, vertices ) ;
```

The first argument in these function calls is the number of parameters for each vertex (except in the case of glNormalPointer(), for which you can have only three arguments for each glNormal3f() command); the second argument tells OpenGL what C-type the array elements are, such as floating-point numbers or integers; the next argument (the 0 in all four of these functions) specifies that the arrays are tightly packed with no gaps between consecutive vertices; the last argument is the actual address of the array.

Having set up all these arrays and pointers, we can draw our object with just one OpenGL call:

```
glDrawElements ( GL_TRIANGLES, NUM_VERTS, GL_UNSIGNED_SHORT, indices ) ;
```

The first argument is whatever value you'd have given to glBegin(). The second argument is the number of vertices to draw. The third parameter is the C-type of the array you are passing as the fourth argument.

That final argument (the indices array) allows you to decide the order in which the vertices in the array will be drawn. In the general case, you'll find that you can reduce the size of your data arrays (and perhaps speed up rendering) by reusing the same vertex data more than once in a single glDrawElements() call.

This feature also allows you to use enormous data arrays—perhaps containing every vertex in an entire game level. If you take this approach, you'll only need an index array and a call to glDrawElements() for each object, saving you the cost of all those gl*Pointer calls.

Another aspect of vertex arrays that some people find useful is that the glVertexPointer(), glColorPointer(), glNormalPointer(), and glTexCoordPointer() routines have a "stride" parameter (which in the previous example was set to 0). This parameter makes it possible to interleave the vertex, color, normal, and texture coordinate data for a single vertex into consecutive memory locations, which is convenient for some applications.

DRAWING WITH TRIANGLE STRIPS AND FANS

Until now, our simple program example has been drawn using GL_TRIANGLES, which draws one triangle for every three vertices you send to OpenGL. This is rarely the most efficient thing to do: The problem is that a real tetrahedron has only four vertices, yet we are sending 12 vertices to OpenGL for each frame. In this example, all 12 vertices turn out to be necessary because we don't want all three triangles that meet at a vertex to be the same color or to have the same surface normal or texture coordinate.

However, if you were drawing something like a globe (a sphere textured with a map of the earth), at every vertex of the triangles that approximate that sphere, you'd want the same surface normal, the same color, and the same texture coordinate. In the case of a densely tessellated sphere, you may have six triangles meeting at each vertex, which means that, by using GL_TRIANGLES, you'd be sending each vertex to OpenGL six times!

A better approach is to use triangle strips or triangle fans. In both cases, you send three vertices to describe the first triangle, but each subsequent triangle is connected to the first along a shared edge. In the case of a triangle strip, you send vertices A, B, and C (which forms the first triangle). When you send vertex D, OpenGL draws a triangle between the last three points you sent—and so connects points B, C, and D. If you add a fifth point, you'll get a third triangle formed by points C, D, and E, and so on. With triangle fans, OpenGL remembers the first point you sent and uses the two most recent ones to form each triangle. Hence, sending vertices A, B, C, D, and E creates three triangles: A, B, C; A, C, D; and A, D, E.

If your strips or fans contain enough triangles, using this approach, you can get down to an average of just over one vertex per triangle—a lot more efficient than the three vertices per triangle you have to specify with GL_TRIANGLES.

Although OpenGL also provides GL_QUADS and GL_QUADSTRIP, most OpenGL implementations are heavily optimized for GL_TRIANGLE_STRIP and GL_TRIANGLE_FAN. You would do well to have your software use those two elements as its main geometric primitive in addition to GL_LINES and GL_POINTS.

ADDING TEXT

Eventually, you'll want your game to include onscreen help instructions, credits, high-score tables, and such. If you are using GLUT, and if you don't need to do smooth motion while the text is onscreen, you can use the following command:

```
glutBitmapCharacter(font,character);
```

In this syntax, font is one of the following values:

Value	Meaning
GLUT_BITMAP_9_BY_15	Bitmapped 9x15
GLUT_BITMAP_8_BY_13	Bitmapped 8x13
GLUT_BITMAP_TIMES_ROMAN_10	10-point Times Roman font
GLUT_BITMAP_TIMES_ROMAN_24	24-point Times Roman font
GLUT_BITMAP_HELVETICA_10	10-point Helvetica font
GLUT_BITMAP_HELVETICA_12	12-point Helvetica font
GLUT_BITMAP_HELVETICA_18	18-point Helvetica font

The character parameter can be any regular ASCII character. You choose a color for the text and position it like this:

```
glColor3f ( 1, 0, 1 ) ;
glRasterPos2f ( 100, 150 ) ;
while ( *s != '\0' )
{
     glutBitmapCharacter ( GLUT_BITMAP_9_BY_15, *s++ ) ;
}
```

Make sure that you have the Projection matrix set up in orthographic mode.

The GLUT text-rendering routines are handy, but they are quite slow on hardware OpenGL accelerators, and the limited range of fonts can get boring. GLUT fonts are also displayed at a constant size (in pixels), so they can be rather tiny on modern high-resolution displays. A better approach is to draw each letter as a separate texture-mapped quadrilateral. That way, you can paint any font you like into the texture and scale or rotate the characters using the usual glScale() and glRotate() commands.

> ## CAUTION
>
> Don't put each character into a separate texture map. The time consumed in switching from one texture map to another (between one character and the next) will kill your performance. Instead, put all your characters into a single large map and use the glTexCoord2f() command to tell OpenGL which part of the texture map to use for each character.

UNDERSTANDING MATRICES

At first sight, matrices are hard to understand. Even people who know all the rules for using matrices don't always know what all the numbers inside the matrix really mean.

The 16-element array that OpenGL uses to represent matrices is easy to decode (at least for the majority of matrices that represent a rotation, a translation, or a combination of the two).

The way to imagine what the matrix does is to think about a little cube with one corner at the origin and aligned to the positive X, Y, and Z axes. Assume that the little cube is one unit across in each direction. Now let's label some vertices: The vertex that is touching the origin we'll call O; the vertices that are at (1,0,0), (0,1,0), and (0,0,1) we'll call X, Y, and Z respectively.

What happens to this cube when it's transformed by a matrix? Well, the corner of the cube that was at the origin (O) ends up at the coordinate defined by the right-hand column of the matrix (array elements 12, 13, and 14 in the OpenGL array).

The first three columns of the matrix tell you where (relative to that first corner of the cube) the rest of the object will be. The first column (array elements 0, 1, and 2) tells you where X is relative to O. The second column (array elements 4, 5, and 6) tells you where Y is relative to O. The third column (array elements 8, 9, and 10) is the coordinate of Z relative to O.

Pictorially, OpenGL array indices are laid out like this:

```
0 4 8 12
1 5 9 13
2 6 10 14
3 7 11 15
```

The functions of these indices look like this:

```
Xdx Ydx Zdx Ox
Xdy Ydy Zdy Oy
Xdz Ydz Zdz Oz
0   0   0   1
```

The original points of the cube—O, X, Y, and Z—undergo these transformations:

```
O    (0,0,0) -> (Ox,Oy,Oz)
X    (1,0,0) -> (Ox+Xdx,Oy+Xdy,Oz+Xdz)
Y    (0,1,0) -> (Ox+Ydx,Oy+Ydy,Oz+Ydz)
Z    (0,0,1) -> (Ox+Zdx,Oy+Zdy,Oz+Zdz)
```

It's pretty easy to see how to map any point to its destination after it has been transformed by the matrix:

```
P (p,q,r) -> (Ox+p*Xdx+q*Ydx+r*Zdx,
    Oy+p*Xdy+q*Ydy+r*Zdy,
    Oz+p*Xdz+q*Ydz+r*Zdz)
```

In essence, the columns of the matrix define a new coordinate system into which objects are drawn. Understanding how that matrix is put together is key to understanding transformations in OpenGL.

I'm sure that you noticed that we have talked about only the first three elements of each column of the matrix. The bottom element of each row isn't relevant to simple rotate/translate matrices, so these matrices are always set so that elements 3, 7, and 11 are 0 and element 15 is 1.

An interesting consequence of understanding what the various rows of the matrix contain is that you can make up matrices that OpenGL cannot directly generate with the API. For example, you can make a "shear" matrix by having the first and second columns of the matrix represent vectors that are not perpendicular. Apply one of these matrices using `glLoadMatrix()` or `glMultMatrix()`, and all your squares will come out in a diamond shape.

WORKING WITH PLANE EQUATIONS, LINE EQUATIONS, AND DISTANCES IN 3D

If you intend to get seriously into 3D graphics, it's unavoidable that you'll need a certain amount of mathematics. I'll explain some of the most important equations and algorithms here, but realize that there are always more equations to learn.

One useful concept, the *surface normal*, was explained in Chapter 6—along with a function you can use to compute the surface normal from the three vertices of a triangle. The normal is a 3D vector that is one unit long and points in a direction at right angles to the plane of the polygon. All polygons that are parallel to one another have the same surface normal. A useful extension of this concept is the *plane equation*, which is a set of four numbers that describe an infinite plane in 3D. It's composed of the surface normal (three numbers) and the distance from the plane to the origin at the closest point. These four numbers are called A, B, C, and D (where A, B, and C are the surface normal vector and D is the distance to the origin). These values obey this relationship for every (x,y,z) that lies on the plane:

```
A * x + B * y + C * z + D == 0
```

Hence, if you know the surface normal of a triangle (by using the algorithm in Chapter 6), you can find D by substituting one of the triangle's vertices into the plane equation:

```
D = - ( A * x + B * y + C * z )
```

When you compute it like this, D is a signed quantity that is positive if the origin is on one side of the plane and negative if it lies on the other. That's a useful fact and leads to this equation:

```
d = A * x' + B * y' + C * z' + D
```

Where (x',y',z') is any point in space and D is the signed distance to that point from the plane. Now, armed with the plane equation, you can easily compute whether some other point lies on the plane, behind the plane, or in front of the plane—and by how much (using OpenGL's counterclockwise convention discussed in Chapter 6).

Just as there are plane equations, so there are also equations that describe lines in 3D. These equations are generally in parametric form:

```
x = e * t + x1 y = f * t + y1 z = g * t + z1
```

Where E,F,G is a vector (one unit in length) describing the direction along the line, (x1,y1,z1) is one point on the line, (x,y,z) is another point on the line, and t is the distance between the two points. The sign of the equation depends on which side of (x1,y1,z1) the point (x,y,z) is.

If you know two points that lie on a line, you can work out the distance between them and reverse the equations above to compute (e,f,g).

Another important thing is to be able to measure distances in 3D. The distance between two points is calculated in 3D using the Pythagorean theorem (just as it is in 2D):

```
dx = x1 - x2 ;
dy = y1 - y2 ;
dz = z1 - z2 ;
dist = sqrt ( dx * dx + dy * dy + dz * dz ) ;
```

Two other operations are commonly found. Mathematicians call them by the names *dot-product* and *cross-product* (which are typically uninformative names). The *dot-product* operation is between two length-one vectors that produces the cosine of the angle between them:

```
dot_product = x1 * x2 + y1 * y2 * z1 * z2
```

In this syntax, (x1,y1,z1) and (x2,y2,z2) are both vectors of length 1.0.

The *cross-product* of two unit vectors is another vector that's at right angles to the first two. We already used a cross-product operation to calculate the surface normal of a triangle:

```
cross_x = y1 * z2 - z1 * y2 ;
cross_y = z1 * x2 - x1 * z2 ;
cross_z = x1 * y2 - y1 * x2 ;
```

Many of these algorithms need so-called *unit vectors*—that is, vectors whose length is 1. The act of taking an arbitrary vector and changing its length to 1.0 without altering its direction is called *normalizing*. All you have to do to normalize a vector is to divide the three components of the vector by the length of the vector:

```
float length = sqrt ( x * x + y * y + z * z ) ;
float one_over_length = 1.0f / length ;
x *= one_over_length ;
y *= one_over_length ;
z *= one_over_length ;
```

Now you know the most common 3D mathematical operations; almost all 3D algorithms use these operations in various combinations.

USING BILLBOARDS TO SIMULATE 3D

In many games, you need to draw very complex objects such as trees that, to represent accurately in 3D, would require thousands or even millions of polygons. (Did you know that a typical European Oak tree has more than a half-million leaves?) Even with the wonders of modern 3D graphics hardware, it would be a while before you could draw even a single mature tree as a true 3D object.

The usual graphical trick to get around this is to paint a 2D picture (or photograph) of a tree into a texture map and set the parts of the map that are not part of the tree to be fully transparent. This single texture map can then be applied to a single polygon—and as long as you don't look too closely, you'll see a tree!

The snag is that it's really only a cardboard cutout of a tree: If you walk around it, the 2D nature of the tree will be obvious. Therefore, we have to rotate the tree to face the camera, so that no matter where you stand, you see the same picture of a tree.

You can do this by calculating the position of the tree and the position of the camera and applying a glRotate() command, but there is an easier way. Because OpenGL keeps the camera at (0,0,0), all you really have to do to keep something facing the camera is to model it in the X,Y plane and avoid rotating the model at all.

That's easier said than done because by the time we get to render the tree, we'll have the OpenGL matrix stack piled high with transformations that deal with the position of the camera relative to the world and so on. One way to deal with that is to ask OpenGL what the current rotation matrix is and then erase the rotation part of that matrix when we render the tree:

```
float matrix [ 16 ] ;

glPushMatrix () ;
glGetFloatv ( GL_MODELVIEW_MATRIX, matrix ) ;

matrix[ 0 ] =matrix [ 5 ] = matrix[ 10 ] = matrix[ 11 ] = 1.0f ;
matrix[ 1 ] = matrix[ 2 ] = matrix[ 3 ] = matrix  4 ] = 0.0f;
matrix[6] = matrix[7] = matrix[8] = matrix[9] = matrix[11] = 0.0f ;

 /* Elements 12, 13, 14 are the translate component of the matrix - leave those
alone! */
glLoadMatrixf ( matrix ) ;

/* Draw billboard polygons */
glPopMatrix () ;
```

However, this isn't quite the right thing. The preceding code rotates the tree's billboard so that the billboard exactly parallels the screen—which is fine for a cloud or a beach ball, but you don't want a tree to lean backward if your virtual camera happens to be high above the tree. You really only want the tree's billboard to rotate around the vertical axis.

To do this, we need to look at where the Y axis of the model ends up because that's not changed by the billboarding process. If we know that, then we know that the X axis should be at right angles to it—as well as at right angles to the Z axis. That is what a cross-product can do for you.

NOTE

You may want to have another surface perpendicular to the main billboard if you ever have the situation where you view the object from above.

The last step is to figure out where the new Z axis should go, which should always be at right angles to the other two axes. This location is something that a second cross-product can achieve:

```
float x_axis [ 3 ] ;
float y_axis [ 3 ] ;
float z_axis [ 3 ] ;
float matrix [ 16 ] ;

glPushMatrix () ;

glGetFloatv ( GL_MODELVIEW_MATRIX, matrix ) ;
```

```
z_axis [ 0 ] = 0.0f ;
z_axis [ 1 ] = 0.0f ;
z_axis [ 2 ] = -1.0f ;
y_axis [ 0 ] = matrix[4] ;
y_axis [ 1 ] = matrix[5] ;
y_axis [ 2 ] = matrix[6] ;

VectorProduct ( x_axis, z_axis, y_axis ) ;
VectorProduct ( z_axis, y_axis, x_axis ) ;
Normalize ( x_axis ) ; Normalize ( z_axis ) ;

/* Now we know where we want the three axes to end up, change the matrix to make
it so. */
matrix[ 0] = x_axis [0] ;
matrix[ 1] = x_axis [1] ;
matrix[ 2] = x_axis [2] ;
matrix[ 8] = z_axis [0] ;
matrix[ 9] = z_axis [1] ;
matrix[10] = z_axis [2] ;

glLoadMatrixf ( matrix ) ;

/* Draw billboard polygons */
glPopMatrix () ;
```

This example uses two functions we talked about earlier:

```
void VectorProduct ( float *dst, float *a, float *b ) {
     dst[0] = a[1] * b[2] - a[2] * b[1] ;
     dst[1] = a[2] * b[0] - a[0] * b[2] ;
     dst[2] = a[0] * b[1] - a[1] * b[0] ;
}

void Normalize ( float *v ) {
     float length = sqrt ( v[0] * v[0] + v[1] * v[1] + v[2] * v[2] ) ;
     float one_over_length = 1.0f / length ;
     v[0] *= one_over_length ;
     v[1] *= one_over_length ;
     v[2] *= one_over_length ;
}
```

WORKING WITH PARTICLES

Many graphical effects in games need fluid motion to reproduce the look of spraying water, swirling or drifting smoke, dust, little magical sparkles, and so on. These effects are generally handled by rendering small "particles" of whatever material is being simulated. By using the first version of the billboard code that causes objects to turn to face the camera, we can render each particle as a tiny texture-mapped shape (typically either a single triangle or at most a quadrilateral). After you have established the special billboard matrix on the OpenGL ModelView stack, you can rapidly render a large number of particles in a 3D volume.

The rules for moving the particles from one frame to the next can range from the very simple (gravity acting on water droplets in a fountain) to something much more complex (a full fluid-dynamics model that makes fog swirl as a character walks through it). The particle-moving basics are much the same for all these effects. Keep track of the coordinates of your particles in a large array and then zip quickly through that array: In each frame, you update the position of each particle.

You'll also want to add rules for creating new particles and destroying old ones. For a fountain, for example, you might want to delete water droplets that hit the ground and create new ones with an appropriate upward velocity at the fountain's outlet even as old droplets die.

Even systems with just a handful of golden "glow" particles that swirl in a spiral can create wonderful magical effects that can help cue the player that something special has just happened.

When a character jumps into water, you can create a handful of splash particles. If someone gets shot, a little shower of blood droplets can add greatly to the goriness of the game! If your character is running quickly and comes to a sudden stop, you can launch some tiny dust clouds from his feet and let them settle to earth.

DETECTING COLLISIONS

It's generally necessary to provide several types of 3D collision-detection sequences so that you can tell when the player walks into a wall or is hit by a weapon. In games where the player can walk or drive on uneven ground, you'll also have to detect the height and slope of the terrain beneath his feet or wheels.

These related problems are enough to completely kill your frame rates because they are mathematically complex to resolve and may require you to test often for each frame of graphics.

Imagine a case of a thin brick wall and a car driving along at high speed. It could be that the car is entirely on one side of the wall at the start of one frame—and entirely on the other side of it at the start of the next frame. In a game situation, it would be possible to drive right through a brick wall if the user is driving fast enough!

There are two solutions to that problem. One is to divide up the time span of one graphics frame into sufficiently small intervals so that the car does not move more than its own length during each interval. The other approach is to pretend that the length of the car is equal to its real length *plus* the distance it's about to travel in that frame.

To calculate whether two polygonal shapes have collided is quite tricky and very time-consuming. If you tried to test every polygon of your player's character against every polygon in the game level, you'd be doing millions or perhaps billions of calculations per frame.

SIMPLIFY THE SHAPES YOU TEST

The key to making collision detection work in real time is to simplify the shapes you test against. You should then use refined, detailed tests only if coarser, simpler tests suggest the possibility of a collision.

You can start off by imagining an invisible sphere surrounding each object in the scene and another sphere surrounding the player. It's easy to use the Pythagorean theorem in 3D to figure out the distance between the centers of two spheres. If that distance is less than the sum of the two radii, then the spheres overlap and the objects have collided. However, square roots are a costly math operation; it's cheaper to compare the square of the distance to the square of the sum of the radii. Here's a suggested series of equations your program can process to detect whether two objects are in contact:

```
struct Sphere { float x, y, z ; /* Center */
                float r ;       /* Radius */ } ;
#define sq(x) ((x)*(x)) int isOverlapping ( struct Sphere *s1, struct Sphere *s2 )
{
    float d_sqd ;
    d_sqd = sq(s1->x - s2->x) + sq(s1->y - s2->y) + sq(s1->z - s2->z) ;
    return d_sqd < sq(s1->r + s2->r) ;
}
```

If the Objects Are Close, Test Again

When you know that two objects are close enough that their bounding spheres overlap, you can look inside each object and see whether their polygons overlap. This is a *much* nastier test. First, you'll really want to test each triangle; you'll have to split the polygons into individual triangles before you start.

The steps to test a triangle against a sphere are complex:

- Compute the plane equation of the triangle. If the distance from the center of the sphere to the plane containing the triangle is greater than the radius of the sphere, they can't be touching, so we can stop the test.
- If we get this far, we know that the sphere is crossing the plane of the triangle, but we still don't know whether the sphere is a million miles away from the triangle itself. However, if we were to construct three more planes—each at right angles to the plane of the triangle, and each of which runs through one side of the triangle, facing outward—we could measure the signed distance from the center of the sphere to these three new planes. If that distance is greater than the radius of the sphere, it's a miss, and we don't need to look any further.
- Unfortunately, we still aren't there yet. There are still cases in which the sphere can overlap both the "fence" planes and the plane of the triangle and still not intersect the triangle. However, if the center of the sphere is inside the fence planes, then it's a definite hit and we need look no further.
- If the sphere penetrates the plane of the triangle and the plane of one or more of the fence planes, we can use the Pythagorean theorem to determine whether the sphere actually intersects that edge between the plane and the triangle. If the distance from the center of the sphere to the plane of the triangle (squared) plus the distance to the plane of the fence (squared) is less than the radius of the sphere (squared), then it's a hit. If this value is greater than the radius of the sphere (squared), it's a miss.

Whew! Well, if you think the effort to code all of *this* is complex, wait until you get to the next test—intersecting the actual triangles of one object against the triangles of another!

Rather than attempting to convey that in enough detail to allow you to reproduce it (which would fill several more chapters with ugly mathematics), I'll refer you to the code in my own OpenSource scenegraph library. This library contains the code for all of this nastiness and is the subject of the next section.

FOLLOW SURFACE CONTOURS

The other thing you know is how to make an object follow the contours of a surface (a vehicle driving over hilly terrain, for example). You need to find out the height of the surface along with its orientation so that you can rotate the vehicle to sit on top of it.

Using the kinds of intersection techniques described in the preceding section, you can identify the polygon in question. Then you can use the plane equation to find the Y coordinate of a point on the plane that corresponds to the X and Z coordinates of the object. That gives you the height of the polygon, which you can use with `glTranslate()` to position your vehicle at the desired height. The surface normal of the polygon—plus a little trigonometry—gives you the rotation angles.

THE NEXT LAYER: SCENE GRAPH APIS

In the preceding chapter, we took a swift gallop through the OpenGL API without too much concern for how you apply this technology to games. Now we'll take a step back and see how to apply what we've learned.

One thing that I'm sure you are thinking about is the amount of information it took to draw something as simple as a tetrahedron. Just how much would it take to draw the Enterprise and four Romulan WarBirds? The simple tetrahedron contained four triangles, with three vertices each; each vertex had a `glColor()`, `glNormal()`, `glTexCoord()`, and `glVertex()` command. That's about 36 numbers for each triangle! When you consider a game like *Quake* and see an individual monster that's drawn with a thousand or more triangles, it's readily apparent that you are not going to be typing all those vertices and commands by hand!

In practice, you'll hardly ever enter vertex data by hand. It's much more likely that you'll use a kind of specialized CAD program called a *modeler*. There are several cheap (or even free) modelers for Linux, including Blender, AC3D, PrettyPoly, and Moonlight Creator. These programs allow you to enter 3D models in a fairly natural way, without too much typing. It's interesting that all four of these programs are written using OpenGL.

Although modelers help you do the detailed work of creating the 3D models, you will still need to load those models into your program from data files on disk.

> **NOTE**
> You can find Blender and PrettyPoly on the CD accompanying this book.

OpenGL was designed without a native file format because it's focused on an efficient and flexible rendering mechanism. This means that if you want to load models from disk, you'll either have to use a library that's layered on top of OpenGL or write the code to parse the data files yourself.

There is really no single standard for storing 3D models on disk (although several formats such as VRML try to take on that mantle). Worse still, there are really no 3D model loaders that are analogous to libpng, libjpeg, and libgof for 2D images. The reason for that is that there is also no standard data structure for storing 3D models in memory after they are loaded. To store a simple 2D image, on the other hand, you need little more than a 2D array of pixel values.

I will not attempt to describe 3D file formats in detail; there are plenty of descriptions of them on the Web. Instead, I'm going to talk about using a library layered on top of OpenGL to structure the storage of models—and hence to provide a framework around which you can write standardized file loaders. Such libraries are sometimes called *game engines*, but that term covers a multitude of other functions. A more concise term is *scene graph API* because most of these libraries store the 3D scene in some type of directed graph or tree structure.

> **NOTE**
>
> A good place to find out about file formats of any type is **http://www.wotsit.org**.

FIELD-OF-VIEW CULLING

When you have the models you need stored in memory, it's tempting to just place them all in their correct positions in each frame using `glRotate()` or `glTranslate()` and let OpenGL get on with the business of drawing the models. Doing that would certainly work—providing that your game is simple enough and your computer is fast enough. But to make the best use of your machine, you'll need to help out OpenGL.

One thing you can do to help is to try not to give OpenGL things to draw that are obviously off the edge of the screen. Precisely how you do this depends on the nature of your game. You might be able to say that all the monsters that are not in the same room as the player don't have to be drawn (well, unless the doors are left open). You might also be able to discard objects that are behind you because they can't be seen. In general, anything that lies outside your field of view (FOV) is not needed and doesn't have to be drawn.

Clearly, OpenGL is itself already doing these kinds of tests, but it is forced by the nature of its API to test every single vertex of every triangle to see whether the triangle is on the screen or not. Inside *your* application, however, you can test whole objects with a simple test and toss out thousands of polygons without even looking closely at them. One way to do that is to store a bounding box or bounding sphere that tightly encloses each of the objects in your 3D scene and just test those simple shapes against the field of view. You can test a sphere against the field of view with just a handful of operations (it's even faster than testing a single triangle). This is why it makes sense to "cull" the scene to the field of view before you pass anything on to OpenGL.

Scene graph APIs often store the 3D scene in a tree structure; a bounding sphere (or cube) at every node surrounds all the polygons that are beneath that node in the tree. Thus, a space game might have a bounding sphere around each spacecraft model; that sphere would contain a number of sub-objects (the engine, the weapons, the cockpit, and so on), each of which would have its own bounding sphere. With one test, the scene graph API can toss out the entire spaceship if it's not anywhere close to being on-screen; alternatively, it can draw the spacecraft unconditionally if the entire bounding sphere is clearly on-screen. If the bounding sphere lies part inside and part outside the field of view, the API can look at each part of the spaceship in turn, accepting or rejecting each small group of polygons as it comes to it.

STATE MANAGEMENT

Another aspect of OpenGL that needs careful attention if you want the best performance is state management. As you saw in the last chapter, you can have a significant number of calls to glEnable() or glDisable()—along with glMaterial(), glBindTexture(), and other functions that have to be set up before you can draw a triangle. It's tempting to simply run through all of the things that a triangle needs, and to set them up before you do the glBegin() and glEnd() sequence. However, these so-called *state changes* take time to execute—and sometimes a relatively innocuous change can have a horrible impact on performance.

There are two things you can do about this: First, you can perform "lazy" state changes, making changes only when you absolutely have to. If two consecutive groups of polygons have the same glMaterial() and glBindTexture() needs, you can test for this and avoid repeating those calls unnecessarily. Second, you can even go so far as to sort your polygons into groups that share the same textures, material settings, and such so that they are all drawn together, requiring fewer state changes.

SCENE GRAPHS

Getting all of this together is a little complicated, but fortunately there are several OpenSource scene graph API libraries you can pick up and use or rip apart and learn from. Probably the two most popular scene graph APIs for games under Linux right now are CrystalSpace and my own PLIB/SSG. Both are pre-installed on most complete Linux distributions and can be downloaded from the Web with full source code if you prefer to get the absolute latest and greatest version. Each has a thriving newsgroup and developer community, so you'll always have someone you can ask for help.

The general style of programming a scene graph API is very different from the OpenGL approach, although most of these libraries use similar terminology and even allow you to mix raw OpenGL and higher-level constructs.

In PLIB/SSG for example, you construct your 3D scene as a collection of C++ class objects organized into a tree structure. The leaves of the tree contain polygons, lines, and points as well as pointers to structures containing the OpenGL state elements. Leaf nodes are grouped into higher-level objects (called *branch nodes*), which are grouped in turn into yet higher-level objects until, at the root of the tree, is a node that contains the entire virtual world and all the information that's needed to draw it.

From that point on, the entire scene can be efficiently drawn with a single call to the scene graph API.

For the game software to interact with this virtual world, you use various special nodes in the tree that allow objects or subobjects to be rotated or positioned within the scene. Other nodes allow you to automatically draw simpler versions of objects when they are farther away so that you can save your precious polygon-generating capacity for drawing things in more detail closer to the camera. You can also select different versions of objects under program control so that you can have things look different after they've been destroyed or after a key has been turned in a lock.

All of this flexibility allows the game programmer to concentrate on the higher-level aspects of game play, leaving it to the scene graph API to handle the ugly details of drawing the pictures.

Let's look at a simple example using the PLIB/SSG scene graph. PLIB is a suite of portable game libraries designed to work well with OpenGL; SSG is a Simple Scene Graph. Because SSG works well with GLUT and relies on OpenGL behind the scenes, much of what follows should be familiar. This example is written in C++ because PLIB/SSG is a C++ library:

```
#include <math.h>
#include <GL/gl.h>
#include <GL/glut.h>

void redisplay () ;
void init_graphics () ;

int main ( int, char ** ) {

    glutInit ( &argc, argv ) ;
    glutInitDisplayMode ( GLUT_RGB | GLUT_DOUBLE | GLUT_DEPTH ) ;
    glutInitWindowSize ( 640, 480 ) ;
    glutCreateWindow ( "My First OpenGL Program" ) ;
    glutDisplayFunc ( redisplay ) ;

    ssgInit () ;

    init_graphics () ;

    glutMainLoop () ;

    return 0 ;
}
```

The main program is quite similar to the OpenGL examples in Chapter 6. There is a new initialization routine, called ssgInit(), that sets up the SSG library.

Initializing the graphics system entails some OpenGL setup:

```
ssgRoot *scene = NULL ;
ssgTransform *transform = NULL ;

void init_graphics () {
    ssgEntity *object = ssgLoad ( "my_object.ac" ) ;

    scene = new ssgRoot ;
    transform = new ssgTransform ;

    scene -> addKid ( transform ) ;
    transform -> addKid ( object ) ;
```

```
        glClearColor ( 0.0f, 0.5f, 0.0f, 1.0f ) ;

        glEnable ( GL_DEPTH_TEST ) ;

        ssgSetFOV ( 60.0f, 40.0f ) ;
        ssgSetNearFar ( 1.0f, 700.0f ) ;
        sgVec3 pos ;
        sgSetVec3 ( pos, 0.2f, -0.5f, 0.5f ) ;

        ssgGetLight ( 0 ) -> setPosition ( pos ) ;
}
```

The ssgLoad() function loads a 3D model from a file on disk into an ssgEntity class object. The code then creates a scene into which we can insert the object. You can have any number of independent scenes—for example, one for each of the different levels in a game.

The next line creates another type of SSG object, a transform. These three objects are then connected into a tree containing parent and child nodes. First, we add the transform as a child of the whole scene; then connect the object we loaded underneath the transform.

In fact, there will be more than just these three levels in the scene graph because ssgLoad() will probably have created several dozen more objects that are connected as kids of object.

The remainder of the function sets up the usual OpenGL states: the perspective parameters (the field of view and the near and far clip planes), and one of the OpenGL light sources.

The third function is the redisplay() function, and it works just like the examples in Chapter 6:

```
void redisplay () {
        #define ROTATION_SPEED 1.0f
        static float a = 0 ;
        sgCoord campos ;
        sgCoord objpos ;

        /* Spin Tux, make the camera pan sinusoidally left and right */
        sgSetCoord ( & campos, 0.0f, -5.0f, 1.0f, 0.0f, 0.0f, 0.0f ) ;
        sgSetCoord ( & objpos, 0.0f, 0.0f, 0.0f, a, 0.0f, 0.0f ) ;
        ssgSetCamera ( & campos ) ;

        transform -> setTransform ( & objpos ) ;
```

```
        glClear ( GL_COLOR_BUFFER_BIT | GL_DEPTH_BUFFER_BIT ) ;

        ssgCullAndDraw ( scene ) ;

        glutPostRedisplay () ;
        glutSwapBuffers () ;
}
```

This example creates two sets of positional coordinates: one for the camera and another for the object. sgSetCoord() calls set up the X, Y, Z, coordinates and the heading, pitch, and roll values for both the camera and the model. Unlike OpenGL, SSG lets you specify the camera position simply and directly. The ssgSetCamera() call positions the camera. The transform->setTransform() statement sets the location of all the child nodes beneath transform in the scene graph. In this example, this call positions the object node and everything inside it.

After the screen has been cleared, the entire process of drawing the scene requires just one SSG call: ssgCullAndDraw() walks through the scene graph, drawing just those parts of the scene that appear on-screen.

SSG is a part of a larger suite of graphics and sound libraries that includes code to load and draw fonts and to create simple graphical user interfaces, all using OpenGL.

A full discussion of SSG (or any other scene graph for that matter) would fill a book in itself. However, this brief introduction should be enough to encourage you to visit **http://plib.sourceforge.net** to find out more about PLIB/SSG.

PLIB/SSG: HTTP://PLIB.SOURCEFORGE.NET

MOVING THE CAMERA

For some 3D games, the "camera" is attached to the player's character. For these kinds of first-person games, there is really no problem in deciding where to place the camera. In games such as *Quake*, this is the preferred mechanism. However, other styles of game such as racing games and third-person adventure/RPG games, the camera must be moved intelligently by the game software to keep the player's character in view—without being moved behind obstacles or ending up embedded in the scenery.

Moving the camera is a deep subject, and one that many third-person games come *far* from getting right. The problem is that you wind up having to play the roles of Hollywood cinematographer and director all rolled into one. One strategy that seems to work is to make a list of good places for the camera to be in each room or other area of your game level and to move the camera smoothly between those positions depending on where the player's character is at the time. If, in testing the game, you find that there is a place to which the player can go where he's hidden from the camera, you can simply add another camera position closer to the player that does have a good view.

Another approach is to allow the player some control over the camera. You have to be careful not to allow him to move the camera somewhere where he may see something that he shouldn't (for example, he should not be able to move the camera inside a locked room to which he doesn't yet have the key). If you restrict the player's ability to move the camera only to places where the camera has a clear line of sight to the player, this flexibility should be a fairly safe gambit.

For racing games, it's tempting to place the camera at a fixed position behind the player's vehicle. However, this tends to look very artificial because the vehicle ends up nailed to the center of the screen, and you only see it exactly square-on from the rear. A better approach is to remember the position of the player in every frame and to position the camera back where that position was (say) a half-second ago. This simple trick works surprisingly well; as the player turns, you see the effect of that turn on-screen immediately, and a half-second later, the camera catches up and follows. Similarly, if you brake suddenly, the camera will come in closer to the vehicle; as you accelerate, the camera will fall behind.

Even in this case, it's nice to provide the player with a little camera control (for example, you can allow the player to control the amount of delay in camera positioning, which, in effect, moves it in closer or farther away).

One problem with this approach is that if the player stops dead, the camera will crash into him a half-second later. This condition requires a little adjustment to the code so that it can detect when the player stops moving and can then stop remembering old positions when that happens. Now the camera will stop moving whenever the player does.

ADVANCED LIGHTING

The current spate of First Person Shooter (FPS) games is mostly set in dark, dungeon-like locations with flickering torchlight and brightly glowing energy weapons shooting along corridors.

The standard OpenGL lighting model really doesn't cater to lighting of this sophistication. If you need shadows in OpenGL, you need to model them yourself—probably as dark, translucent polygons that overlay the walls and floors. The current generation of FPS games uses a technique called *light-mapping* to apply custom-made texture maps that mimic shadows to otherwise normally lit walls.

One serious problem with OpenGL's standard lighting model is that it's computed *before* texturing is applied to the model. Because textures have to modulate the results of lighting, there is no way for any amount of light to brighten up the dark parts of your texture map. This can cause serious problems for some kinds of objects.

In my games that star Tux, the Linux penguin, I use textures to map Tux's features. However, the black feathers that cover most of a penguin's body need to be shiny. However, no matter how shiny you make his body, the resulting white polygon colors are multiplied by the black texels in the map, and the result is always black.

The solution is to render the textured polygons and then to draw them again as *untextured* black polygons with white specular colors. Setting the OpenGL glBlendFunc() function to add the incoming color to the color already drawn results in only the shiny spots in the second pass showing.

It's possible to produce all kinds of interesting effects with these kinds of multilayered rendering techniques. However, on older graphics cards, these effects can be considerably expensive because you wind up drawing each polygon several times, often with the least-efficient pixel-blending modes.

Fortunately, some modern 3D cards implement OpenGL extensions to render and combine multiple texture maps at the same time. This certainly avoids the cost of transforming the geometry several times, but the fill rates for many cards slow down proportionately to the number of texture maps that are being applied, so the net gain in fill rate may be close to zero.

PUTTING IT ALL TOGETHER

The following sample code demonstrates most of the techniques discussed in this chapter. It can be found on the CD-ROM, along with a Makefile to compile it.

```
#include <math.h>
#include <GL/gl.h> /* Include definitions of the OpenGL API */
#include <GL/glut.h> /* Include definitions of the GLUT API */

extern void redisplay ( void ) ;
extern void initCamera ( void ) ;
extern void loadTextures ( void ) ;

int main ( int argc, char **argv )
{
    glutInit ( &argc, argv ) ;
    glutInitDisplayMode ( GLUT_RGB | GLUT_DOUBLE | GLUT_DEPTH ) ;
    glutInitWindowSize ( 640, 480 ) ;
    glutCreateWindow ( "My First OpenGL Program" ) ;
    glutDisplayFunc ( redisplay ) ;
```

```
    loadTextures () ;
    initCamera () ;

    glEnableClientState ( GL_NORMAL_ARRAY ) ;
    glEnableClientState ( GL_COLOR_ARRAY ) ;
    glEnableClientState ( GL_TEXTURE_COORD_ARRAY ) ;
    glEnableClientState ( GL_VERTEX_ARRAY ) ;

    glutMainLoop () ;

    return 0 ;
}

unsigned char texture [ 16 ] =
{
    0xFF, 0x00, 0x00, 0xFF, 0xFF, 0xFF, 0xFF, 0xFF,
    0xFF, 0xFF, 0xFF, 0x00, 0xFF, 0x00, 0x00, 0xFF
} ;

unsigned int texture_handle ;

void loadTextures ( void )
{
    glGenTextures ( 1, & texture_handle ) ;
    glBindTexture ( GL_TEXTURE_2D, texture_handle ) ;

    gluBuild2DMipmaps(GL_TEXTURE_2D,GL_RGBA, 2, 2,
GL_RGBA,GL_UNSIGNED_BYTE,texture);

    glTexParameteri ( GL_TEXTURE_2D, GL_TEXTURE_MAG_FILTER, GL_NEAREST ) ;
    glTexParameteri ( GL_TEXTURE_2D, GL_TEXTURE_MIN_FILTER,
GL_LINEAR_MIPMAP_LINEAR ) ;
    glTexParameteri ( GL_TEXTURE_2D, GL_TEXTURE_WRAP_S, GL_REPEAT ) ;
    glTexParameteri ( GL_TEXTURE_2D, GL_TEXTURE_WRAP_T, GL_REPEAT ) ;

    glBindTexture ( GL_TEXTURE_2D, 0 ) ;
}
```

```c
void initCamera ( void )
{
    /* Select the Projection matrix */
    glMatrixMode ( GL_PROJECTION ) ;
    glLoadIdentity();
#if 0
    glOrtho(-1,1,-1,1,-1,1);
#else
    gluPerspective ( 40.0, 1.333, 0.1, 100000.0 ) ;
#endif
    /* Go back to the ModelView matrix */
    glMatrixMode ( GL_MODELVIEW ) ;
}

#define NUM_VERTS (3*4)
float normals [ 3 * NUM_VERTS ] =
{
    0.000000f,-0.707107f, 0.707107f,
    0.000000f,-0.707107f, 0.707107f,
    0.000000f,-0.707107f, 0.707107f,
    0.816497f, 0.408248f, 0.408248f,
    0.816497f, 0.408248f, 0.408248f,
    0.816497f, 0.408248f, 0.408248f,
    -0.816497f, 0.408248f, 0.408248f,
    -0.816497f, 0.408248f, 0.408248f,
    -0.816497f, 0.408248f, 0.408248f,
    0.000000f, 0.000000f,-1.000000f,
    0.000000f, 0.000000f,-1.000000f,
    0.000000f, 0.000000f,-1.000000f
} ;

float colors [ 3 * NUM_VERTS ] =
{
    1.0f, 0.0f, 0.0f, /* Red */
    1.0f, 0.0f, 0.0f,
    1.0f, 0.0f, 0.0f,
    0.0f, 1.0f, 0.0f, /* Green */
    0.0f, 1.0f, 0.0f,
    0.0f, 1.0f, 0.0f,
```

```
    0.0f, 0.0f, 1.0f, /* Blue */
    0.0f, 0.0f, 1.0f,
    0.0f, 0.0f, 1.0f,
    1.0f, 1.0f, 0.0f, /* Yellow */
    1.0f, 1.0f, 0.0f,
    1.0f, 1.0f, 0.0f
} ;

float texcoords [ 2 * NUM_VERTS ] =
{
    0.0f, 0.0f,
    -5.0f, -5.0f,
    5.0f, -5.0f,
    0.0f, 0.0f,
    5.0f, -5.0f,
    0.0f, 5.0f,
    0.0f, 0.0f,
    0.0f, 5.0f,
    -5.0f, -5.0f,
    -5.0f, -5.0f,
    0.0f, 5.0f,
    5.0f, -5.0f
} ;

float vertices [ 3 * NUM_VERTS ] =
{
    0.0f, 0.0f, 0.0f,
    -1.0f, -1.0f, -1.0f,
    1.0f, -1.0f, -1.0f,
    0.0f, 0.0f, 0.0f,
    1.0f, -1.0f, -1.0f,
    0.0f, 1.0f, -1.0f,
    0.0f, 0.0f, 0.0f,
    0.0f, 1.0f, -1.0f,
    -1.0f, -1.0f, -1.0f,
    -1.0f, -1.0f, -1.0f,
    0.0f, 1.0f, -1.0f,
    1.0f, -1.0f, -1.0f
} ;
```

```
unsigned short indices [ NUM_VERTS ] =
{
    0, 1, 2, 3, 4, 5, 6, 7, 8, 9, 10, 11
} ;

void redisplay ( void )
{
#define ROTATION_SPEED 1.0f
    static float a = 0 ;
    float white [ 4 ] = { 1.0f, 1.0f, 1.0f, 1.0f } ;
    float black [ 4 ] = { 0.0f, 0.0f, 0.0f, 1.0f } ;
    float pos [ 3 ] = { 1000.0f, 5000.0f, 0.0f } ;
    float dim_white [ 3 ] = { 0.3f, 0.3f, 0.3f } ;

    glEnable ( GL_LIGHTING ) ;

    glMaterialfv ( GL_FRONT_AND_BACK, GL_EMISSION, black ) ;
    glMaterialfv ( GL_FRONT_AND_BACK, GL_SPECULAR, white ) ;
    glMaterialf ( GL_FRONT_AND_BACK, GL_SHININESS, 5.0f ) ;
    glEnable ( GL_COLOR_MATERIAL ) ;

    glColorMaterial ( GL_FRONT_AND_BACK, GL_AMBIENT_AND_DIFFUSE ) ;
    glLightfv ( GL_LIGHT0, GL_AMBIENT , dim_white ) ;
    glLightfv ( GL_LIGHT0, GL_DIFFUSE , white ) ;
    glLightfv ( GL_LIGHT0, GL_SPECULAR, white ) ;
    glEnable ( GL_LIGHT0 ) ;

    glEnable ( GL_BLEND ) ;
    glEnable ( GL_ALPHA_TEST ) ;
    glAlphaFunc ( GL_GREATER, 0.01f ) ;
    glBlendFunc ( GL_SRC_ALPHA, GL_ONE_MINUS_SRC_ALPHA ) ;
    glEnable ( GL_DEPTH_TEST ) ;

    glClearColor ( 0.0f, 0.5f, 0.0f, 1.0f ) ; /* Dark Green */
    glClear ( GL_COLOR_BUFFER_BIT | GL_DEPTH_BUFFER_BIT ) ;

    a += ROTATION_SPEED ;
```

```
    glLoadIdentity () ;

    glTranslatef ( 0.0f, 0.0f, -10.0f ) ;

    glLightfv ( GL_LIGHT0, GL_POSITION, pos ) ;
    glRotatef ( a, 0.0f, 0.0f, 1.0f ) ;

    /* Pick a texture */
    glEnable ( GL_TEXTURE_2D ) ;
    glBindTexture ( GL_TEXTURE_2D, texture_handle ) ;
    glColorPointer ( 3, GL_FLOAT, 0, colors ) ;
    glTexCoordPointer ( 2, GL_FLOAT, 0, texcoords ) ;

    glNormalPointer ( GL_FLOAT, 0, normals ) ;
    glVertexPointer ( 3, GL_FLOAT, 0, vertices ) ;

    glDrawElements ( GL_TRIANGLES, NUM_VERTS, GL_UNSIGNED_SHORT, indices ) ;

    glutSwapBuffers () ;
    glutPostRedisplay () ;
}
```

Hopefully by now you should be able to handle most of the graphics requirements for your future hit games; however, you might want to try adding some funky graphical effects. If so, you may want to visit some Web sites, such as **http://www.opengl.org** and **http://www.flipcode.com**.

On the OpenGL Web site, there are links to Mark Kilgard's Web site (which moves once in a while, depending on his current employer). This Web site is filled with various OpenGL tutorials for use in all sorts of applications.

CHAPTER 8

SOUND UNDER LINUX

This is where things start to get tricky. Sound under Linux is a tough thing to do if you don't have the right libraries. Fortunately, Loki makes an OpenGL-like API called OpenAL that makes your audio life a lot easier. Of course, SDL also provides simple sound support.

OpenAL

OpenAL (Open Audio Library) is an OpenSource 3D sound library with an API similar to OpenGL (Open Graphic Library). 3D surround sound is pretty much essential in today's games, allowing total immersion into the environment. You can download OpenAL from **http://www.openal.org** or use the version in the libs directory on the CD-ROM that accompanies this book. At the time I am writing this, the documentation for OpenAL is less than complete, but hopefully someone will complete it before too long.

OpenAL: HTTP://WWW.OPENAL.ORG

If you plan to port your game to other platforms, OpenAL is the perfect choice for the audio API because it compiles for various operating systems, including Windows and the Mac.

A Simple OpenAL Application

OpenAL coding is as easy as eating pie. (For you non-American readers, that means it's very easy. Just look at Elvis.) If you've read the last two chapters, you should already be familiar with the basic functions (just replace the gl at the beginning of the function name with al, and you're away).

Okay, it's not quite that easy, but it's not far from the truth. The following sections are dedicated to the basics of OpenAL, ranging from loading a WAV file to achieving full 3D surround sound.

Initializing and Loading Samples

The first thing your OpenAL application must do is create a *rendering context*. This is achieved with the function alcCreateContext(). The function prototype for this is as follows:

```
ALAPI void * ALAPIENTRY alcCreateContext(ALint *attrlist);
```

This function returns a context identifier that will be used later in the program. The `attrlist` argument is an array of attributes to use in creating the attribute list. You can use a combination of several options for this argument, as listed in the following chart:

Attribute Name	Description
ALC_FREQUENCY	The frequency of the sound to use, followed by the frequency to use.
ALC_RESOLUTION	The resolution of the soundform, followed by the bit rate to use.
ALC_BUFFERSIZE	The size of the sound buffer, followed by the size in bytes of the buffer. The larger the buffer, the longer the delay in playing the sound, but the smoother the results.
ALC_CHANNELS	The number of sound channels to use.
ALC_INVALID	End of the attribute list.

The use of these attributes varies slightly from most APIs. The following code sample demonstrates how to implement these attributes:

```
#include <AL/al.h>
#include <AL/alc.h>
#include <AL/alut.h>

int main(int argc, void **argv)
{
    // Use 22khz samples
    ATuint *attributes = {ALC_FREQUENCY, 22050,
        ALC_INVALID};
    void *context = NULL;
    // XXX1

    // Attempt to create the OpenAL context
    context = alcCreateContext(attributes);
    if (context == NULL) {
        fprintf(stderr, "Can't create context");
        return 1;
    }

    // XXX2

    // Clean up
    alcDestroyContext(context);
    return 0;
}
```

This simple sample creates an audio context and then destroys it. Useful, no? Well, not really. Now we actually need to play some sounds!

CREATING LISTENERS

Before we can set up a sound source, we first need to tell OpenAL where exactly the listener is in the scene. We do this in the same way that we'd set up a camera position in OpenGL before drawing any tetrahedrons. We establish the position of the listener using a series of calls to a function called alListenerfv(). This function is similar in many ways to the OpenGL vertex and lighting functions.

> **NOTE**
>
> You are limited to only one listener per scene, but you can move the current listener around to create the illusion of multiple sound sources.

The function prototype for alListenerfv() is as follows:

```
ALAPI void * ALAPIENTRY alListenerfv(ALenum pname, ALfloat *param);
```

The first argument, pname, is the name of the property we want to change. There are three possible options here: AL_POSITION (the position of the listener), AL_ORIENTATION (the direction), and AL_VELOCITY (the speed). The properties we're interested in at the moment are the first two, the position and direction of the listener.

Where our little sample code has the comment XXX1, add the following two lines of code:

```
ALfloat listener_pos[3] = {0.0f, 0.0f, 0.0f};
ALfloat listener_dir[3] = {0.0, 0.0, 1.0f, 0.0f, 1.0f, 0.0f};
```

These statements specify the coordinates (the middle) and the direction of the listener (facing forward). Before these values are used by OpenAL, you need to inform the API of these little, but important, facts. Add the following code to where the comment reads XXX2:

```
    // Set up the listener
    alListenerfv(AL_POSITION, listener_pos);
    alListenerfv(AL_ORIENTATION, listener_dir);
    // Stationary listener, so no Doppler shift needed
    alListener3v(AL_VELOCITY, 0.0f, 0.0f, 0.0f);
```

LOADING A SOUND FILE

We're almost ready to play a sound (not really), but first we have to load a sound into memory. There are a number of ways to do this, but I will focus on the more complicated method here. I'm not just being sadistic; later in this chapter, I will talk about streaming buffers, and you will need to know how to load the samples without assigning a buffer to them to do that.

The function `alutBufferAndConvert_LOKI()` (in the file `alext.h`, which is an extension to the API added by Loki) converts a WAV file loaded into memory into an audio buffer that can be used by OpenAL. The function prototype is shown here:

```
ALAPI ALboolean alutBufferAndConvert_LOKI(ALuint ALbid, void *data,
                                          ALboolean dummy, ALuint size);
```

The first argument is the buffer identifier of the sample to convert. These are user-definable, and used when assigning the buffer to a source. The next argument is the WAV sample data to convert, and the final argument is the size of the data (in bytes). The `dummy` argument is exactly that: a dummy argument that should be set to `AL_TRUE` just to be safe.

The following code demonstrates how to load a WAV file into a buffer. Add it to our evolving sample program after the block of code that set up the listener.

```
fp = fopen("boom.wav", "rb");
if (!fp) {
    // Clean up and quit
    fprintf(stderr, "Can't load file boom.wav\N");
    alcDestroyContext(context);
    return 1;
}

// Read the WAV data
data_len = fread(data, 1, DATABUFFERSIZE, fp);
fclose(fp);

if (!alutBufferAndConvert_LOKI(sound_buffer, data,
    AL_TRUE, data_len)) {
    fprintf(stderr, "Invalid file format\n");
    return 1;
}
```

Add the following lines at the XXX1 comment:

```
// A 2MB sound buffer
#define DATABUFFERSIZE (2048*1024)
void *data = (char *)malloc(DATABUFFERSIZE);
int data_len = 0;
int sound_buffer = 0;
```

CREATING SOUND SOURCES

Now that we've loaded a sound sample into a buffer, we have to create the sound source that will be playing the sound. The sound sources are created in a similar way to listeners, but the functions (there are more than one this time) are called alSourcefv() and alSourcei(). Before you can define the position of the source, however, you must first generate the source. The function alGenSources() does this for you.

```
ALAPI void ALAPIENTRY alGenSources(ALuint n, ALuint *sources);
```

The first argument, n, is the number of sources you want to create. The second and final argument is an array containing the source identifiers you want to use. In our example program, we need only one source.

After you have generated the source, you must define the position of the source using the same method you used to set up the listener. In addition to setting up the position, direction, and velocity of the sound source, you also must specify which sound buffer the source will be playing. This is defined by the AL_BUFFER property.

Add the following code to the sample program after we load the sound file to generate the single sound source:

```
// Generate a single source
alGenSources(1, &source);

// Set up the source details
alSourcei(source, AL_BUFFER, sound_buffer);
alSourcei(source, AL_SOUND_LOOPING, AL_FALSE);
alSourcefv(source, AL_POSITION, source_position);
alSource3v(source, AL_VELOCITY, 0.0f, 0.0f, 0.0f);
```

If you're wondering what that extra property, AL_SOUND_LOOPING is, it's a flag to specify whether or not to loop the sound. If you want the sound source to loop (as you would with background music, for example), set the third argument of alSourcei() to AL_TRUE.

Before this section of code is finished, we have to define the source number. Add the following lines of code to the variable declarations:

```
int source = 0;
ALfloat source_position[3] = {-1.0f, 0.0f, 1.0f};
```

PLAYING SOUNDS

Now that we've finally set up everything for playing the source, we can actually play something. To play a source, you use the function alPlaySource(), which takes a single argument: the source identifier (in our example, this value is 0, or the identifier source).

Add the following code to our sample program, after the source we set up in the previous section:

```
// Start playing the source
alPlaySource(source);
```

GETTING THE STATE OF THE SOUND

Under certain circumstances, you may want to check whether a source is currently playing a sound or not. This is an important task if you ever want to delete a source because you can delete a source only when the source is inactive (that is, not playing).

To read the state of a given source, you can use the function alSourcei() with the property AL_SOURCE_STATE and a pointer to an integer as the property value. The variable pointed to by the third argument will specify whether the current source is being used.

Add the following code to our sample program, after we start playing the source:

```
int state = AL_ACTIVE;

// Loop while the sound is playing
while (state == AL_ACTIVE) {
    // XXX3
    alSourcei(source, AL_SOURCE_STATE, &state);
}
```

STOPPING SOUNDS

If you ever have to stop a sound prematurely, you can use the function alStopSource(). This function takes a single argument: the source number to stop playing.

DELETING A SOURCE

When you have finished with a source, you can safely destroy it by calling alDestroySources(). This function takes the same form as alGenSources(). Add the following code after the while loop we just created to test the state of the source:

```
// Delete the sources
alDestroySources(1, &source);
```

MOVING THE SOURCE

Although the sample program will play a sound as it is currently written, the code doesn't exploit any of the decent capabilities of OpenAL. Without improving the code, we might as well stream raw audio data to /dev/audio (which is a bad thing).

One of the attractions of OpenAL is its 3D sound capabilities (*stereo sound* for those who don't like sales pitches). OpenAL makes integration of audio features with OpenGL a breeze; I'll cover the more complex stuff later.

If you look at the sample program as it is currently written, you should notice that the position of the listener is slightly off center. This was done for a reason. The next block of code we'll add to the sample will bounce the source around the screen to demonstrate the stereo capabilities of OpenAL.

For this trick, we have to declare another variable. Add the following code to the declarations at the top of the main() function:

```
AUfloat move = 0.05;
```

To actually move the source, all we have to do is alter the AL_POSITION property. This is done with the following block of code, which should be inserted where the XXX3 comment is located:

```
// Bounce the source around
if (source_position[0] > 1.0f ||
    source_position[0] < -1.0f) move = -move;

// Update the source position
source_position[0] += move;
alSourcefv(source, AL_POSITION, source_position);
```

COMPILING THE SAMPLE

We've finally completed our simple OpenAL application; now we can compile it. Use the following gcc command line to do this:

```
gcc -Wall -L/usr/local/lib -I/usr/local/include -lal \
    -o aldemo1 aldemo1.c
```

> **NOTE**
>
> The OpenAL libraries install to
> /usr/local/lib and
> /usr/local/include by default. If
> you installed them to a different direc-
> tory, you will have to replace these val-
> ues with the location to which you
> installed them.

ADVANCED OPENAL

Now that we have covered the basics of OpenAL, we can start looking at some of the more advanced features, such as reverb and Doppler shift. Because it is a complete 3D sound library, OpenAL has more capabilities than you can shake a big stick with pointy bits at.

VOLUME CONTROL

The first "advanced" OpenAL feature we're going to look at isn't really that advanced; it's volume control.

Because different sources may require different levels of volume in the game (a silenced machine gun, for example), OpenAL provides the functionality to give each source a different volume. You can also control the volume of the listener itself.

If you've ever played around with any "real" audio equipment, you may have noticed a gain knob that affects the amplification of the sound. OpenAL uses a similar pre-amplification gain control to alter the volume of music.

Each source has a property, AL_GAIN_LINEAR, which is basically the volume at which you want to play the sample. You use the function alSourcef() to set this value:

```
alSourcef(source, AL_GAIN_LINEAR, 1.0f);
```

The reason "volume" is not really a suitable term here is because OpenAL uses a 3D environment. In that environment, two sources can have the same gain, but be at different volumes as far as the listener is concerned (depending on the position of the sources relative to the listener).

VELOCITY AND DOPPLER SHIFT

If you've ever been watching a race on TV, or even been trackside during a race, I'm sure you've noticed that *voo-roooom* sound the cars make as they approach you. However, if you were inside the car, that noise is more of a steady *vooooooo* without the *rooom* bit of the sound.

The spectator hears the *voo-rooooom* because of something called the *Doppler effect* or *Doppler shift.* Doppler shift affects just about everything that moves in waves, be it light or sound.

Doppler shift works like this: Consider a moving object that is generating sound (a car). This sound moves at a fixed speed (about 330 meters per second through air), but because the source of the sound is also moving, the sound interferes with itself as a newer part of the sound wave arrives at the same position as an "older" part of the wave.

This Doppler shift is what causes a sonic boom: the sound you hear when an object is moving so fast that all the sound it generates occupies the same point in the universe, and the universe doesn't know what to do with all the built-up energy.

OpenAL has a feature to simulate the Doppler effect; you control it by using the AL_VELOCITY property of the sources and listeners. If you remember your high school physics class, you know that velocity is a vector (a speed in a single direction). It is important to remember this fact when trying to work out why your racecars don't *vooo-rooooom* like they should.

In the sample application we built earlier in this chapter, we used 0s for the velocity of both the listener and the source. We can, however, make the code more realistic by introducing Doppler shift into the equation.

Add the following new variable to the sample code with the other variables so that we can start implementing Doppler shift into our sample program:

```
ALfloat source_velocity[3] = {0.0f, 0.0f, 0.0f};
```

As the source bounces around the screen, we should update the velocity to contain the current direction of the source (although the speed of the source remains constant, the direction in which the source is travelling doesn't, so the velocity variable has to take this into account). Add the following code just before we update the position of our source:

```
// Update the velocity of the source
source_velocity[0] = move;
alSourcefv(source, AL_VELOCITY, source_velocity);
```

HEAR NO DIFFERENCE?

If you don't actually hear any change when you compile and run this revised program, that may be because the sound scale that OpenAL is using isn't really suitable for the amount of movement going on.

According to the OpenAL documentation, there isn't a function for setting the scale of the universe, but according to the header files, there is such a function. The convert function is alDopplerScale(), which takes a single argument:

```
void ALAPIENTRY alDopplerScale(ALfloat value);
```

Because the OpenAL documentation is so sketchy as I write this, I can't find a point of reference for what the scaling system is. However, we do know that the default is 1.0, whatever that means. Through trial and error, you can find the best value for alDopplerScale() in your application.

REVERB AND ECHO

Although there is no official support for reverberation and echo features in OpenAL, there are some temporary Loki extensions in the library that do the job. The OpenAL documentation recommends that you don't use these functions, but it is possible to hack your program to support both the current functions as well as the functions in the stable release.

The Loki-specific functions you shouldn't use are called alReverbScale_LOKI() and alReverbDelay_LOKI(). Each of these functions takes two arguments: the source that generates the effect and a floating-point value.

The second argument in alReverbScale_LOKI() specifies the amount of gain to use as the sample reverberates; the second argument in alReverbDelay_LOKI() specifies the delay between "echoes."

If you decide to use these functions in your program, you may want to use the following macros to call them so that your code is more maintainable when the new functions are implemented in the API:

```
// Macros for OpenAL reverb functions
#define alReverbScale(sid, value) alReverbScale_LOKI(sid, value)
#define alReverbDelay(sid, value) alReverbScale_LOKI(sid, value)
```

STREAMING BUFFERS

If you are generating audio on-the-fly or are decompressing a large audio file and don't want to store it all in memory, you may want to use a *streaming buffer*. Streaming buffers provide a constant stream of input instead of a single sample. You can stream the audio from several sources, such as an MP3 file, a CD-ROM, or off the Internet (think voice-chat).

When you want to create a streaming buffer, you must use the function alGenStreamingBuffer():

```
ALAPI void ALAPIENTRY alGenStreamingBuffers(ALsizei n, ALuint *samples);
```

The first argument for alGenStreamingBuffers() is the number of buffers you want to create, followed by a pointer specifying the buffer identifiers you want to generate.

When you want to add data to a streaming buffer, you must use the function alBufferAppendData(). This function works in a similar fashion to the function alutBufferAndConvert():

```
ALsizei alBufferAppendData(ALuint buffer, ALenum format,
        ALvoid *data, ALsizei size, ALsizei freq);
```

The first argument, buffer, specifies which streaming buffer to add the data to. This argument should be one of the values you used in alGenStreamingBuffers(). The next argument, format, is one of the types listed in the following chart.

> **NOTE**
>
> At the time I am writing this, the alBufferAppendData() function isn't actually in the API, but it *is* in the documentation. There is, however, a function called alBufferAppendData_LOKI() that takes the same arguments as alBufferAppendData().

Name	Description
AL_FORMAT_MON08	8-bit mono sample
AL_FORMAT_MON016	16-bit mono sample
AL_FORMAT_STERE08	8-bit stereo sample
AL_FORMAT_STERE016	16-bit stereo sample

The next two arguments, data and size, specify the sample and the size of the sample to append to the buffer. The final argument, freq, is the frequency of the sample you are adding to the buffer.

When you want to attach the buffer to a source, you use the same method you use for a normal, non-streaming sample.

SDL Audio

If you find OpenAL a little too complex, powerful, or unfinished for your project, SDL also has a simple audio layer that can handle sound effects. The SDL audio layer is slightly more complex to set up than an OpenAL equivalent, but if you don't like the idea of using libraries that are still in heavy development, it's perfect for you.

Starting an Audio Session

When you start SDL with SDL_Init() (as explained in Chapter 4), you must specify an extra argument, SDL_INIT_AUDIO in your initialization. Assuming that you have done this, the next thing you need to do is set up the audio device. The function that does this is SDL_OpenAudio():

```
int SDL_OpenAudio(SDL_AudioSpec *desired, SDL_AudioSpec *obtained);
```

The first argument, desired, is the type of audio device you want to use; the second argument, obtained, is what you've actually got. The SDL_AudioSpec structure looks something like this:

```
typedef struct {
    int freq;
    Uint16 format;
    Uint8 channels;
    Uint8 silence;
    Uint16 samples;
    Uint32 size;
    void (*callback)(void *userdata, Uint8 *stream, int len);
    void *userdata;
} SDL_AudioSpec
```

The following chart describes the various members of the SDL_AudioSpec structure:

Name	Description
freq	Audio frequency in samples per second
format	Format of audio data
channels	Number of channels (1=mono, 2=stereo)
silence	Assigned by SDL
samples	Audio buffer size in samples
size	Audio buffer size in bytes
callback()	Function for filling the audio buffer
userdata	Data to be passed to the callback() function

The following sample code demonstrates how to open an audio device:

```
#include <sdl.h>

// Function to play audio
void audio_func(void *userdata, Uint8 *stream, int len) {
    // XXX
}

int main(int argc, char **argv) {
    SDL_AudioSpec *des_audio, *real_audio;

    // Fire up SDL
    if (!SDL_Init(SDL_INIT_AUDIO)) {
        return 1;
    }

    atexit(SDL_Quit);

    // Allocate memory for the audio specs structures.
    des_audio = (SDL_AudioSpec *)malloc(sizeof(SDL_AudioSpec);
    real_audio = (SDL_AudioSpec *)malloc(sizeof(SDL_AudioSpec);

    // Set up the audio spec
    des_audio->freq = 22050    // 22khz samples
    des_audio->format = AUDIO_S16LSB;
```

```
    des_audio->samples = 1024;
    des_audio->callback = audio_func;
    des_audio->user_data = NULL;

    // Try and open audio device
    if (!SDL_OpenAudio(des_audio, real_audio)) {
        fprintf(stderr, "Error: %s", SDL_GetError());
        return 1;
    }

    // Clean up and quit
    SDL_CloseAudio();
    return 0;
}
```

The format member of SDL_AudioSpec can be one of several options, as shown in the following chart:

Name	Description
AUDIO_U8	8-bit unsigned samples
AUDIO_S8	8-bit signed samples
AUDIO_U16LSB	16-bit unsigned samples (little-endian)
AUDIO_S16LSB	16-bit signed samples (little-endian)
AUDIO_U16MSB	16-bit unsigned samples (big-endian)
AUDIO_S16MSB	16-bit signed samples (big-endian)
AUDIO_U16	Same as AUDIO_U16LSB
AUDIO_S16	Same as AUDIO_S16LSB

The final member of the SDL_AudioSpec structure that is of interest at the moment is the samples member. This member specifies the size of the sample buffer in samples. The larger the buffer, the longer the wait until a new sample is played; the smaller the buffer, the shorter the wait, but there is more chance of "choppy" sound with a small buffer.

To figure out the exact size of the buffer you want to use, consider the following equation:

```
time in milliseconds = (samples/1000) * freq
```

The SDL documentation recommends a buffer somewhere between 512 and 8,192 samples.

LOADING SAMPLES

After you have set up the audio device (or before you have done that, if you feel so inclined), you can start loading WAV files with the function SDL_LoadWAV():

```
SDL_AudioSpec *SDL_LoadWav(const char *file, SDL_AudioSpec *spec,
    Uint8 **audio_buf, Uint32 *audio_len);
void SDL_FreeWav(Uint8 *audio_buf);
```

The first argument of SDL_LoadWav() is the file you want to load, followed by an SDL_AudioSpec structure to be filled with details about the WAV format. If you want, you can use the structure that was returned with SDL_OpenAudio(), but that doesn't give you as much flexibility.

The next argument, audio_buf, is a pointer to an area of memory that will contain the actual audio data. This memory space is allocated by SDL, so you don't have to worry about it. What you do have to worry about, however, is calling SDL_FreeWAV() when you have finished with the sample.

When SDL_LoadWAV() succeeds, it returns a pointer to an SDL_AudioSpec structure (it also assigns the spec argument to the same structure); it returns NULL on an error.

Add the following code to our sample program, after we initialize the audio:

```
// Attempt to load a sample.
if (!SDL_LoadWAV("./boom.wav", des_spec,
    wav_buffer, &wav_len)) {
    SDL_CloseAudio();
    fprintf(stderr, "Error: %s", SDL_GetError());
    return 1;
}

// Unpause the audio
SDL_PauseAudio(0);
```

We also need a couple of global variables assigned to store the sample data:

```
// Data for the WAV file
Uint8 **wav_buffer;
Uint32 wav_len;
Uint32 wav_pos;
```

Using the Audio Callback Function

Actually, playing a sound under SDL isn't as easy as it is under OpenAL. With SDL, you have to use a callback function and calculate the current position of the sample you are playing.

If you look at our sample program as it is currently written, you will notice that we already have a callback function that is ready to be coded: audio_func(). This function has three parameters. The first is a pointer to some user-defined data that is set when you call SDL_OpenAudio() in the userdata member of the SDL_AudioSpec structure.

The second argument is a pointer to the audio stream. This is where you actually send data when you want it to be played. More on this later. The final argument for the callback function is the length of the audio buffer in bytes.

Playing a Sample

To copy a sample to the audio stream, use the function SDL_MixAudio(), which takes care of everything. Although you can do things manually, I don't recommend doing that.

```
void SDL_MixAudio(Uint8 *dst, Uint8 *src, Uint32 len, int vol);
```

The first argument to SDL_MixAudio() is the destination sound buffer, which can be the actual audio stream. The second argument is the sample you want to play. The third argument is the size of the audio sample to play, followed by the volume at which you want to play the sample.

The volume can be any value between 0 and 128, but you should use SDL_MIX_MAXVOLUME if you want to play the sample at full volume.

In our sample program, replace the empty callback function with the following code:

```
// Function to play audio
void audio_func(void *userdata, Uint8 *stream, int len) {

    // Check if the buffer is big enough for the whole sample
    if (len >= (wav_len - wav_pos)) {
        // Play whole sample
        SDL_MixAudio(stream, (wav_data + wav_pos),
            (wav_len - wav_pos), SDL_MIX_MAXVOLUME);
        wav_pos = 0;
    } else {
```

```
        // Only fill the audio buffer
        SDL_MixAudio(stream, (wav_data + wav_pos),
            len, SDL_MIX_MAXVOLUME);
        wav_pos += len;
    }
}
```

The callback function will be called whenever the audio stream is empty.

Now that we have written our callback function, we have to add a loop to the main program. After we load the WAV file, add the following code:

```
    // Do nothing while the sample is playing.
    while(SDL_GetAudioStatus() != SDL_AUDIO_STOPPED) {
        SDL_Sleep(100);
    }
```

PAUSING THE AUDIO STREAM

When you open the audio device, SDL assumes that you want to pause the buffer until you have loaded some samples. Before anything is played, you must "unpause" the device by calling SDL_PauseAudio(). This function takes a single argument: a Boolean flag to say whether you want the audio stream paused or not.

When the audio stream is paused, the buffer is continuously filled with silence until the stream is unpaused.

CLEANING UP

When you have finished with the audio layer of SDL, you must call SDL_CloseAudio(). This function doesn't take any arguments. You must also remember to free any samples you have used.

MIXING DIFFERENT SAMPLES

If you want to play more than one sample at a time, you will have to mix them before sending them to the audio buffer. To do this, you may want to create a simple function that handles this for you, as shown here:

```
char *mix_samples(char *sample1, char *sample2,
    int len, int vol) {
    char *dest = malloc(len);

    // Copy sample1 to new sample so we don't break it
    memcpy(dest, sample1, len);

    // Mix second sample in, using the standard SDL call
    SDL_MixAudio(dest, sample2, len, vol);

    // We're done.
    return dest;
}
```

This simple function allows the mixing of two different samples without overriding either of the original samples.

CD Audio

Playing an audio CD is probably as low-level as you will need to go when playing a game.

Using the `ioctl()` Function

The function `ioctl()` allows access to various pieces of hardware, ranging from the sound card to network interfaces. There are very few occasions when you really need to use it, but playing audio CD-ROM discs is one of those occasions.

```
int ioctl(int d, int request, ...)
```

The first argument is an open file descriptor describing the character device (such as a mouse or disk drive) you want to access. The second argument is the type of request you want to make, followed by any arguments that may or may not be required.

In the include file `cdrom.h` (usually accessible from `/usr/include/linux`) are several of the different types of requests you can perform on a CD-ROM drive using `ioctl()`.

OPENING THE DEVICE

The CD-ROM device we are interested in is usually /dev/cdrom. To start playing a CD, we must open a file descriptor to the device using open().

```c
#include <stdio.h>
#include <linux/cdrom.h>

int main(int argc, char **argv) {
    int fd_cd;

    // Open the CD device
    fd_cd = open("/dev/cdrom", O_RDONLY | O_NONBLOCK);

    if (!fd_cd) {
        perror("Error: ");
        return 1;
    }

    // XXX5

    // Close the CD device
    close(fd_cd);

    return 0;
}
```

GETTING A TRACK LISTING

Before we can start playing a track, we should first check to see whether the track we want to play actually exists. We do this by sending the request CDROMREADTOCHDR.

Where our code has the comment XXX5, add the following code:

```c
    // Read the track information.
    ioctl(fd_cd, CDROMREADTOCHDR, &track_list);
```

This request retrieves the numbers of the first and last tracks on the CD and stores them in the address pointed to by track_list. The track_list structure is of type cdrom_tochdr.

```
struct cdrom_tochdr {
    u_char cdth_trk0;      // First track
    u_char cdth_trk1;      // Last track
};
```

Before we are ready to continue, we must declare the variable in which ioctl() will store the track information. Add the following line to the start of the main() function:

```
    struct cdrom_tochdr track_list;
```

PLAYING A CD

To play a CD, we use the request CDROMPPLAYTRKIND, which uses a structure of type cdrom_ti as an argument.

```
struct cdrom_ti {
    u_char cdti_trk0;      // First track to play
    u_char cdti_ind0;      // First index to play
    u_char cdti_trk1;      // Last track to play
    u_char cdti_ind1;      // Last index to play
};
```

TRACKS AND INDICES

The difference between *tracks* and *indices* is hard to explain, but I'll have a go at it. Audio tracks can be divided into several minitracks. Home CD players usually play whatever data is located at index 1 and continue until they reach the next track (even if that means going through the second index and so on).

A good example of this can be seen on the "Right" CD of the Nine Inch Nails album, *The Fragile*. Located at track 5, index 0 is a sample of another Nine Inch Nails song (called "10 Miles High," available on *Things Falling Down*). It is almost impossible to get to this track using normal methods, but some CD players let you "rewind" to the start of the index.

SOME CODE

Now we are going add some code to our sample to play the track "10 Miles High." If you don't own *The Fragile* album, don't worry. This is only some sample code; you can modify it for other CDs.

Add the following variable definition to the start of our main() block:

```
struct cdrom_ti tracks;
```

Now we actually need to fill that structure and play some tracks. Add the following code after the last call to ioctl() in the current program:

```
// Check if there are enough tracks on the CD
if (trak_list.trk0 > 5) {
    // What tracks do we want to play?
    tracks.trk0 = 5;    // Start on track 5, index 0
    tracks.ind0 = 0;
    tracks.trk1 = 5;    // End on track 5, index 1
    tracks.ind1 = 1;

    // Start playing the CD
    ioctl(fd_cd, CDROMPLAYTRKIND, &tracks);
}
```

STOPPING A CD

After you have started the track playing, you might have to stop the CD for some reason (such as to read data from it). You can stop the CD from playing by calling the ioctl() function with the request CDROMSTOP. This request takes no arguments.

CHAPTER 9

NETWORKING

I n today's Internet society, very few games will pass public muster unless they include some form of multiplayer entertainment. Even so, a small number of PC games are released without the ability to compete or cooperate with other human beings. At the other extreme are games designed as pure multiplayer experiences, offering very little in the way of single-player entertainment.

INTRODUCTION TO MODERN NETWORKING

Networking today is very different from the way it was in the early days. In recent years, traditional technologies such as IPX have been superceded with widely accepted standards such as TCP/IP.

Even the physical design of a network has changed. Old, thin Ethernet systems have been replaced with the more reliable Cat-5 structure, which adopts a format similar to that of the Internet. The "star" topology is probably the most-used type of network today—and with good reasons. However, I'm not here to teach you how to set up networks, but to focus on the software side of things.

When it comes to adding network support to any type of software, there are certain things you need to consider before writing any code. The first thing you have to consider is what sort of network architecture you want to use. There are two types worth considering: peer-to-peer and client/server.

PEER-TO-PEER NETWORKING

Peer-to-peer applications are programs in which all systems on the network communicate, with no central point of contact. Although many people shun this system, if your game has only a few players, this could be your best option.

Peer-to-peer games work by transmitting data to all other clients connected to the game. If there are more than four players in the game, the peer-to-peer architecture is unsuitable, but for a few players, it's perfect.

Each client in the system also acts as a server, telling all the other systems what it is doing at that precise moment in time. At the same time, that machine is being told by all the other systems what's happening. This simultaneous communication can lead to problems keeping all the clients synchronized, but these problems can be navigated with a little bit of hard work.

CLIENT/SERVER NETWORKING

The other main network architecture in use today is the client/server method. This approach makes use of a dedicated server to which all the clients connect. Instead of communicating with other clients, the client sends a message to the server; the server then passes that message to the other clients involved in the game.

The client/server model makes it easier to communicate with the other clients because there is only one address to send the data to. However, this model does double any latency that may occur. There are not many ways around the latency problem, and this delay can kill the success of a game in no time flat.

THE TCP/IP STACK

Most networks work using the TCP/IP stack. This collection of protocols is designed to isolate applications from the underlying hardware. There are several layers, ranging from the physical layer (data going over the cable) to the application layer (what programs actually send).

The layers of interest to us are the transport layer (which includes the TCP, UDP, and ICMP protocols) and the application layer. The application layer is completely undefined and can be used to transmit any data you want, in whatever format you want.

> **NOTE**
> ICMP (Internet Control Messaging Protocol) is a very simple protocol that can only be used for a few things, and are not really usable in games.

The transport layer, on the other hand, offers several options for transmitting the data.

TCP

TCP (Transport Control Protocol) is a reliable system that incorporates error checks to the data. These error checks increase the size of the packet headers, and therefore reduce the amount of data you can send in a single packet (different connection types have different MTUs (Maximum Transmission Units). PPP connections, for example, have an MTU of 500).

Unlike UDP connections (which are explained in the following section), TCP connections establish a connection to the other machine and send data directly there. This approach reduces the amount of work you have to do while coding your program.

TCP is generally slower than UDP because of the error checks involved, so it's not suitable for urgent data (such as game data), but it is perfect for applications that need reliability over speed.

UDP

The other option, UDP (User Datagram Protocol), is as low-level as you could ever want to go (trust me on that). It's a fast, efficient system, but it's not too safe. All the UDP packet header contains is the destination address for the packet (which is all it really needs to know). However, if a packet is dropped or becomes corrupted en route, it is lost for good.

UDP is used for games much more than TCP is because of the performance enhancements UDP sports. A good comparison between the two protocols can be seen in the differences in lag time between *Quake Deathmatch* and *QuakeWorld*. Originally, *Quake* used TCP connections to transmit data, which resulted in a major latency problem. This issue was fixed to some degree with *QuakeWorld*, which used UDP instead.

SOCKET PROGRAMMING

Socket programming can be quite easy at times, a nightmare at others, depending on what you want to do. Unfortunately, the TCP option is easier (in my opinion) than UDP, but there are some functions that apply to the whole area of socket coding.

OPENING A SOCKET

The function call socket() opens the initial socket for you. This function simply describes the type of socket you want and returns a socket descriptor. These socket descriptors can be used as normal file descriptors (for example, such as the ones returned by open()) and demonstrate the UNIX philosophy of "everything's a file" quite well. The function prototype for socket() is shown here:

```
int socket(int domain, int type, int protocol)
```

The first argument, domain, specifies the protocol family to use. This should be either PF_INET or PF_INET6 (for IPv6 sockets, which are going to be in use in several years' time). There are several other options, but these are out of the scope of this book.

The next argument, type, is the transport layer type you want to use. Again, although there are several possibilities, you'll probably want to use SOCK_STREAM (for TCP) or SOCK_DGRAM (for UDP).

The final argument, protocol, is the type of protocol to use. It can be either IPPROTO_TCP or IPPROTO_UDP.

The socket() function returns a valid socket descriptor on success; it returns –1 on failure.

CONNECTING THE SOCKET

When you have successfully opened a socket, you must specify where exactly you want it to go. You do this with the connect() function. Note that you call connect() only if you are using a TCP socket. UDP is a connectionless protocol and does not require this call.

```
int connect(int sockfd, struct sockaddr *serv_addr, int addrlen);
```

The first argument, sockfd, is the socket descriptor returned by socket(). You will use this value again throughout the program. The next argument, serv_addr, is a pointer to a structure containing details about the address to which you want to connect. Although the function prototype uses a structure of the type sockaddr, you'll need to use the structure sockaddr_in and cast it to the correct type when you call the function. The members of this structure that are of interest are sin_addr->saddr and sin_port. The first one is the address of the machine to which you want to connect. You can determine this address by calling the function inet_aton(), which takes as arguments the IP address (as a string) of the host to connect to, followed by a pointer to the address at which you want to store the resulting in_addr structure.

The sin_port member is the port number to which you want to connect, which must be specified in network-byte order.

> **NOTE**
> When specifying any sort of numbers, remember to use the htons() function, which converts the host-specific number to network-byte order.

The following sample code demonstrates how to connect to a remote machine with TCP:

```c
#include <sys/socket.h>
#include <sys/types.h>

#define HOST "127.0.0.1"
#define PORT 80

int main(int argc, char **argv) {
    int sock;
    struct sockaddr_in *server;

    // Open the socket
    sock = socket(PF_INET, SOCK_STREAM, IPPROTO_TCP);

    if (sock == -1) {
        perror("Socket error:");
        return 1;
    }

    // Where do we want to connect to?
    inet_aton(HOST, &(server->sin_addr));
    server->sin_port = htons(PORT);
    server->sin_family = AF_INET;

    // Attempt to establish connection
    if (connect(sock, server, sizeof(sockaddr_in)) == -1) {
        perror("Socket error:");
        return 1;
    }

    // We're done.
    close(socket);
    return 0;
}
```

SENDING DATA

When you have successfully established a socket, you can go ahead and send data to it. There are several ways to do this, depending on the type of socket, ranging from standard file I/O calls to TCP-specific I/O functions, and everything in between.

OPENING A SOCKET AS A FILE STREAM

I mentioned earlier in this chapter that the socket descriptor is the same as a standard file descriptor created by a call to open(). This similarity allows you to use the function fdopen() to access the standard file I/O functions, such as fprintf() and fgets().

```
FILE *fdopen(int filedes, char *mode);
```

This function works exactly the same as fopen() except that you specify a file descriptor (or a socket descriptor, in this case) instead of a filename. Depending on the type of access you want, the mode string can be any of the standard fopen() mode strings (see fopen man page for details).

When you want to send data to the socket, you can use the standard file I/O functions to write data to the file stream by using fprintf() for raw text (which is useful for clear-text protocols, such as HTTP) or fwrite() (for more complex data types).

USING THE send() FUNCTION

If you have opened a TCP socket, you can use the function send() after you have established a connection to the remote end. The send() function takes four parameters: a socket descriptor, the data to send, the length of the data, and some flags.

```
int send(int s, const void *msg, int len, unsigned int flags);
```

The flags parameter can consist of a combination of the following predefined values:

Name	Description
MSG_OOB	Send out-of-bounds data.
MSG_DONTROUTE	Ignore routing tables; usually used by routers and diagnostic tools.
MSG_DONTWAIT	Don't block if the data is too big to be sent in a single packet.
MSG_NOSIGNAL	Don't generate a SIGPIPE in the event of a socket error.

If the call to send() succeeds, it returns the number of bytes sent; it returns a –1 on error.

THE sendto() FUNCTION

If you are using a UDP socket (or a TCP socket if you like the added hassle of the extra sendto() parameters), you can't use send() to send data. You have to use sendto() instead.

```
int sendto(int s, const void *msg, int len,
    const struct sockaddr *to, int tolen, unsigned int flags);
```

The extra two arguments, to and tolen, specify the destination address of the message being sent. This information is presented in the same format as the address you used when calling connect(); you can reuse it here.

If you are writing a UDP server that maintains connections, you should keep a list of connected clients and refer to that list when sending them data. Alternatively, you can give each separate client its own thread (as explained later in this chapter).

A MINI-EXERCISE

To the program we are developing in this chapter to connect to the server, add some code to send the following string to the server:

```
GET / HTTP/1.0\n\n
```

The actual code required to accomplish this task is shown later in this chapter. By the end of the chapter, we should have created a simple (understatement of the century) Web browser that is capable of retrieving the index page of a Web server located on the local machine (assuming that you're running one on your Linux box).

RECEIVING DATA

Receiving data is slightly more complicated than sending data. Because you don't know when data is ready to be received, and because the receive functions block the current thread, you could run into some problems here. A solution to this snag is to use the select() function, which is covered later in this chapter.

THE recvfrom( ) FUNCTION

For receiving messages on both TCP and UDP sockets, you have to use the recvfrom( ) function. Note that this wasn't always the function you called to receive data. A now-redundant function, recv( ) (similar to recvfrom( ) but without the address details), simply called recvfrom( ) with NULL specified for the unnecessary arguments. The recv( ) function may be removed from future versions of the BSD socket library, so if you do decide to use it, I will also demonstrate a simple macro to emulate it here.

```
// Macro to emulate recv() - not really needed in
// current versions of the TCP/IP stack
#define recv(s, msg, len, flags) recvfrom(s, msg, len, flags,\
    NULL, NULL);

int recvfrom(int s, void *msg, int len, unsigned int flags,
    struct sockaddr *from, int from_len);
```

The first argument, s, specifies the socket to receive data on; the next argument is a pointer to some memory in which to store the data. This memory *must* be allocated beforehand, or your program will most likely crash with a possible buffer overflow. Because this is a network socket, a buffer overflow is a major problem because it could allow remote attackers full access to the client PC.

The len argument is the size of the allocated buffer into which you want to receive data. The flags argument can be a combination of the following predefined macros:

Macro Name	Description
MSG_OOB	Receive out-of-bounds data.
MSG_PEEK	Don't remove the message from the queue; this macro can help find the amount of memory you need to store the message in.
MSG_WAITALL	This flag causes recvfrom( ) to block until the operation is completed.
MSG_NOSIGNAL	This flag prevents a signal from being generated in the event of a socket error.

The final two arguments, from and from_len, specify where to store the source details and the size of the address details, respectively. Although the prototype claims that you should use a structure of type sockaddr, you should use sockaddr_in (as you do when connecting) instead.

On success, recvfrom( ) returns the size of the message received; it returns –1 on an error.

THE select() FUNCTION

As mentioned in the preceding section, recvfrom() is a *blocking function*, meaning that it causes the current thread to wait before continuing. This is not what you want your application to do in the middle of a busy combat sequence. To counter this problem, you can use the function select() to determine whether there are any incoming messages before calling recvfrom().

```
int select(int n, fd_set *readfds, fd_set *writefds,
    fd_set exceptfds, struct timeval *timeout);
```

The first parameter, n, is the highest number of file descriptors in any of the three sets plus 1. The next three arguments are blocks of file descriptors for data to be read, data to be written, and data containing exceptions respectively. The final argument, timeout, is how long to wait before returning. This argument should be 0 (return immediately), but you can choose to wait here. Be sure that you do not set this argument to NULL or select() will wait indefinitely before returning.

The file descriptor blocks, or FD_SETs, are controlled by a set of macros. You should never try editing these blocks yourself. The macros are listed here:

```
FD_CLR(int fd, fd_set *fds)     // Remove fd (filesdescript) from fds (fd_set)
FD_ISSET(int fd, fd_set *fds)   // Check if fd is in fds
FD_SET(int fd, fd_set *fds)     // Add fd to fds
FD_ZERO(fd_set *fds)            // Empty fds
```

The select() function returns the number of descriptors contained with activity; it returns 0 if nothing happens before the function times out. If –1 is returned, an error has occurred.

ANOTHER MINI-EXERCISE

Before reading the following block of code, add to the evolving application in this chapter a loop that prints all incoming data to stdout. Use the select() function where necessary.

THE COMPLETE MINI-WEB BROWSER

```c
#include <sys/socket.h>
#include <sys/types.h>
#include <stdio.h>
#include <string.h>
#include <malloc.h>

#define HOST "127.0.0.1"
#define PORT 80
#define BUFFERSIZE 1500

int main(int argc, char **argv) {
    int sock;
    struct sockaddr_in *server;
    char *request = {"GET / HTTP/1.0\n\n"};
    char *buffer;
    fd_set *readfd;

    // Open the socket
    sock = socket(PF_INET, SOCK_STREAM, IPPROTO_TCP);

    if (sock == -1) {
        perror("Socket error:");
        return 1;
    }

    // Where do we want to connect to?
    inet_aton(HOST, &(server->sin_addr));
    server->sin_port = htons(PORT);
    server->sin_family = AF_INET;

    // Attempt to establish connection
    if (connect(sock, server, sizeof(sockaddr_in)) == -1) {
        perror("Socket error:");
        return 1;
    }
```

```
    // Send an HTTP request
    send(sock, http_request, strlen(http_request), 0);

    // Set up file descriptors for select()
    FD_ZERO(readfd);
    FD_SET(sock, readfd);

    // Allocate some memory for receiving data
    buffer = (char *)malloc(BUFFERSIZE);

    // Message receive loop
    while (1) {
        if (select(2, readfd, NULL, NULL, 0)) {
            // Message to be read...
            recvfrom(sock, buffer, BUFFERSIZE, 0, NULL, NULL);
            fprintf(stdout, buffer);
        }
    }

    // We're done.
    close(socket);
    return 0;
}
```

CREATING A SERVER

A server isn't that different from a client, except that a bit more effort goes into the initialization process for a server. Depending on the type of server you're working with (TCP or UDP), there are a number of extra functions you have to call before your program is ready to start serving data.

BINDING THE SOCKET

Instead of connecting to a server after you create the socket, you have to bind the socket to a specific port. This is achieved using the bind() function if you are using TCP. If you are using UDP, no action is needed at this point.

```
int bind(int sockfd, struct sockaddr *my_addr, int len);
```

The first argument is the more-than-familiar socket descriptor. The next argument, my_addr, is a pointer to a structure containing information about the local address. You set up this structure in the same way as when you are establishing a socket using connect(), except that you set the sin_addr member of the sockaddr_in structure to INADDR_ANY. The final argument for bind() is the size of the local address descriptor.

USING THE listen() FUNCTION

After you have bound the socket to a port, you must tell the TCP/IP subsystem that you are willing to accept connections. This is achieved with the function listen():

```
int listen(int s, int backlog);
```

This first argument is—yep, you guessed it—the socket descriptor. The next argument specifies how many connection requests can be queued at any one time.

The listen() function returns a 0 on success or a –1 on error.

ACCEPTING CONNECTIONS

After you have called listen(), you can start your main server loop. Incoming connections can be received by calling the function accept().

```
int accept(int s, struct sockaddr *addr, int *addrlen);
```

I really don't think I need to say what the first argument is, so I'll move on to the second. The sockaddr structure is where to store the address of the remote client. Depending on how you implement your server, you may want to store this information in a linked list of other addresses, or pass this value on to a new thread to handle that client's information.

The accept() function is a blocking function, so you may want to use the select() function described earlier to check whether there are any incoming connections before calling accept(). In this scenario, the socket is regarded as data to be read.

From here on in, the rest of the server operations are pretty much identical to client operations, such as sending and receiving data.

NOTE

Because **UDP** is a connectionless protocol, anyone can send data to a UDP server. This means that all you have to do is to create the socket in the same way you would for a client and then wait for incoming data using `recvfrom()`. The server is not notified of an incoming connection because there are no connections to be established. The only time a UDP server knows about the clients is when the clients actually transmit some data to the server.

Because of this, you may want to keep a list of all **UDP** clients that have sent data to the server. When you have to notify all clients about a change in the game environment, you can refer to the list of connected machines to get the details about the remote clients.

Because **UDP** is faster than TCP—and because speed is essential in real-time applications—writing the code for game servers can be a lot of hard work. It can also be quite rewarding at the same time. Ask not what your client can do for you, but what you can do for your client.

THREADS AND NETWORKING

Because a network subsystem is relatively independent from the rest of your game, you may want to use another thread for processing network traffic. Depending on the type of application you are working with (client or server), there are different approaches to use.

At this point in the book, I want to introduce a library called pthreads (POSIX threads). You can use this library to create extra threads within an application. It is included with most Linux distributions.

The most useful function in the pthread library is `pthread_create()`, which creates a new thread within a process. The function prototype for `pthread_create()` is shown here:

```
int pthread_create(pthread_t *thread,
    pthread_attr_t *attr,
    void *(*start_routine)(void *),
    void *arg);
```

The first argument, thread, is a pointer to where you want to store an identifier for the newly created thread. The next argument, attr, contains the attributes for the thread. For now, it's safe to specify a value of NULL for this argument (this is a chapter on networking, not threads). The third argument, start_routine, is a pointer to a function that will be started in the separate thread. The final argument, arg, specifies any arguments you want to pass to the thread function.

When you want to end the thread, you end the thread function just as you would a normal function: by calling return. For more details on the pthreads library, see the man pages.

Clients

When it comes to client-side networking, it's a damned good idea to isolate the game logic and rendering from the network code—unless your game is 100 percent dependant on the network data (which is unlikely). By running the network code in a separate thread, you don't have to worry about calls such as sendto() causing an interruption to the game. Remember that sendto() blocks, and there are few ways to prevent that from happening.

If you decide to run the network code in a separate thread, you must provide a way for the two threads (the game thread and the network thread) to communicate. The first method I will demonstrate is the use of flags to signify important events, such as quitting the game.

Using Flags to Communicate between Threads

In the thread that processes user input, you might have an event such as quitting. This even sets a global variable that is checked within the network thread loop, like this:

```
extern bool quit_game;
extern int thread_count;

void *network_thread(void *data) {
    // Increase the thread count
    thread_count++;

    // Connect to server here

    // Main thread loop
    while(!quit_game) {
        // Do network stuff here
    }
```

```
    // End network stuff here

    // Reduce the thread count
    thread_count--;

    return NULL;
}
```

In the game thread, the code to cause the thread to quit would look like this:

```
bool quit_game = 0;
int thread_count = 0;

void main_loop() {
    pthread_t *net_thread;

    // Create network thread
    pthread(net_thread, NULL, network_thread, NULL);

    // Do game stuff here
    while(1) {
        // Loop until quit
    }

    // Tell all threads to finish
    quit_game = 1;
    while(thread_count > 0)
        ;

    // Do quit stuff here
}
```

NOTE

Novell suggested this method for closing all threads that are running on the server at the 1999 NetWare Developers Conference. If Novell thinks it's the best way to do it, there must be some merit in it. On a side note, if you ever go to a NetWare Developers Conference, don't eat the food. It put me in bed for a week.

USING MESSAGE QUEUES TO COMMUNICATE BETWEEN THREADS

The other method of interthread communication I will discuss here is a message queue. If you've ever done any Windows programming, you'll have a basic understanding of how the message retrieval system works.

Basically, all messages are stored in a queue. When you want to receive a message, you call GetMessage() or PeekMessage() to get the next message to be processed. These functions pull the next message from the message queue and allow you to act on it. We'll use this identical idea for our multithreaded program.

I won't go into too much detail about queues, but I'll demonstrate the basic usage here. You'd place this code somewhere in the network receive loop in the function network_thread().

```
extern void *message_queue[QUEUE_SIZE];
extern int queue_position;

        // Get message from receive queue
        recvfrom(sock, buffer, BUFFERSIZE, 0,
            from, &from_len);

        // Add message to queue to be processed
        if (++queue_position > QUEUE_SIZE)
            queue_position == 0;
        message_queue[queue_position] = buffer;
```

In our game loop, the queue would be read as follows:

```
void *message_queue[QUEUE_SIZE];
int queue_position = 0;
int queue_start = 0;

        // Read next message from queue
        if (queue_start != queue_position) {
            // New message in queue, so process it
            process_message(message_queue[queue_start++]);

            if (queue_start > QUEUE_SIZE) queue_start = 0;
        }
```

That simple (and probably very buggy) implementation of a message queue system should demonstrate how to allow messages received from the network thread to be read from the game thread itself. With this approach, the network thread can do what it does best: be a network thread.

SERVERS

In addition to the methods discussed in the preceding section regarding clients, there are a few more tricks to lighten the load when it comes to server programming. The most common trick is the use of a separate thread for each client; then you can use the interthread communication methods described in the preceding section to pass messages between the threads.

When a connection is requested with accept(), you pass the new socket descriptor associated with the fresh client as the argument to the client's own thread. This approach removes the need to keep a database of sockets (which can be a pain in the backside to maintain).

The following code demonstrates this theory:

```
// Accept the new connection
new_sock = accept(sock, NULL, NULL);

// Create a new thread for said client
pthread_create(client_thread, NULL, client_func, &new_sock);
```

PINGS

Every so often during a game, a client may be disconnected from a server. This can cause problems because there is no way to automatically detect this situation. To combat it, you must keep track of player activity using a number of methods. The easiest method is to keep a timer of how long it has been since the last message was received from a particular client. If the timer exceeds a specified time, that client is removed from the game.

Note that this approach isn't necessarily the best course of action to take. If a client is not doing much at that point of the game (dare I say that he might be camping?), he probably won't appreciate being kicked out of the game for it. Another approach is to send regular pings to all the clients.

A *ping* is a simple message that contains the time the message was sent. When the client receives the message, it sends the message back unchanged. The server can then keep track of these ping times and base the timeout value on the time between pings being returned to the server. Again, this approach might cause problems with players who are suffering high latency (but if the latency is that bad, the game would probably be pretty unplayable as it is).

You might also want the client to use a keep-alive system to make sure that it is still sending and receiving data to and from the server.

NETWORKING IN GAMES

All the stuff in this chapter up to this point is pretty generic and can be used in any application. The next sections cover some systems that are applicable only in games, such as sending only user input between the clients.

DEAD RECKONING

In fast-paced action games such as *Quake*, latency on the network can cause major problems with the game. Latency can be combated somewhat by the use of dead reckoning on the clients.

When the client isn't receiving messages from the server, it continues processing the game logic based on the last known data until it receives an update from the server. This is fine for games played in a low-latency range, but if you've ever played *Quake* at a medium-ping range, you may have noticed characters suddenly jump around the screen.

This jumpy behavior is caused by the client assuming that the character will take a different action than the server thinks the character will take. Because the server has full control of the gaming environment, what the server says is gospel.

When the server updates the client machine with the game state, it sends only the information that has changed since the last update. At other times, it only sends minor changes that affect play, such as a player changing direction or firing a weapon. The client bases its logic on a continuation of the last action sent.

There are further complications to this system, such as the infamous "death by lag" scenario. If player Bob is running towards a corner, and player Jim suddenly encounters some lag, Jim may see Bob running straight into a wall; he may then fire a few missiles and relax. Meanwhile Bob, who isn't affected by the lag, runs around the corner, sees Jim just standing there, and opens fire.

Because the server processes only the data it has received, it considers Bob's kill to have happened and updates all the clients with that version of events.

SENDING CONTROLLER INPUTS

If you have a server controlling the state of game, why bother sending every single piece of data that the client generates to the server? A better method is to send only what the user presses on the keyboard and to let the server run the main logic.

This approach not only reduces the amount of traffic being sent over the network, but allows the server full control of the game. Note that there are some problems with this system, especially for players experiencing a bit of lag. Such players may find that the server processes their input a long time after they responded. This problem was prevalent in the original *Quake Deathmatch* (not *QuakeWorld*). If you had about 200ms of lag, you felt like you were on ice. Your player would slide all over the place because the packet spent too long updating your current direction (in *Quake Deathmatch*, the client handled all the looking around).

Although this wasn't a major problem, it did get annoying at times, and it's something you should remember when designing your games.

LOBBIES

It's not much use giving the user the ability to play multiplayer games if he doesn't know where to find a server running the game. This is where lobbies come into play. *Lobbies* act as directories of active game servers, allowing players to search a database of games and choose the one he wants to play. Some lobby servers also offer a pregame chat system and staging areas where people can plan tactics before being thrown head-first into a combat scenario.

Most current lobby APIs are limited to a single platform, restricting players to competing against other people using the same platform. APIs such as DirectPlay and Kage (DreamCast) also offer proprietary game protocols, adding a further barrier to interoperability.

WHAT IS OPENLOBBY?

OpenLobby (available at **http://www.thisisnurgle.org.uk/openlobby**) is the first part of a project to eliminate the proprietary-ness of networking APIs for games. With an open protocol and an OpenSource client API (to allow porting to various platforms), OpenLobby is almost guaranteed to provide the interoperability that cross-platform development requires—even if you don't need to use it on other platforms. :)

OPENLOBBY: HTTP://WWW.THISISNURGLE.ORG.UK/OPENLOBBY

Although it's still in early phases of development, OpenLobby promises to offer many features, from persistent users to multiple chat rooms that permit users to socialize before killing each other in a shower of blood and bullets.

USING LOBBY SERVER

Connection to the lobby server is a two-stage process. First, you must connect to a central lobby server (the server software is included with the client API), and then you must log in to the server.

CONNECTING TO THE LOBBY SERVER

Before you can even think about looking for games, you must establish a TCP connection to the server. The function ol_Connect() does this for you. It takes two arguments: the IP address of the server and a port number. On success, it returns a connection object containing all the details about the lobby server, as well as game data (which is established later on). The following sample code demonstrates the use of ol_Connect():

```
#include <olobby.h>
#include <stdio.h>

int main() {
    olServer *server = NULL;

    // Connect to lobby server
    server = ol_Connect("127.0.0.1", 9090);

    // Check that the connection was established
    if (!server->socket) {
        fprintf(stderr, "Connection to server failed");
        return 1;
    }

    // XXX
}
```

The olServer structure contains various details about the server, and its definition is shown here:

```
typedef struct {
    int socket;              // Server socket
    char IPv4[4];            // Server IP address
    unsigned int port;       // Port on server
    unsigned int user_id;    // User id
    unsigned int game_id;    // Game id
} olServer;
```

The member of interest at this point is the socket member. This is a run-of-the-mill TCP/IP socket descriptor (OpenLobby uses TCP, not UDP). On BSD systems, this value is 0 on failure.

LOGGING IN TO THE LOBBY SERVER

After you have successfully connected to the server, you must log in and identify the game you are planning to play. This process is handled by another function, ol_Login(). This function is slightly more complicated than ol_Connect() because it passes several things (well, the server does several things; the client always sees the same thing). The function prototype for ol_Login() is as follows:

```
unsigned int ol_Login(olServer *session,
    unsigned int user_id,
    unsigned char user_name[16],
    unsigned char password[16],
    unsigned int game_id);
```

The first argument is the session returned by ol_Connect(). The next is the user identification number. If this value is 0, a user name must be specified. If a user name is specified, a new user is created on the server database (depending on the implementation). The next argument is the password, which is always required. If a new user is being created, this password is assigned to the user, otherwise it must be the previously assigned password.

The final argument is the unique game identifier. This identifier takes a similar format to the GUID (Globally Unique Identifier) used by DirectPlay and is compatible with UIDs from other platforms (assuming that they are 32-bit identifiers). This value is used to identify games of the same type.

ol_Login() returns the user ID on success; it returns 0 on failure.

In the previous sample of code, replace the comment XXX with the following code:

```
// Login to the server
uid = ol_Login(server, 0, "New Player", 1);

// Make sure that an error didn't occur
if (uid == 0) {
    ol_Bye(server);
    fprintf(stderr, "Error login in");
    return 1;
}
```

FINDING GAMES

Assuming that you've successfully logged on to the server, you can start looking for games. OpenLobby uses an enumeration callback to get the game names; you specify this function with the ol_FindGames() function call. This function takes two arguments: the session pointer and the address of the callback function.

The callback function takes only one argument: a pointer to a game definition (of type olGameDef). The prototype for this function is as follows:

```
void (*FindGameEnum)(olGameDef *gamedef);
```

The olGameDef structure contains details about the games, including name, IP address, and number of players. The structure definition looks like this:

```
typedef struct {
    unsigned int game_id;
    unsigned char game_name[32];
    unsigned char IPv4[4];
    unsigned char IPv6[6];          // For future use
    unsigned int port;
    unsigned int max_players;
    unsigned int num_players;
} olGameDef;
```

Add the following block of code to the start of our little sample program (after the #include statements):

```
olGameDef *my_game;

void FindCallBack(olGameDef *gamedef) {
    if (gamedef->num_players < gamedef->max_players) {
        fprintf(stdout, "Game name: %s\n" gamedef->game_name);
        fprintf(stdout, "Play this game (y/N)?");
        if (fgetc(stdin) == 'Y') {
            memcpy(gamedef, my_game, sizeof(olGameDef));
        }
    }
}
```

This simple enumeration prints the name of the available games and offers the user an option to play the game. Before this code can be called, however, we have to start the enumeration process with the following line of code. Insert it after the sample code logs in to the server:

```
ol_FindGames(&FindCallBack);
```

After the user has selected a game, OpenLobby no longer plays a part in the communication process. Everything from here on in depends on the game. However, a generic network game API is planned after the OpenLobby API is complete; this generic network game API will handle connections and the passing of data between clients. Details about this project are posted on the OpenLobby home page at **http://www.thisisnurgle.org.uk/openlobby/**.

> **NOTE**
>
> Because the OpenLobby enumeration calls are nonblocking, you may want to force a wait before continuing on to the next stage of the process.

CREATING GAMES

It's all very well being able to find the games, but before they can be found, they must be created. This process is handled by a single function, ol_UpdateGame(), which also handles the changing of details about the game, such as the current number of players.

ol_UpdateGame() takes two arguments: a session pointer and an olGameDef structure containing all the relevant details about the game. Only the creator of a game can update the game. The function prototype for ol_UpdateGame() is as follows:

```
void ol_UpdateGame(olServer *session, olGameDef *gamedef);
```

This function also allows you to change the address of the game server, if you need to change the host, for example. You do this by simply updating the IPv4 member of the game definition structure. Clients already in the game must be notified by some other means, however.

You call ol_UpdateGame() whenever something in the game changes, such as the number of players. This is an important call to make because things can become very confusing for the users if more players are in the game than the users are lead to believe there are.

ENDING GAMES

To remove a game from the lobby server's directory, simply call ol_EndGame(). This function takes a single argument: the session pointer from ol_Connect(). Like the other OpenLobby functions, this function doesn't notify clients that the game has ended; this notification must be handled by the game server itself, not the lobby API.

CHATTING IN THE LOBBY

Like any good lobby provider, OpenLobby includes support for a rudimentary chat system. Unlike other chat systems, however, OpenLobby chat is completely isolated from the rest of your networking code. There is no need to check for chat messages because OpenLobby notifies the program using a callback function; that function also contains the chat messages.

LISTING CHAT ROOMS

The process of finding an OpenLobby chat room works almost identically to finding an OpenLobby game. Unlike ol_FindGames(), the chat system lists every chat room on the server. Although this request can result in a very long list of rooms, a system exists to narrow down this list. Like ol_FindGames(), the chat callback function for finding rooms gives information about the chat rooms.

The function for finding chat rooms is ol_FindChatRooms(). Like ol_FindGames(), it takes two arguments: a session pointer and a callback function. The prototype of the callback function is slightly different than the one used in ol_FindGames(), however:

```
void (*FindRoomCallback)(olChatRoom *roomdef);
```

The roomdef argument contains details about the chat room, such as the room name and the number of members. The structure definition for olChatRoom is as follows:

```
typedef struct {
    unsigned int room_id;
    unsigned char room_name[16];
    unsigned int num_users;
}
```

When ol_FindChatRooms() is called, it starts returning the list of chat rooms. Not included in the details, however, are the names of the participants in the chat. This information is sent when the user joins the room in a packet similar to the IRC NAMES packet.

It is a good idea to store the list of rooms so that you can allow the user to select the one he wants to join.

JOINING AND LEAVING ROOMS

When you want to join a chat room, you must call the function ol_JoinRoom(). The prototype for ol_JoinRoom() is as follows:

```
void ol_JoinRoom(olServer *session,
    usigned int room_id,
    void (*callback_func)(char *message));
```

The third argument of ol_JoinRoom() is a function pointer that points to the function that will receive and process the chat messages. An example of this function is shown here:

```
void ChatMessage(char *message) {
    char sender[16], message[256];

    // Break the message into two parts, sender and text
    sscanf(message, "<%s> %s", &sender, &message);

    // Display our reformatted message
    fprintf(stdout, "%s: %s", sender, message);
}
```

It's really that easy. Okay, it's not. Your games will probably have a fancy chat window to display the message in, but the message should get across. The OpenLobby chat system is stupidly easy to use because all the complex stuff such as attaching user names to messages and the like is handled by the server.

When you join a room, the client is sent a single chat message that looks something like this:

```
:NAMES User1 User2 User3
```

This message is a list of the users in the room. Whenever the message is sent, the client should update the list of users in the room (if there is such a list) or simply ignore it. OpenLobby has a number of messages like this, and they're fully documented in the OpenLobby documentation.

Leaving a room is just as simple; a call to `ol_PartRoom()` does the job. It takes two arguments: the session pointer and the ID of the room you want to leave.

SENDING CHAT MESSAGES

Now that we know how to join a chat room and receive messages, things are looking good. But our chat system is missing one small thing: the ability to send messages. Never fear! As are the rest of the chat features, sending messages is handled by a function, `olChatSend()`.

`ol_ChatSend()` takes three arguments: the session pointer, a room number, and the actual message to send. The OpenLobby server prepends the sender's name to the message so there is no need to handle that aspect of the message on the client.

If the client tries to send a system message (for example, a message beginning with the character `:`), the server either rejects the message or removes the offending character. Only a server can send system messages because these kinds of messages can affect the clients in various ways.

CLEANING UP

When you have finished with OpenLobby, it is wise to call `ol_Bye()`, with the single argument being the session pointer. This function causes you to leave any chat rooms in which you were participating and closes the connection. The server should detect a dead client after a short while, but this approach results in unwanted packets being sent to the user for an unspecified period of time.

SECURITY ISSUES

There are a variety of security issues involved with multiplayer games, ranging from buffer overflows to denial-of-service attacks. Recently, there has been some exposure on the Security Focus mailing lists about these issues. As a developer you should do your best to make sure that your clients and servers are as secure as is humanly possible.

BUFFER OVERFLOWS

A *buffer overflow* occurs when the program tries to store too much data in an array that hasn't been allocated enough space. In most circumstances, the program just crashes, but some buffer overflows are *exploitable*, meaning that remote users can send code to be executed on the target computer.

To prevent a buffer overflow, always make sure that your program doesn't make assumptions about the size of data being copied. Use functions where you can specify the amount of data to copy, such as `memcpy()` and `strncpy()`.

DENIAL-OF-SERVICE ATTACKS

Because most game servers run UDP, it is possible for someone to spoof your IP address and cause a flood of packets to be sent to a target computer. This isn't an easy attack to prevent, but there are methods.

Have your clients establish a TCP connection to the server so that you can first authenticate their IP addresses; only after the connection has been confirmed should you then send UDP data. In this way, you can make it a lot harder to achieve the kind of attack just described.

CHAPTER 10

Artificial Intelligence

The time has come, my friends, to add an element of surprise to the lives of the poor victims who will play our games. Yes, it's time for artificial intelligence.

BASIC ARTIFICIAL INTELLIGENCE

Unless you're writing a simple puzzle game, you will need some form of artificial intelligence to get your game to do some "thinking." Although you may not need AI that is capable of "learning" (which is covered in the second half of this chapter), your game will probably need the capability to do some problem solving.

ROUTE FINDING

One of the most common pitfalls of game programming is the route-finding system used. A bad algorithm here can ruin an otherwise brilliant game. Picture this situation: You're running away from a lethal enemy, but when you turn around, you see it tripping over a step (or running straight off a cliff, which was quite common in *Quake*).

STATE-TREES

State-trees have many uses, the most common of which is route finding, but they can be used to solve quite a few other problems. The idea behind a state-tree involves the use of a tree of nodes; the root node is the starting point, and the tree slowly branches toward one of several destinations based on choices made along the way.

Imagine that we have the following problem: We are at point A, and we want to get to point D. There is only one possible route to point D, and that is to go through C. Point A has a path to point B, as well as to point C. Point B leads to point E. The route we want is pretty simple: A-C-D (see Figure 10.1).

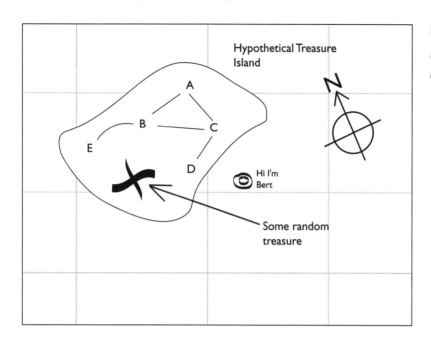

Figure 10.1

Hypothetical treasure map.

GENERATE THE STATE-TREE

The first step is to generate a state-tree of all the possible routes that can be taken on the minimap. This is a relatively simple task and can be achieved easily using a series of linked lists (with a previous-node pointer instead of a next-node pointer). Assume that our state structure looks something like this:

```
struct MapState {
    unsigned char NodeName;
    void *prev_node;
};
```

Our root node (A) would have prev_node pointing to NULL. Using this system, we end up with a tree of all the possible nodes on all the available routes (nodes B and C point to node A; and nodes D and E point to node C and B, respectively). When trying to decide the route your AI is going to take, it is simply a matter of selecting the destination node and walking backwards to find the node it must go to next.

This approach is fine when there is only one possible route to a single destination, but what if there is more than one route or more than one possible destination?

MODIFY THE TREE TO ACCOMMODATE MULTIPLE ROUTES

To change the AI system so that it can take into consideration more than one possible route, we need to modify our tree structure to allow for multiple routes. Change the tree definition to the following:

```
struct MapState {
    unsigned char NodeName;
    void *prev_node[4];
    int num_parents;
};
```

Adding new nodes gets slightly more complicated than adding a single node, but there are two possible ways to do this. The first is to use an array of a fixed size to store the previous node pointers. The second is to allocate the memory needed each time a node is added. The first way is the simplest because very few systems will require more than a finite number of routes to get to a certain point.

The following function demonstrates how to add a node to the tree:

```
void AddNode(void *node, void *parent) {
    if ((((struct MapState *)node)->num_parents == 4) return;
    ((struct MapState *)node)->prev_node[++numparents] = parent;
}
```

SEARCH THE TREE

Now that we can construct a tree, how do we search it? This is where things get icky. The system I will demonstrate now isn't the best, but it's the easiest to understand. The more complex your node tree, the longer the system will take.

To search the list, we need a recursive function that searches all possible routes that the AI can take. We also need a history of nodes already searched (to avoid backtracking) as well as a current route. To do this, we will need two separate linked lists.

First of all, let's create our linked-list system. The following code snippet allows you to create a simple one-way linked list:

```
// Linked list data type
typedef struct link_list {
    void *data;
    void *next;
}


// AddNode() - Adds a node to the linked list
void AddNode(link_list *root, void *data) {
    link_list *me = root, *new;

    while (me->next != NULL)
        me = me->next;

    new = (link_list *)malloc(sizeof(link_list));
    new->data = data;
    me->next = new;
}


// FindNode() - Finds a node on a linked list
link_list *FindNode(link_list *root, void *data) {
    link_list *me = root;

    while (me->next != NULL) {
        if (memcmp(data, me->data, sizeof(len)) == 0) {
            return me;
        }
        me = me->next;
    }
    return NULL;
}
```

Now that we have a minilibrary for the linked lists, we can actually construct a function to find the route we want to take. Following is a very basic function that is no way near perfect. It does, however, demonstrate what you need to do, but I wouldn't try this in a real game.

```
link_list *history;
link_list *route;

char found_route = 0;

void find_route(MapState *start, MapState *dest) {
    link_list *me;

    // A route has been found, so stop searching
    if (found_route) return;

    AddNode(history, start);

    // Check if we've been here before
    me = FindNode(history, start, sizeof(MapState));
    if (me->next != NULL || start->num_parents == 0) {
        return;
    }

    // Search for route in all available subpaths
    for (i = 0; i < start->num_parents; i++) {
        AddNode(route, start->next);
        find_route(start->next, dest);

        // Route found, stop searching
        if (found_route) break;

        // Not valid route, jump back to start
        me = FindNode(route, start->next, sizeof(MapState));
        me->next = NULL;
    }
```

```
// Did we find what we are looking for?
if (!FindNode(route, dest)) {
    return;
}

// Yes we did.
found_start = 1;
}
```

CAUTION

This code is purely for demonstration purposes. It contains a nasty memory leak that could do nasty things. You have been warned!

When using this system, you must `free()` link nodes as they are removed from the current route list.

The search works by generating a map of every possible route the AI system can take until it finds its final destination. It stops searching as soon as it finds a plausible route; if there is more than one route, the system always uses the first one (even if there is another, shorter route possible). Like I said, it's not a perfect algorithm, but it is simple and easy to enhance.

THE NURGLE METHOD

Now that we've discussed the most commonly used method of route finding, I'll teach you about a system I developed myself. The Nurgle method uses a grid system, making it ideal for strategy games such as *Command & Conquer*. Each location on the grid has a score assigned to it, and that score is defined by type of terrain, risk factor, distance from target, and various other factors.

Here's how the system works: When you are initializing the game, you run a test to see what sort of terrain is on each grid section. Each of the types of terrain is assigned a value, terrain that's easier to pass has a low value, while the tougher stuff gets a higher value. In addition to the terrain value, each grid has a number associated with the distance from the target point. The farther away from the target the grid section is, the higher the value. The distance value is stored in another array, separate from the terrain value.

Movement is simple. The first check you perform is to find which adjacent grid section has the lowest distance value. (You *do* want your AI to move toward the target, don't you?) When you have a list of potential squares to move into, you check to see which has the lowest terrain value. Simple, no?

However, there is another factor worth considering. Imagine the situation in which you've sent a group of artillery to attack the enemy base but your attack team is wiped out in a vicious retaliation. Do you want the artillery to go back to the same spot? Of course not. If you consider that the attack means the terrain is more difficult to cross, and adjust your terrain table accordingly, the artillery should (in theory) take a safer route instead.

Another trick you can do with this method is to normalize the terrain array whenever it changes, to allow units to take clear paths around the targets. Normalization can be performed using the following method:

```
for (x = 0; x < MAP_WIDTH; x++)
    for (y = 0; y < MAP_HEIGHT; y++)
        terrain_score[x][y] = (terrain_score[x-1][y-1] +
                                terrain_score[x][y-1] +
                                terrain_score[x+1][y-1] +
                                terrain_score[x-1][y] +
                                terrain_score[x+1][y]) +
                                terrain_score[x-1][y+1]) +
                                terrain_score[x][y+1]) +
                                terrain_score[x+1][y+1]) / 8;
```

This system, in essence, smoothes the terrain ratings and prevents erratic movement from the units, which results in more fluid motion.

GROUPING

When dealing with more than one AI opponent, it would be nice if those opponents actually used some form of tactic or strategy when attacking. For example, it would be very, very cool in *Quake* if the zombies actually had a formation when they were throwing their limbs at you instead of standing in a nice straight line, waiting for your stream of rockets to hit them. This is where *grouping* comes into play (not *groping*, you pervert). Although many games can get by without any intelligent tactics, the more fun games behave a little better.

A good example of a grouping system can be seen when dealing with archers in good ol' medieval England. There were basically two formations they used: One was to stand in a straight line, firing volley after volley at the incoming enemy; the other formation was a diamond, in which pikemen were ready to take care of any inconvenient horseman who was stupid enough to attack.

Unfortunately, grouping varies from game to game, so I can't really give you any code samples in this section, but I will explain how the concept works.

Imagine that you have a soccer team which has several possible tactics (5-3-3, 4-4-3, 3-4-4, and so on). Each player on the pitch has an assigned position (defender, left-midfield, right-midfield, and so on). Under different conditions, each player uses a different tactic to reflect the current state of play (attack or defense).

By using a two-state logic system, we can switch the grouping of the players depending on whether they are attacking or defending. For example, each defender has two wait positions: one toward the halfway line for attack, and one near the goal for defense. Keeping track of the current state of play (which half of the field the ball is in and which team has the ball) is a relatively trivial task. By storing positions for each of the possible states, you can group the players depending on the current state of play.

This logic isn't limited to a soccer pitch with fixed positions. If, instead of soccer players, you have a unit of troops with an assigned leader, the positions of the troops could be relative to the leader. If you are attacking, you stand in a line moving forward; if you're defending, you crawl away from the enemy.

Although this method of grouping may seem obvious, you'd be surprised at the number of email messages I've received asking how to do that sort of thing.

PROBLEM SOLVING

Not every AI system used in games relates to units. Some AI systems are for games like chess or *Tetris*, which require a whole new school of thought if they are to run efficiently. I'm going to cover two of the many methods used for these sorts of games, but there are many, many more out there in the great, wide world.

TRIAL AND ERROR

Everyone in the world has heard of the trial-and-error method (if not, is there room under your rock for me?). The principle behind it is this: You try something, it doesn't work, so you try something else. Couldn't be easier, no?

Just about every form of AI uses some form of trial and error, but there are specific uses for this method, such as in guessing games. Everyone has coded a "what number are you thinking of?" game (if you haven't, your rock must be getting very crowded by now).

In the number-guessing game, you have two variables: a minimum and a maximum number. Each time the computer guesses the number, the user responds whether the secret number is higher or lower than the computer's guess. If it is higher, the number last guessed is stored in the minimum variable, and if it's lower, the last number guessed is stored in the maximum variable.

For the next number the computer will guess, it calculates the mean average of the minimum and maximum variables ((min+max)/2). This concept is used all sorts of search algorithms (when the search data is sorted, that is), and this approach can zero-in on a number very quickly sometimes.

The following code demonstrates the simple guessing game just described:

```
void main(void) {
    char high = 100, low = 0, guess;

    puts("Think of a number between 0 and 100.");
    while ((high - low) > 1) {
        guess = ((low + high) / 2);
```

```
        printf("Is the number higher or lower than %d?\n", guess);
        switch (guess) {
        case 'h':
        case 'H':
            low = guess;
            break;
        case 'l':
        case 'L':
            high = guess;
            break;
        case ' ':
            puts("Woohoo! Aren't I clever?");
            return;
        }
    }
}
```

This stupidly simple example demonstrates the concept of trial and error perfectly. Although it's not a perfect representation of a trial-and-error system that can be used in most types of games, it's perfect for simple kids' games (edutainment), and the concept can be easily expanded to cover more complex problems, such as a *Towers of Hanoi* game.

MIN-MAX TREES

The final aspect of basic artificial intelligence I'm going to cover is the infamous min-max tree idea. This is how most single-player puzzle/board games work, such as chess and tic-tac-toe games. The idea is to keep your opponent from winning at any possible cost. Winning the game is only an afterthought when it comes to min-max trees.

THE THEORY BEHIND THE TREE

The aim of a min-max tree is to keep your score as high as possible, while keeping your opponent's score as low as possible. For each possible action, we calculate the possible results of the follow-up actions. This approach makes this system perfect for turn-based games such as chess or tic-tac-toe.

Here's how the idea works: In a turn-based game, there are two objectives. The first is to maximize your own score, and the second is to keep your opponent's score as low as possible. Although the first objective requires very little thought, the second requires some planning to predict what possible moves the other player can take.

Figure 10.2 shows the first few moves you might take in a tic-tac-toe game. By the time the moves are completed, there are three states left (in a real game, there would be more, but my paper isn't that big). In the first option, the Os are playing defensively; in option 3, the Os are playing more aggressively (in option 2, the Os are being completely stupid). If we were to give each option a score between 1 and 3 (3 being the highest), option 1 would score a 3 (the Os blocked the opponent as well as positioned themselves for possible victory in a single move). Option 2 would score a 1 (the opponent can win in the next turn), and option 3 would score a 2 (the Os have a chance of winning in the next turn if the opponent is a complete idiot).

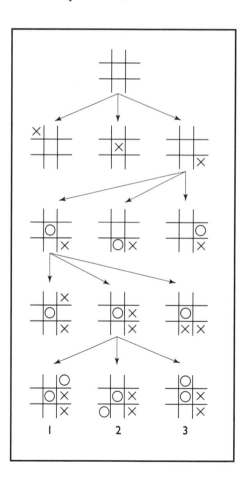

Figure 10.2

Possible tic-tac-toe moves.

PUTTING IT INTO PRACTICE

In tic-tac-toe, the objective is to get three of your symbols (an X or an O) in a row while preventing the other player from doing so. This objective must be considered for our scoring system. How can that be achieved? Well, before you can get three in a row, you must get two in a row. That's a good starting point. What other factors are involved? If the opposition has two in a row, we need to block his move, preventing him from placing a symbol in the winning cell. Although this move rarely offers us an advantage, it ensures that the opponent has to try a different pattern, therefore lowering his possible score when he moves. So we have our scoring system: the number of symbols you have in a row.

Now that we've decided on a scoring system, we need to build a tree that holds all the possible states for the next couple of moves. Although we could, in theory, hold *all* possible states for *every* single game, that's not really practical and takes the fun out of it (the game would always end in a draw or a victory for the computer, *a la* Deep Blue versus Kasporov).

So what information is our min-max tree going to hold? Well, there are nine possible places for each symbol in the game, with each cell being one of three values (X, O, or unused). In theory, we could use a 24-bit variable to store the game data (two bits for each cell require a total of 18 bits), but that's a bit of overkill. A simpler option is to use an array of nine characters.

Using the tree system from our path-finding examples earlier in this chapter, we can incorporate the nine-character array into our game using the following structure:

```
typedef struct GameBoard {
    char cells[9];
    char my_score, their_score;
    GameBoard *children[9];    // There are a total of 9 possible moves
};
```

The next stage is to calculate the moves that the computer player can take. This is slightly more complicated. In this example, assume that the computer is the O player. The following code generates the first set of moves based on the current grid:

```
void CalculateMoves(GameBoard *board, int flag) {
    int NumCells = 0, cell_num = 0;
    GameBoard *NewBoard, *orig_board;
```

```
    // Copy original board for future use.
    memcpy(orig_board, board, sizeof(GameBoard));

    // Count the number of possible moves
    for (int i = 0; i < 9; i++) {
        NumCells += (board->cells[i])?0:1;    // Only count empty cells
    }

    // For each available cell, generate the possible moves
    for (i = 0; i < FreeCells; i++) {
        // Move to next empty cell
        while(board.cells[cell_num])
            cell_num++;

        NewBoard = (GameBoard *)malloc(sizeof(GameBoard);
        NewBoard = memcpy(orig_board, NewBoard, sizeof(GameBoard));
        board->children[i] = NewBoard;
        NewBoard->cells[cell_num] = (flag)?'O':'X';

        // XXX

        // If I'm calculating my moves, work out possible
        // moves the opponent can make
        if (!flag) CalculateMoves(board, 1);
    }
}
```

Ignoring the XXX comment for now (we'll get back to that later), let's take a block-by-block look at this function as it stands.

The first thing the function does is count how many cells are available. Why does this have to be done? Well, there are only nine possible cells that you can move into at the start of the game. On every subsequent turn, there is one less cell to move into. Although we could just ignore the cells that are used when we generate the new game boards, counting the remaining cells at each turn helps optimize the code a little, and that's good practice.

The main block of code generates the board for the next possible move. This is done by allocating a block of memory big enough to hold a board data cell and then copying the original board into it. Just pointing the new data to the same old memory won't work because we'd end up overriding what we've done before. Because we are allocating memory, make sure that you free the memory when you've finished with it later in the game.

After we have generated a possible move, we check to see who we're generating the move for. If it's for ourselves (flag would be O), then we generate the next set of moves; otherwise, we don't. You can skip this step if you want to generate a map of all possible moves for the rest of the game, but that would take quite a bit of time (and memory), and make the game almost impossible to win.

The only thing left to do in this game is to decide which move to take. This is where things get a little more interesting, and this is where we bring in a classic "artificial life" example called the *Game of Life*. If you've never seen it, it basically generates a population model over time based on the number of neighbors each cell has. If the cell has too many neighbors, that cell dies; if the cell has too few neighbors, it dies. It's a bit of a morbid program when you think about it, but the idea behind it can help us work out the "score" for each possible move in the tic-tac-toe game.

Replace the XXX comment with the following code, which calculates the score for the move:

```
for (int c = 0; c < 9; c++) {
    if ((NewBoard->cells[c] == 'X') {
        if ((NewBoard->cells[(c<9)?c+1:c-1] == 'X') ||
            (NewBoard->cells[(c>1)?c-1:c+1] == 'X') ||
            (NewBoard->cells[(c<9)?c+4:c-4] == 'X') ||
            (NewBoard->cells[(c>1)?c-4:c+4] == 'X') ||
            (NewBoard->cells[(c<7)?c+3:c-3] == 'X') ||
            (NewBoard->cells[(c>3)?c-3:c+3] == 'X'))
                NewBoard->my_score++;
    } else if ((NewBoard->cells[c] == '0') {
        if ((NewBoard->cells[(c<9)?c+1:c-1] == 'X') ||
            (NewBoard->cells[(c>1)?c-1:c+1] == '0') ||
            (NewBoard->cells[(c<9)?c+4:c-4] == '0') ||
            (NewBoard->cells[(c>1)?c-4:c+4] == '0') ||
            (NewBoard->cells[(c<7)?c+3:c-3] == '0') ||
            (NewBoard->cells[(c>3)?c-3:c+3] == '0'))
                NewBoard->their_score++;
    }
}
```

Some of you may be thinking that this system doesn't take the edges of the board into account, but there is a reason for this. As well as aiming for a win, the system also considers a draw to be a reasonable result. This code takes that into account by allowing certain checks to wrap.

If, for example, you have control of cells 3, 4, and 9, there is only one way for the opponent to win, and that's by going straight down the middle. However, if you calculate what the AI player would try to do for his next turn, the most profitable square to take would be square number 5 (with three neighbors), forcing a draw.

Now that we have our next two turns planned out, we need to decide which one we want to do. There are two ways to make this decision. The first is to just go for whichever move gives us the highest score, and the other is to work out which gives us the highest score *and* prevents the opponent from winning in his next turn.

The easiest way to do this is to sort the scores from the first test and then select the highest score that also has the lowest score from the second test.

Advanced Artificial Intelligence

Now we are going to take the concept of artificial intelligence one step further. Yes, my friends, we are going to create our own pet Frankenstein. Although a deep understanding of human anatomy isn't required for this exercise, some knowledge of biology, such as genetics and neural chemistry, will help.

Genetic Algorithms

The first high-level AI we're going to look at is a genetic algorithm. Genetic algorithms are considered *non-symbolic*, meaning that the behavior is not hard coded but is learned using a vague form of fuzzy logic. Based on Darwin's Theory of Evolution, genetic algorithms "evolve" over time, adapting to the task at hand.

MEMES

Memes are a small subset of the subject known as universal Darwinism. Darwin applied his theories only to biological evolution, but what if ideas could evolve too? The theory of evolving ideas is relatively new. So how did the meme come about?

In the middle of the last century, Richard Dawkins wrote a book called *The Selfish Gene*. In this book, Dawkins presented a new theory that ideas, like genes, evolve each time they move between carriers (similar to the way Chinese whispers "evolve" as the original phrase is passed from ear to ear in a group of people). Many people picked up on the idea after this book was published. (Dawkins was, in fact, debunking the idea, but many people misunderstood his point, and in true meme style, the information was passed on.)

When you explain an idea to someone, he will make certain modifications to the original idea and spread his version. The more realistic version of the idea has a greater chance of "replicating" between carriers (a *carrier* can be a human, a book, a Web site—in fact, anything that passes information between people).

Consider a joke. People say that it's not the joke that's funny, but the way it's told. When people repeat jokes, the delivery method is slightly different each time. If someone screws up the delivery, the joke is consigned to oblivion, but if someone tells it well, the listeners will repeat the joke. In other words, the stronger joke survives, while the weak one fades out of existence.

"How can memes be put into games?", I hear you asking. It's not as hard as it may at first appear, and I'm surprised that people haven't tried it much.

THE GENEBOT

A few years ago, I was toying with the idea of world domination through the use of a computer virus. (Have fun with the CD! *evil grin*) The way the virus worked was like this: Every time the virus replicated, it randomly modified parts of itself. Some children of the virus would just crash, and others would be slightly better than the parent virus. However, before I could put my plans for global conquest into action, something terrible happened: *Quake*.

For months, I played *Quake*, not doing any programming or school work. The only word in my vocabulary was *Quake*. But, like any game with no longevity, I got bored. (I had only a 14.4 Kbps modem at the time, so *Deathmatch* was out of the question.) Fortunately, I discovered *QuakeC*. Using this language, I had fun creating python-esque patches. But fish grenades and dog launchers can add only a bit of amusement to *Quake* and add no real challenge. Then I created the Genebot. About two weeks later, I lost it in a hard-disk crash. But it's the thought that counts.

Although the original Genebot was created in the C-bastardization of *QuakeC*, I have since converted the system to C++. Why C++? Because of the nature of computer AI, all bots share some characteristics, but other aspects of the bots will be different. The inheritance features of C++ allowed me to keep things simple and to maintain readability in what could turn into some very complex code.

The idea behind the Genebot is quite simple. You have a pool of memes (I called them *genes* originally because I hadn't yet heard of memes at that time) that control the bot's behavior. Each meme has a different purpose (for example, one meme for sniping, one meme for grouping, and one for aggression). When the bot is first created, it selects random memes from the pool. When a bot is respawned, however, it inherits memes from its parent bots. This evolutionary approach causes the bot to adapt to the player's style over time.

Now on to some code. The following class framework defines the bot's behavior. Each meme has a function pointer assigned to it to aid in code reusability.

```cpp
// Bot.h - Class definitions for genetic AI

// Number of genes
#define    MAX_GENES    8

// Gene data
typedef struct {
    void * (function_ptr)(void *);
} Genedata;

// Genepool containing reference counters and function pointers
typedef struct {
    int gene_count[MAX_GENES];    // Gene usage count
    Genedata genes[MAX_GENES];
} Genepool;

// Class definition
class Bot {
private:
    Genepool *my_pool;
public:
    Bot(Genepool *my_pool_);
    ~Bot();
    void Respawn(void);
    void RunAI(void);
};
```

```cpp
void Bot_InitPool(Genepool *new_pool);
void Bot_EndInitPool(Genepool *new_pool);
```

The next source file defines the functions used in the bot.

```cpp
// Bot.cpp
#include "Bot.h"

// Bot_InitPool(new_pool)
// Initializes a new gene pool - Call before creating the bot
// for the first time
void Bot_InitPool(Genepool *new_pool) {
    for (int i = 0; i < MAX_GENES; i++) {
        if (new_pool->genes[i].function_ptr)
            new_pool->gene_count[i] = 1;
    }
}


// Bot_EndInitPool(new_pool)
// Finishes initialization of a new gene pool
void Bot_EndInitPool(Genepool *new_pool) {
    for (int i = 0; i < MAX_GENES; i++) {
        if (new_pool->genes[i])
            new_pool->genes[i]--;
    }
}


// Bot::Bot(my_pool_)
// Called when creating a new bot for the first time
Bot::Bot(Genepool *my_pool_) {
    my_pool = my_pool_;

    for (int i = 0; i < MAX_GENES; i++) {
        if (my_pool->usage_count[i] && ((rand() % 10) > 5)) {
            my_genes[i] = 1;
        }
    }
}
```

```
// Bot::Respawn()
// Called when respawning a bot
void Bot::Respawn(void) {
    for (int i = 0; i < MAX_GENES; i++) {
        if (my_genes[i]) {
            my_pool->usage_count[i]--;
        }
    }

    for (int i = 0; i < MAX_GENES; i++) {
        if (my_pool->usage_count[i] && ((rand() % 10) > 5)) {
            my_genes[i] = 1;
        }
    }
}


// Bot::~Bot()
// Called when deleting a bot
Bot::~Bot() {
    for (int i = 0; i < MAX_GENES; i++) {
        if (my_genes[i]) {
            my_pool->usage_count[i]--;
        }
    }
}


// Bot::RunAI()
// Called every frame to process the bot's AI
void Bot::RunAI(void) {
    for (int i = 0; i < MAX_GENES; i++) {
        if (my_genes[i]) {
            (my_pool->genes.function_ptr)(this);
        }
    }
}
```

This simple framework cannot work as it stands. This is the reason for developing it in C++. By building a less-generic class on this class framework, we can tailor each bot to a specific purpose while still ensuring that it will learn with the rest of the bots.

This next example is based on a *Half-Life* mod called *Frontline*, which uses three different types of classes (scout, assault troops, and heavy weapons troops). In this code, we extend the Bot class to create three new classes, starting with the scout.

```
class BotScout : Bot {
private:
    int x, y, z;     // Bot positions
    int ammo_prim;   // Primary weapon ammo
    int ammo_sec;    // Secondary weapon ammo
    int health;      // Bot's health
public:
    void Respawn(void);
    void RunAI(void);
}

void BotScout::Respawn(void) {
    ::Respawn();

    // Set the bot's starting position
    x = rand() % map_width;
    y = rand() % map_height;

    // Set the amount of ammo we have
    ammo_prim = MAX_PRIMARY;
    ammo_sec = MAX_SECONDARY;

    // Restore scout's health
    health = 50
}
```

```
void BotScout::RunAI(void) {
    // First of all check if this bot takes the fastest route to
    // the target. If not, then take the safest route
    if (!my_genes[FASTEST]) {
        FindSafestRoute(this);
    }

    ::RunAI();
}
```

This fictitious example demonstrates how the new BotScout class overrides the simple generic routines in the original Bot class to allow the scout to carry out more specific tasks, such as capturing a flag or assassinating the enemy VIP.

Actually, calling this class framework from the game is quite simple. In your game initialization, you include something like this:

```
Genepool ScoutGenes;

ScoutGenes->genes[FASTEST].function_ptr = FindFastestRoute;
ScoutGenes->genes[GROUP].function_ptr = ScoutGroupFunc;
ScoutGenes->genes[CAMP].function_ptr = ScoutCamp;

Bot_InitPool(ScoutGenes);

for (int i = 0; i < NUM_SCOUTS; i++) {
    Scouts[i] = new BotScout(ScoutGenes);
}

Bot_EndInitPool(ScoutGenes);
```

Each of the genes mentioned (FASTEST, GROUP, and CAMP) are, in fact, function pointers that take the address of the class that is calling it as an argument. Because each bot can store the details of the genes, the gene functions must use the address of the calling class to find the locations of these values. An example of one of the genes, FASTEST, is demonstrated here:

```
void FindFastestRoute(void *caller) {
    int bot_x = ((BotScout *)caller)->x;
    int bot_y = ((BotScout *)caller)->y;

    // Do some funky route finding

    // Let the bot know where it is
    ((BotScout *)caller)->x = bot_x;
    ((BotScout *)caller)->y = bot_y;
}
```

Our hypothetical scout bot is almost complete. The only thing we have left is to process the AI in each frame and to respawn the bot occasionally. Both of these tasks couldn't be easier. The functions BotScout::RunAI() and BotScout::Respawn() handle these tasks for you. All you have to do is call the RunAI() function every frame; that function takes care of everything for you.

NEURAL NETWORKS

Neural networks are what make up the very essence of the soul. You are controlled by a series of chemical reactions that send electrical impulses around the brain. These reactions are what make up the very essence of emotion. But how do they work?

Imagine a transistor. A transistor acts as a switch; when two inputs are activated, it sends a current out of an emitter. Now imagine a whole network of transistors, with some connected to inputs (such as light sensors and contact switches), and some connected to outputs (such as motors and speakers). By carefully arranging the transistors, you can create an "artificial brain" that has preprogrammed responses to certain stimuli. If you add some variable resistors, you'll be able to fine-tune the network.

This oversimplified example is pretty much how the brain works, except that there are more than two inputs to each node on the network. But how does the network learn? This is where things get complicated. As each path on the network is activated, the path becomes easier to traverse—much like a footpath through a forest becomes easier to navigate as more people walk along it, even if the path is completely unmaintained.

ARTIFICIAL NEURAL NETWORKS

Artificial neural networks are really quite simple (in the same way that genetic algorithms are simple). However, a complicated system can be quite processor intensive. Even if your artificial neural network isn't that complicated (unless you're a big fan of multithreaded applications), the system can still make a significant impact on performance if it is not thought out carefully.

For this example, we're going to use a fictitious table of data that we want the network to learn from. Table 10.1 shows a series of dog-fighting tactics and how successful they are.

Before I go into the details about Table 10.1, I'll explain what each of the tactics mean. Table 10.2 does this succinctly.

In a perfect world, you want to use tactics that result in the enemy being killed while minimizing damage to yourself. However, some tactics result in damage to yourself while still killing the enemy, so these tactics can be considered okay but not as desirable. If we were to hard-code the logic, we would end up with something like this:

```
if ((ENEMY_HIT || ENEMY_KILLED) && !(ME_DEAD)) {
    // do something here
}
```

Table 10.1 Dog-Fighting Tactics and Success Rates

Name	Successful Hit	Successful Kill	Took Damage	Was Killed	Mission Success
Immelman	0	0	0	0	0
Scissors	0	1	0	0	1
Inverted scissors	0	0	1	1	0
Low yo-yo	1	0	0	0	0
Hi yo-yo	1	1	0	0	1

Table 10.2 Definitions of Dog-Fighting Tactics

Name	Description
Immelman	Pull back on the stick to fly inverted, then rotate the aircraft 180 degrees.
Scissors	Fly downward while in a barrel roll.
Inverted scissors	Similar to Scissors tactic, but performed while flying upward.
Low yo-yo	Point nose of aircraft down, then pull up to attack the target from below.
Hi yo-yo	Pull nose of aircraft up, then attack the target from above.

This is all well and good, but after a while, a player may realize how the AI works and may use the same trick over and over again to always win. Now, what if the AI-controlled opponent could learn as it went along, on a mission-by-mission basis, and could analyze the results between missions (hence using less CPU time during the fight)?

This dynamic learning behavior can be achieved using a weighting system that performs some simple math in each AI frame. By using weights, you can cut down on your use of some large if-else blocks as well, which is another advantage. To create this weighting system, CPU-heavy algorithms come into play.

Software-based neural networks work by analyzing each situation and adjusting the weights so that a suitable outcome is achieved. Some pseudo-code that demonstrates this logic follows. The inputs are prefixed with an i (i1 is a successful hit, i2 is a successful kill, and so on); outputs are prefixed with an o. The weights associated with each input are prefixed with a w.

```
// repeat for all scenarios until no changes are made
if ((i1 * w1) + (i2 * w2) + (i3 * w3) + (i4 * w4) > threshold)
    if (!o)    // event shouldn't happen under these input
        w1 = w1 - (i1 * 0.2)
        w2 = w2 - (i2 * 0.2)
        w3 = w3 - (i3 * 0.2)
        w4 = w4 - (i4 * 0.2)
    end if
```

```
else
    if (o)      // event should have happened, but it didn't
        w1 = w1 + (i1 * 0.2)
        w2 = w2 + (i2 * 0.2)
        w3 = w3 + (i3 * 0.2)
        w4 = w4 + (i4 * 0.2)
    end if
end if
```

If you apply this algorithm to the criteria defined in Table 10.1, your weights end up with the values [w1=0.3, w2=0.7, w3=0.1, w4=0.1]. Now that your computer pilot has been "taught" which tactics work and which tactics don't, you have to tell it when to use them.

In your AI loop, multiplying the weights against the input criteria for each tactic (such as whether to perform an Immelman or not) results in a value to be compared against a threshold value (I usually use 0.5 for this value, but it can be any number). The comparison tells you how successful that tactic has been in the past. If the calculated value is greater than the threshold, the tactic can be beneficial to use; otherwise, it isn't.

The following C code demonstrates how to use this theory in practice. I'll start by defining some variables and a macro that will simplify use of the neural code.

```
#define     TACT_IMMELMAN       0
#define     TACT_SCISSORS       1
#define     TACT_LOYOYO         2
#define     TACT_HIYOYO         3
#define     TACT_INVSCISSORS  4
#define     TACT_NUMTACTICS   5

signed float weights[4];
bool tactics[NUM_TACTICS][5];

#define     DoNeural(x) \
    (((weights[0] * tactics[x][0]) + \
    (weights[1] * tactics[x][1]) + \
    (weights[2] * tactics[x][2]) + \
    (weights[3] * tactics[x][3])) > 0.5)
```

The next code segment demonstrates the use of this macro in the code itself.

```
// check whether it's a good idea to do an Immelman
if (DoNeural(TACT_IMMELMAN)) {
    // do some funky stuff
} else if (DoNeural(TACT_SCISSORS)) {
    // do some funky stuff
} else            // and so on...
```

After you have set up your basic node on the network, creating a more complex network is simply a case of adding more input variables based on the output of other nodes.

Changing the Behavior of the Network

As time goes on, different tactics will have different results. If you update the tactics tables whenever a result that wasn't expected occurs (such as a successful kill from an Immelman), you can continue to use the table. This gives the table a slightly dynamic property as time goes on.

However, when you regenerate the weights at the end of a mission, some results are undesirable (such as getting killed). You must check the desired outputs when you recalculate the weights, and then update the weights accordingly. In a perfect world, the weights for undesirable actions would be negative to make sure that they always put off potentially bad events.

Personality

A slightly cool thing about neural networks like these is that you can create "personalities" for each AI opponent simply by modifying the threshold that checks to see whether a node should be activated.

If, for example, you have a paranoid pilot who doesn't take any risks, increasing the threshold value results in less-fancy dog-fighting tactics (and in a faster kill for the pilot). As time goes on, pilots using that higher threshold would start using riskier tactics as the data table evolved.

Likewise, if you lower the threshold, pilots would take more risks when choosing tactics, choosing to risk their pseudo-lives more frequently just to get that one extra kill.

CHAPTER 11

OpenSource: Friend or Foe?

In recent years, OpenSource has been in the spotlight. Although it's been heralded as a new age of software development, is it really all people claim it can be, or is it just another form of communism in disguise?

WHAT IS OPENSOURCE?

The idea behind OpenSource software is simple, yet it involves many complex political issues. Sometimes hailed as "technical communism," other times as "the future of software development," everyone has a different opinion about what OpenSource means. But what *is* it?

The concept is like this: You write a program and release it along with the source code. Now, people have been doing that since long before the OpenSource movement started, so what makes OpenSource different? Traditional source code usually had some restrictions on its use by other people. Early versions of UNIX, for example, included the source code, but those versions weren't OpenSource applications by today's standards.

The license restrictions regulating the use of UNIX meant that only corporations and universities could actually see the source code. Mr. Joe Public didn't have a hope in hell of seeing a single line of code that went into making the monster that was the original AT&T UNIX. Modern OpenSource software is different.

An OpenSource license places no restrictions on who can see the source code or who can redistribute it. This approach allows a single program, released on a simple Web page, to end up on every Linux user's hard drive without any special effort by the original programmer.

However, just releasing the source code to a program doesn't make it an OpenSource application. To be a "proper" OpenSource program, your license agreement must meet certain requirements. Several sample license agreements are presented in Appendix A, but I'll cover some of the more common aspects of all the licenses in the next few sections.

Unlimited Redistribution

Every OpenSource software license must have the provision that anyone can give your software to anyone else, including any modifications they may have made to your original code. Safeguards are in place within the license agreement to protect the author's copyright, preventing someone else from claiming credit for the original coder's hard work. This is one of the key selling points of OpenSource software: the low cost of acquisition.

Ability to Charge for Expenses

Many OpenSource licenses offer an option to charge for the cost of redistribution, such as the price of a CD and manuals. This is how companies such as RedHat and SuSE make their money. Although these companies very rarely develop their own software for the operating system, they make the application available in a nice box, on several CDs, and with printed instruction manuals. If these companies weren't allowed by the rules of OpenSource redistribution to charge for this kind of packaged redistribution, the Linux CDs that get many of us started with the operating system wouldn't exist.

In addition to charging for nicely packaged distribution copies of software, these companies can also charge for support packages, allowing paying customers to get help when they need it, be it through email or telephone support (some companies offer on-site support, but that kind of package tends to cost a small fortune, something that the budget of the average Linux developer can't stretch to include).

The Development Models

So, now we have a vague idea of what OpenSource is, but what is the reasoning behind it? In Eric Raymond's essay called "The Cathedral and the Bazaar," he describes the two main software development models, based on community centers around the world.

The Cathedral

A *cathedral* is a place where many people can go, but where only a select few can address the masses. This development model represents commercial, closed-source software such as *Windows* and *Quicken*. These programs are written and controlled by a relatively small group of people, yet hundreds of people use them without any say in the future of the product.

This development model is like religion in many ways: Priests or ministers tell people what a particular god says, and the "little people" (that is, the people who pay the leaders' wages) must do what they're told. Although this is a mildly cynical view of both religion and software, it sums up a large percentage of the commercial software industry pretty well. How often has a vendor actually listened to your recommendations and acted on them?

THE BAZAAR

A *bazaar* is an open marketplace, bustling with people haggling over prices and lined with stalls set up and run by anyone who has something to sell. Trading takes place between the stalls, and there is a sense of an informal community about the place. People get to know other people's names, and friendships are formed.

If you replace the marketplace image with the Internet, and the goods and services being sold with various globs of source code, you should be able to see the relevance of the bazaar model when it comes to OpenSource. (Don't worry, I don't get it 100 percent either.) OpenSource works like this: You give someone your code for free; in return, they make some modifications, test it, or just spread the word about it, bringing in more users and developers to help with the project.

A large part of the OpenSource community is the word of mouth aspect of it. With sites like Freshmeat and (heaven forbid) Slashdot offering daily coverage of changes to the ever-growing world of Linux, the word of mouth aspect is very, very easy to find. Without it, people wouldn't have heard of projects such as The GIMP and the XFree86 project. By linking from various Web sites, people are finding out about these projects and joining the development teams to fill the holes that may appear in the software.

In addition to the development advantages offered by the OpenSource community, free access to the software also helps raise an army of testers. If you display your contact address in some obvious location in your software, you can be guaranteed to get bug reports in no time flat (take that as you will).

All the community aspects of OpenSource can help create high-quality software. Although this "community development" takes some time in many cases, more often than not, the effort is worth it. Take a look at the FreeCiv project, for example. When I first tried that game, it was, if you'll pardon my French, *merde*. When I tried it again about a year later, it was still bad. But a few months after that, things started improving. Developers started communicating, or a new hot-shot rookie with brilliant art skills had joined the team, because something was better, and that made the game actually enjoyable.

REASONS FOR AND AGAINST OPENSOURCE

There are many reasons why OpenSource can be considered a good thing, ranging from greater security to a development team consisting of thousands of coders. But are these really legitimate claims? In some ways they are, and in other ways they're not, depending on which side of the fence you are standing on.

TEN REASONS TO USE OPENSOURCE

There are many reasons to consider an OpenSource development route for your latest Linux game; the following sections present a small selection of them.

PEER REVIEWS

The first and most pushed reason to go the OpenSource route is that thousands of developers can look at your code and point out errors. This free testing team can help you debug your game much more thoroughly than you ever could on your own.

People become attached to their code and find it hard to test all possibilities because they think that their code is flawless or that a certain situation could never happen. As much as we all wish this were true, it isn't. Your attachment to your code clouds your judgment and can result in a faulty testing process. This is where one of the OpenSource mottoes, "Release early, release often," really comes into play.

SECURITY

The next reason you should consider the OpenSource development route is that it's a lot harder to sneak a back door into a program where it can be easily found. This issue has been raised on the Indrema mailing lists in the past, although when it comes to games, there are few reasons to hide a back door (except for copyright reasons, in which the game reports to the server that it's being used, and the server can check whether that user is allowed). Of course, if your game is OpenSource software, it would be very easy to remove the piracy checks.

AVAILABLE CODE

Another good argument for the OpenSource cause is that other people can learn from your code. This is probably one of the best reasons for OpenSource software: to aid the world in its quest to destroy ignorance in all its forms.

FREE SOFTWARE, FREE INFORMATION

Who said there ain't no such thing as a free lunch? Many OpenSource products are free in more than one sense of the word. In addition to making code available for free (as in free beer), OpenSource also allows another form of freedom. Many people claim that information wants to be free (although how a metaphysical entity can "want" anything is beyond me).

By sharing your code with other people, it can be claimed that you are helping mankind, and in doing so, you are making yourself a better person. Personally, I don't fall for that, but many others have. Who am I to say who's right and who's wrong?

MANY DEVELOPERS

In addition to the peer reviews OpenSource almost guarantees, participating in an OpenSource development approach offers the possibility that other programmers may want to join your project as time goes on. This results in several things (including more free time to enjoy that free beer I mentioned earlier). Your project will gain the skills of someone who may or may not have more experience in developing software than you do.

FAME

Publicity is probably one of the primary factors involved in the OpenSource movement, although many people will disagree with me on that. People love to see their names in the credits of a game, and that may be all the inspiration they need to work with your software, find a few bugs, and fix them. (Obviously, then, your final version of the software will have to include a list of names of people who have helped you in your development efforts.) Although this may be a cynical view of society, I'm a cynical person, and that's what counts.

THE COMMUNITY ASPECT

If there's one thing the OpenSource movement has that closed-sourced developers generally don't have, it's a sense of community. Apart from a few global mailing lists filled with professional developers (in whose company an amateur developer may feel intimidated), commercial developers generally don't help each other out unless they know each other personally from previous experiences.

OpenSource developers are generally much more welcoming of "newbies" than anyone else (although claiming to be female when you're not may get you a few enemies). Finding the help you need in an OpenSource community can prove quite easy, as long as you help out others. An elitist programmer makes few friends in the real world.

AVAILABILITY OF THE SOFTWARE

Commercial games are hard to get on the shelves, trust me. There are so many layers of bureaucracy to get through that you'll need an army of lawyers to handle all the paperwork. That problem doesn't exist with OpenSource. If you write a good game and stick it on a Web site, before you know it, it will appear on every major Linux distribution out there, as well as on FTP archives mirroring those sites.

THE CAUSE

I know some people who refuse to use non-GPLed software, whether it's OpenSource or not. They do this because they believe in "the cause" and because they have the same political beliefs that some other OpenSource gurus like Richard Stallman do. In my opinion, this is probably a bad thing to think.

Just because something happens to fall under the GPL or some other OpenSource license doesn't mean that it's the best thing since sliced bread.

BECAUSE YOU LIKE IT

Many OpenSource developers out there don't really care about the whole OpenSource movement, but they write free games because they enjoy writing them. This is probably one of the best reasons for OpenSource development—not because you follow the same political agenda, or that you worship the ground Richard Stallman walks on, but because you want to, because it makes you feel all warm and fuzzy inside.

TEN REASONS TO WRITE CLOSED-SOURCE SOFTWARE

I'm known for my neutral stance in pretty much everything, and the OpenSource movement is no exception. To balance my list of ten reasons for using OpenSource development, here is another list of reasons for using a closed-source development route. (Note that this list does not present ten reasons against OpenSource development, which is a completely different ball game.)

MONEY

It's very hard to make money from an OpenSource product. If you ever plan to get a publisher for your game, you'll have a tough time convincing them that OpenSource is the way to go. There are too many issues to count, ranging from easy piracy to intellectual property rights. Closed-source software, on the other hand, can make money very quickly if the product is of high-enough quality. Note that many developers have found that people still buy shareware, so contacting a publisher isn't always a requirement for making money from your game.

PARANOIA

Many developers are worried that people will rip off their code, or that their code is of substandard quality and don't want other people to see it. This fear of having code dissected can be found everywhere, even within commercial companies, and is probably one of the main reasons why hobby developers do not release their code.

PLAGIARISTS

A few years ago, when I was in school, people kept asking me for the code to my programs. At first, I had no problem with this, but after a while, I realized that instead of writing their own programs, these people were just copying different bits of my code to make a new program. As soon as I realized that, I decided that I wouldn't give my code out. Instead, I would guide people to the right track when it came to development. I still stick by this philosophy today; programming ignorance is still rampant in the world, and hacked code is frequently of much lower quality than new, original code.

NEW TECHNOLOGIES

Your game might be the foundation of a brand new technology, such as a new 60 frame-per-second ray-tracing engine. Anyone would have doubts about freely releasing that hard-earned technique into the OpenSource arena, and I wouldn't blame them.

New technology is one of the key reasons for closed-source software. In some ways, the fear of making a new technology freely available reflects the paranoia aspect of closed-source development. However, be aware that OpenSource software is responsible for developing some new technologies itself.

CONTRACTS

Some developers work under contract to other companies and don't actually own the code they write. This is also the case in many universities and colleges, where the work you produce as part of your course is actually owned by the institution. In many cases, universities will allow you to release your code; sometimes they won't (if the program is part of an examination, for example). In situations like these, obviously, the OpenSource development route is not an option.

SELFISHNESS

Everyone is selfish in some ways, as much as we hate to admit it. Sometimes this selfishness drives us to not let anyone see our code, even if that code could help people in the future. This short-sightedness is a major obstacle to the OpenSource movement, and one that will be very hard to hurdle.

THE "HE DIDN'T, SO 1 WON'T" ATTITUDE

Sometimes people work solely from the example of others. In some situations, people may think that because Microsoft didn't release its code, why should anyone else? Although this is a good question, it doesn't really mean much in the real world, as everyone is born with free will, and people don't have to live their lives in the shadow of someone else.

POLITICS

Everyone has a political agenda, and sometimes that plays a factor in deciding whether you will allow others access to your source. Some people believe that by keeping their source closed, they can gain ground in the development environment. How can this be, I hear you ask. By developing some funky new graphics engine, people gain the respect of their peers. However, some people believe that this respect would be lost (and that they would therefore have less power) if people knew exactly how the engine was created.

EGO

As described in the example in the preceding section, someone may feel that others won't respect him if they knew exactly how he did something with his code. That person may therefore not want to hurt his fragile ego by releasing his source code. Although this scenario may sound ridiculous, it does happen. The human ego is a dangerous thing, but it's a part of us, and there's nothing we can do to stop it from playing a role in our decision making.

SECURITY THROUGH OBSCURITY

Although many people claim that "security through obscurity" doesn't exist, it does, especially where games are involved. If people can see exactly how something is done, they can change the code to their advantage. This is a serious problem in online games, where people can give their online avatars super-human strength, making them impossible to beat by the average (non-cheating) player.

Also, keeping your game protocols closed means that people can't "sniff" packets to find out certain things about the in-game environment that would give them an unfair advantage.

THE MIDDLE GROUND

If both the OpenSource and closed-source development routes have reasons for their respective development models, is there any way to exploit the advantages from both systems? Of course there is!

FREE CODE, PRIVATE DATA

One way to gain the advantages of both sides of the OpenSource/closed-source argument is to make the source code to your game public but to keep the actual data required to run the game private. This approach has been proven successful many times; id software proved the system to work when it made the *Doom* source code publicly available.

The idea behind the *Doom* license was that although the source code was free, the data files from the registered game weren't. This meant that you still had to buy the game if you wanted to play it (the shareware data files worked just as well, though).

This approach allowed third-party developers to learn from the *Doom* graphics engine while keeping the game itself a commercial (private) product. Since id has done this, many other developers have followed suit; *Alien Versus Predator* is one of the more recent games to follow this pattern.

While many of the examples I cited usually fall into the next category, there is nothing really stopping you from doing this right from the start. In fact, rumor has it that Lionhead Studios will OpenSource its first game, *Black & White*, if the company ever actually releases it.

Another advantage to the free code, private data method is that it allows other developers to port your game to other platforms, giving you a larger user base while maintaining a potential revenue stream.

OpenSource Later

Examples from the free code, private data method described in the preceding section, such as *Doom* and *Descent*, weren't made OpenSource as soon as they were released. Instead, the development companies waited until their next big products were being played (*Quake* and *Descent II*, respectively) before they released the source to the older applications. This approach probably kept the publishers happy because anyone who was going to buy the older games already had them, so no real money was lost from the move.

But there is a potential legal issue involved with trying to use this method. If you sign a publishing agreement, there may be a clause regarding ownership of the code. Many publishers will try to sneak this clause into the contract and pray that no one asks questions. Several development companies have been bitten by similar clauses in publishing agreements. Consider DMA, who created the original *Lemmings* but agreed to give Psygnosis all the intellectual property rights to the application when they signed the publishing agreement (I doubt they'll make that mistake again).

Another factor to be careful about if you plan to wait until your game is no longer commercially viable until you release the code is that sometimes comebacks happen. For example, after several months of zero sales, something could happen, such as an appearance in a film or some fan fiction, that may spark interest in the game, causing people to start buying it once again.

Guessing what the future may bring is a dangerous thing and should be done only with extreme caution. Remember, the best way to know the future is to make the future.

Limited License

Some programs, such as *Povray*, have licenses that actually define how the code can be reused. This license allows the *Povray* code to be used on closed software as long as the original *Povray* code is made available. Another variation on this theme is to restrict the use of the software in certain environments, such as with a "free for noncommercial use" license. Many of the free game engines on the market, such as *Genesis 3D*, have licensing schemes like this.

The limited license is quite common in many areas. It allows amateur developers with little skill to use the engine to practice game development without spending months writing their own 3D engines or spending a few million on a commercial engine. The limited license allows them to focus on other aspects of game development, such as improving the game's artificial intelligence or just creating a good game in general. If the amateur game is of commercial quality, and the programmer decides to sell it, then the license will force royalty payments or lump sums to be paid to the developers of the original engine.

This philosophy is perfect in today's world. Commercial entities that want to use the software for profit have the means to pay for that use and don't want the legal hassle of doing anything to breach the contract (license) supplied with the engine. Amateur developers who don't have the means to develop commercial-quality software are still free to use the engine, and even to redistribute their end products, as long as it isn't for profit.

KEY TECHNOLOGIES

Another option when it comes to games is to keep the actual game logic itself closed, but OpenSource the surrounding technologies, such as sound and 3D engines. This option allows people to learn from your systems and to use them to make their own games, while keeping your game unique.

Alternatively, you can OpenSource the game logic itself, while keeping the engine closed. (This method requires a bit of work because any changes to the logic must be recompiled against the engine.) One method of doing this is to dynamically link the game logic at run time, as is done with *Quake II*, using a shared library and a predefined interface for the functions. Although this method isn't strictly OpenSource, it does allow people to create patches for the game.

Continuing on this theme, you may want to create a separate scripting language for your game, or use a C library that gives you access to another language, such as Python. This method allows you to OpenSource the logic (so that others can create patches and the like) while keeping your development time to a minimum. This does have a slight impact on performance, depending on the language used, but just about everything else in programming does anyway.

THE INDREMA DEBATE

Recently (in December 2000), a question was raised on one of the Indrema mailing lists regarding how the certification program (which Indrema Entertainment Systems requires all programs that run on the console to participate in) would affect the testing of OpenSource software. Traditionally, anyone can help test an OpenSource product, but the certification program prevents this free testing from happening in the usual way.

The certification program works like this: You pay a fee to get a binary file that says the program is allowed to run on the Indrema system. Without this digital signature, a program won't run on the console. This system allows Indrema to recoup the money it lost selling the console at a loss.

Like all other consoles, Indrema has a development kit (at a higher price compared to the console) that can run uncertified games so that people can test the games as they write them. The question about how to get mass testing done *before* the game is submitted to the certification process caused much conflict between OpenSource developers and Indrema.

Several ideas were raised, from big red warnings saying that the game is uncertified to a time-share system for the development kits—and everything in between.

The real problem is that the OpenSource bazaar model isn't compatible with console development as it stands today. People need to rethink the whole process before a solution that everyone is happy with can be found. The following sections present some of the ideas raised during the debate.

Big Red Warning

One of the first ideas in resolving the conflict between OpenSource and the Indrema certification system was to allow games to be "semicertified" for free while they were in development. This approach would allow people to download the game and report bugs back to the author. When the game ran, a big red warning screen would appear, saying that the game was not yet certified and that Indrema wouldn't be held responsible for any incompatibilities with the console.

This suggestion presented several problems for Indrema, the biggest being that no one would actually pay for full certification if you could get it for free, albeit at the expense of a warning screen (but that wouldn't put most people off playing the game). There was also the problem of malicious coders. Because the game would be in development, the minicertificate wouldn't be able to be tied to a single binary and the binary file would be subject to change. A checksum of the binary would have to be regenerated every time the program was compiled. This inconstant checksum could allow anyone to write a trojan that could cause irreparable damage to the end-user's console.

At the time I am writing, many people still think this is one of the better ideas proposed during the debate.

EMULATORS

My contribution to the debate was for Indrema to develop an emulator for the console that could run uncertified games. The emulator wouldn't run on the console itself because that would allow people to use it to play uncertified games.

There are several potential problems with this solution. NTSC and PAL output systems are not the same as those of a normal monitor, and these systems would have to be emulated as well. Televisions can also slightly warp the picture, making color bleed very hard to simulate accurately. Emulation of the console would therefore give an inaccurate representation of the game.

The problem is, the game logic itself can be tested using a normal PC running DV Linux. The only reason an actual console is needed is to test for interface glitches, such as warping caused by televisions or color bleeding that causes severe visual problems. These are the sorts of things that can't be emulated.

TIME-SHARE

One of the suggestions from Indrema's PR representative was to form developer groups that could share the development kits. Although this solution would work if the developers were all located in the same geographic area, this is seldom the case. This method also failed to address the problem of testers, who would still need access to the development kits to test the uncertified titles.

REGISTERED TESTERS

Another suggestion was to allow a select number of testers to run uncertified games on their standard home consoles by having a central database that the DRM (Digital Rights Management) engine would refer to when trying to load an uncertified game.

Although this suggestion puts a limit on the number of testers available, it does help ensure a higher quality of testers because the people registered as testers would have tested other Indrema games before, and therefore have experience in dealing with bug reports and the like.

THE SOLUTION

Currently, Indrema is looking at the first method, a self-certification system that would allow developers and testers to create a time-limited certificate to allow people to run the software without going through the full certification process.

The terms of usage would prevent people from sharing the mini-certificates but would allow developers to release the code and the binaries (as long as they are uncertified). At the time I am writing, it looks like this is the method Indrema is planning to use to keep everyone happy.

WHICH LICENSE TO USE?

There are many kinds of OpenSource licenses, and some people can get quite emotional regarding the issue of licensing. From the "free software fanatics" who consider only a GPL program to be free, to the more open-minded OpenSource zealot who assumes that all closed-source software is dangerous to society, there is a whole range of attitudes towards licensing.

You have several kinds of licenses to choose from, including viral licenses such as the GPL and more open licenses such as the BSD license. A number of the more popular license agreements are printed in Appendix A.

VIRAL LICENSES

Licenses such as the GNU Public License have a clause in them stating that any derivative software must be released under the same license, as must any libraries that the software is linked to. This clause has caused a lot of problems among KDE developers because their commonly used widget library, Qt, used another license.

This conflict has been the topic of a very heated argument, one side arguing that Qt must be re-released under the GPL (or LGPL, a less restrictive version of the license), and the other side claiming that the GPL was the thing that needed changing. This issue has almost been resolved since the Qt libraries were released under a new license, the QPL (Qt Public License), as well as the original license.

But there are further complications involved. Some libraries are released under the GPL (libMPEG being one example); as a result, any program that uses that library must be released under the same license as the library. It is this problem that causes people to consider the GPL to be a virus, infecting anything it comes close to.

Viral licenses are good for keeping things open, however. They do help prevent people from taking parts of one program and cloning them in a proprietary system under a completely new license. (Note that this does happen anyway; there are numerous examples of it, such as an incident where Be Inc. accidentally released a development tool based on a GPLed library.)

OPEN LICENSES

Another type of OpenSource license worth considering is a more open license that allows end users to do more things with the source than a viral license like the GPL permits. The BSD license, for example, allows someone to close the source if they so desire. Although many of the previously mentioned "free software fanatics" would refuse to go near this license, it does open up the prospect of commercial entities taking OpenSource software, adding their own proprietary extensions, and then releasing a closed version of the modified software.

Although many people would argue that this scenario does nothing for the OpenSource movement, they would be wrong. Situations such as this would bring awareness to the movement, and the original software would still be available as OpenSource software. The proprietary extensions a company may add to the software may be specific to that company's uses, such as an employee-tracking system that hooks up to a custom database. Releasing the extensions to allow access to a system nobody has access to would have very little point.

Many OpenSource licenses allow practices like the one just described. In my humble opinion, allowing people to do this is vital to the health of OpenSource in the enterprise environment.

When it comes to games, if you decided to release a small part of your product as OpenSource (such as the graphics engine and nothing else), an open license would allow you to do so. The terms of the GPL dictate that the *entire* program must be made available to OpenSource (or must be dynamically linked to the LGPL library, if you use the lesser version of the license).

CUSTOM LICENSES

Some situations might require you to write your own software license from scratch. This approach can be a problem because you would have to remember to "cross all the *i*s and dot all the *t*s." On the other hand, it allows you to have a license tailor-made to the software you're writing.

If you plan on having a restricted-use license, you will probably have to write your own license. It doesn't have to be stupidly long and complex; it just has to cover all the essential features such as redistribution rights, copyright, and disclaimers.

LIABILITY

One area that most OpenSource licenses don't cover is who is responsible when everything breaks. With off-the-shelf software, you know who you can turn to (and sue) if you lose all your data, but with OpenSource, that safeguard is rarely there.

Although many license agreements include clauses to indemnify the original developers from blame, these clauses offer very little protection under circumstances of gross negligence.

When a company is looking into purchasing software, it has to consider the liability issue. The liability issue is the number-one reason why many people still buy faulty closed-source software: Because there is a single source for fixes and blame. With OpenSource software, nobody knows who is responsible for a certain line of code, or who wrote the bit of code that caused a conflict with another patch.

Although liability isn't really an issue involving games (unless your title happens to be used to pilot planes covertly, which is unlikely), it does affect the business perspective of OpenSource software. Some publishers might want the liability factor to be resolved before any contracts are signed.

APPENDIX A

OpenSource License Agreements

There are more OpenSource license agreements than you can shake a stick at, so I will include only the most popular ones in this appendix. I'll start with the most common, the GNU Public License. This is the license that is distributed with the Linux kernel, as well as the core of most Linux.

GNU GENERAL PUBLIC LICENSE

Version 2, June 1991

Copyright © 1989, 1991 Free Software Foundation, Inc. 675 Mass Ave, Cambridge, MA 02139, USA.

Everyone is permitted to copy and distribute verbatim copies of this license document, but changing it is not allowed.

PREAMBLE

The licenses for most software are designed to take away your freedom to share and change it. By contrast, the GNU General Public License is intended to guarantee your freedom to share and change free software—to make sure the software is free for all its users. This General Public License applies to most of the Free Software Foundation's software and to any other program whose authors commit to using it. (Some other Free Software Foundation software is covered by the GNU Library General Public License instead.) You can apply it to your programs, too. When we speak of *free software*, we are referring to freedom, not price. Our General Public Licenses are designed to make sure that you have the freedom to distribute copies of free software (and charge for this service if you wish), that you receive source code or can get it if you want it, that you can change the software or use pieces of it in new free programs; and that you know you can do these things.

To protect your rights, we need to make restrictions that forbid anyone to deny you these rights or to ask you to surrender the rights. These restrictions translate to certain responsibilities for you if you distribute copies of the software, or if you modify it.

For example, if you distribute copies of such a program, whether gratis or for a fee, you must give the recipients all the rights that you have. You must make sure that they, too, receive or can get the source code. And you must show them these terms so they know their rights.

We protect your rights with two steps: (1) copyright the software, and (2) offer you this license which gives you legal permission to copy, distribute and/or modify the software.

Also, for each author's protection and ours, we want to make certain that everyone understands that there is no warranty for this free software. If the software is modified by someone else and passed on, we want its recipients to know that what they have is not the original, so that any problems introduced by others will not reflect on the original authors' reputations.

Finally, any free program is threatened constantly by software patents. We wish to avoid the danger that redistributors of a free program will individually obtain patent licenses, in effect making the program proprietary. To prevent this, we have made it clear that any patent must be licensed for everyone's free use or not licensed at all.

The precise terms and conditions for copying, distribution and modification follow.

TERMS AND CONDITIONS FOR COPYING, DISTRIBUTION, AND MODIFICATION

0. This License applies to any program or other work which contains a notice placed by the copyright holder saying it may be distributed under the terms of this General Public License. The "Program", below, refers to any such program or work, and a "work based on the Program" means either the Program or any derivative work under copyright law: that is to say, a work containing the Program or a portion of it, either verbatim or with modifications and/or translated into another language. (Hereinafter, translation is included without limitation in the term "modification".) Each licensee is addressed as "you".

   Activities other than copying, distribution and modification are not covered by this License; they are outside its scope. The act of running the Program is not restricted, and the output from the Program is covered only if its contents constitute a work based on the Program (independent of having been made by running the Program). Whether that is true depends on what the Program does.

1. You may copy and distribute verbatim copies of the Program's source code as you receive it, in any medium, provided that you conspicuously and appropriately publish on each copy an appropriate copyright notice and disclaimer of warranty; keep intact all the notices that refer to this License and to the absence of any warranty; and give any other recipients of the Program a copy of this License along with the Program.

   You may charge a fee for the physical act of transferring a copy, and you may at your option offer warranty protection in exchange for a fee.

2. You may modify your copy or copies of the Program or any portion of it, thus forming a work based on the Program, and copy and distribute such modifications or work under the terms of Section 1 above, provided that you also meet all of these conditions:

   a) You must cause the modified files to carry prominent notices stating that you changed the files and the date of any change.

   b) You must cause any work that you distribute or publish, that in whole or in part contains or is derived from the Program or any part thereof, to be licensed as a whole at no charge to all third parties under the terms of this License.

   c) If the modified program normally reads commands interactively when run, you must cause it, when started running for such interactive use in the most ordinary way, to print or display an announcement including an appropriate copyright notice and a notice that there is no warranty (or else, saying that you provide a warranty) and that users may redistribute the program under these conditions, and telling the user how to view a copy of this License. (Exception: if the Program itself is interactive but does not normally print such an announcement, your work based on the Program is not required to print an announcement.)

   These requirements apply to the modified work as a whole. If identifiable sections of that work are not derived from the Program, and can be reasonably considered independent and separate works in themselves, then this License, and its terms, do not apply to those sections when you distribute them as separate works. But when you distribute the same sections as part of a whole which is a work based on the Program, the distribution of the whole must be on the terms of this License, whose permissions for other licensees extend to the entire whole, and thus to each and every part regardless of who wrote it.

   Thus, it is not the intent of this section to claim rights or contest your rights to work written entirely by you; rather, the intent is to exercise the right to control the distribution of derivative or collective works based on the Program.

   In addition, mere aggregation of another work not based on the Program with the Program (or with a work based on the Program) on a volume of a storage or distribution medium does not bring the other work under the scope of this License.

3. You may copy and distribute the Program (or a work based on it, under Section 2) in object code or executable form under the terms of Sections 1 and 2 above provided that you also do one of the following:

   a) Accompany it with the complete corresponding machine-readable source code, which must be distributed under the terms of Sections 1 and 2 above on a medium customarily used for software interchange; or,

b) Accompany it with a written offer, valid for at least three years, to give any third party, for a charge no more than your cost of physically performing source distribution, a complete machine-readable copy of the corresponding source code, to be distributed under the terms of Sections 1 and 2 above on a medium customarily used for software interchange; or,

c) Accompany it with the information you received as to the offer to distribute corresponding source code. (This alternative is allowed only for noncommercial distribution and only if you received the program in object code or executable form with such an offer, in accord with Subsection b above.)

The source code for a work means the preferred form of the work for making modifications to it. For an executable work, complete source code means all the source code for all modules it contains, plus any associated interface definition files, plus the scripts used to control compilation and installation of the executable. However, as a special exception, the source code distributed need not include anything that is normally distributed (in either source or binary form) with the major components (compiler, kernel, and so on) of the operating system on which the executable runs, unless that component itself accompanies the executable.

If distribution of executable or object code is made by offering access to copy from a designated place, then offering equivalent access to copy the source code from the same place counts as distribution of the source code, even though third parties are not compelled to copy the source along with the object code.

4. You may not copy, modify, sublicense, or distribute the Program except as expressly provided under this License. Any attempt otherwise to copy, modify, sublicense or distribute the Program is void, and will automatically terminate your rights under this License. However, parties who have received copies, or rights, from you under this License will not have their licenses terminated so long as such parties remain in full compliance.

5. You are not required to accept this License, since you have not signed it. However, nothing else grants you permission to modify or distribute the Program or its derivative works. These actions are prohibited by law if you do not accept this License. Therefore, by modifying or distributing the Program (or any work based on the Program), you indicate your acceptance of this License to do so, and all its terms and conditions for copying, distributing or modifying the Program or works based on it.

6. Each time you redistribute the Program (or any work based on the Program), the recipient automatically receives a license from the original licensor to copy, distribute or modify the Program subject to these terms and conditions. You may not impose any further restrictions on the recipients' exercise of the rights granted herein. You are not responsible for enforcing compliance by third parties to this License.

7. If, as a consequence of a court judgment or allegation of patent infringement or for any other reason (not limited to patent issues), conditions are imposed on you (whether by court order, agreement or otherwise) that contradict the conditions of this License, they do not excuse you from the conditions of this License. If you cannot distribute so as to satisfy simultaneously your obligations under this License and any other pertinent obligations, then as a consequence you may not distribute the Program at all. For example, if a patent license would not permit royalty-free redistribution of the Program by all those who receive copies directly or indirectly through you, then the only way you could satisfy both it and this License would be to refrain entirely from distribution of the Program.

   If any portion of this section is held invalid or unenforceable under any particular circumstance, the balance of the section is intended to apply and the section as a whole is intended to apply in other circumstances.

   It is not the purpose of this section to induce you to infringe any patents or other property right claims or to contest validity of any such claims; this section has the sole purpose of protecting the integrity of the free software distribution system, which is implemented by public license practices. Many people have made generous contributions to the wide range of software distributed through that system in reliance on consistent application of that system; it is up to the author/donor to decide if he or she is willing to distribute software through any other system and a licensee cannot impose that choice.

   This section is intended to make thoroughly clear what is believed to be a consequence of the rest of this License.

8. If the distribution and/or use of the Program is restricted in certain countries either by patents or by copyrighted interfaces, the original copyright holder who places the Program under this License may add an explicit geographical distribution limitation excluding those countries, so that distribution is permitted only in or among countries not thus excluded. In such case, this License incorporates the limitation as if written in the body of this License.

9. The Free Software Foundation may publish revised and/or new versions of the General Public License from time to time. Such new versions will be similar in spirit to the present version, but may differ in detail to address new problems or concerns.

   Each version is given a distinguishing version number. If the Program specifies a version number of this License which applies to it and "any later version", you have the option of following the terms and conditions either of that version or of any later version published by the Free Software Foundation. If the Program does not specify a version number of this License, you may choose any version ever published by the Free Software Foundation.

10. If you wish to incorporate parts of the Program into other free programs whose distribution conditions are different, write to the author to ask for permission. For software which is copyrighted by the Free Software Foundation, write to the Free Software Foundation; we sometimes make exceptions for this. Our decision will be guided by the two goals of preserving the free status of all derivatives of our free software and of promoting the sharing and reuse of software generally.

11. BECAUSE THE PROGRAM IS LICENSED FREE OF CHARGE, THERE IS NO WARRANTY FOR THE PROGRAM, TO THE EXTENT PERMITTED BY APPLICABLE LAW. EXCEPT WHEN OTHERWISE STATED IN WRITING THE COPYRIGHT HOLDERS AND/OR OTHER PARTIES PROVIDE THE PROGRAM "AS IS" WITHOUT WARRANTY OF ANY KIND, EITHER EXPRESSED OR IMPLIED, INCLUDING, BUT NOT LIMITED TO, THE IMPLIED WARRANTIES OF MERCHANTABILITY AND FITNESS FOR A PARTICULAR PURPOSE. THE ENTIRE RISK AS TO THE QUALITY AND PERFORMANCE OF THE PROGRAM IS WITH YOU. SHOULD THE PROGRAM PROVE DEFECTIVE, YOU ASSUME THE COST OF ALL NECESSARY SERVICING, REPAIR OR CORRECTION.

12. IN NO EVENT UNLESS REQUIRED BY APPLICABLE LAW OR AGREED TO IN WRITING WILL ANY COPYRIGHT HOLDER, OR ANY OTHER PARTY WHO MAY MODIFY AND/OR REDISTRIBUTE THE PROGRAM AS PERMITTED ABOVE, BE LIABLE TO YOU FOR DAMAGES, INCLUDING ANY GENERAL, SPECIAL, INCIDENTAL OR CONSEQUENTIAL DAMAGES ARISING OUT OF THE USE OR INABILITY TO USE THE PROGRAM (INCLUDING BUT NOT LIMITED TO LOSS OF DATA OR DATA BEING RENDERED INACCURATE OR LOSSES SUSTAINED BY YOU OR THIRD PARTIES OR A FAILURE OF THE PROGRAM TO OPERATE WITH ANY OTHER PROGRAMS), EVEN IF SUCH HOLDER OR OTHER PARTY HAS BEEN ADVISED OF THE POSSIBILITY OF SUCH DAMAGES.

GNU LESSER GENERAL PUBLIC LICENSE

Version 2.1, February 1999

(The master copy of this license lives on the GNU Web site.) Copyright © 1991, 1999 Free Software Foundation, Inc. 59 Temple Place, Suite 330, Boston, MA 02111-1307 USA

Everyone is permitted to copy and distribute verbatim copies of this license document, but changing it is not allowed.

[This is the first released version of the Lesser GPL. It also counts as the successor of the GNU Library Public License, version 2, hence the version number 2.1.]

PREAMBLE

The licenses for most software are designed to take away your freedom to share and change it. By contrast, the GNU General Public Licenses are intended to guarantee your freedom to share and change free software—to make sure the software is free for all its users.

This license, the Lesser General Public License, applies to some specially designated software packages—typically libraries—of the Free Software Foundation and other authors who decide to use it. You can use it too, but we suggest you first think carefully about whether this license or the ordinary General Public License is the better strategy to use in any particular case, based on the explanations below.

When we speak of *free software,* we are referring to freedom of use, not price. Our General Public Licenses are designed to make sure that you have the freedom to distribute copies of free software (and charge for this service if you wish); that you receive source code or can get it if you want it; that you can change the software and use pieces of it in new free programs; and that you are informed that you can do these things.

To protect your rights, we need to make restrictions that forbid distributors to deny you these rights or to ask you to surrender these rights. These restrictions translate to certain responsibilities for you if you distribute copies of the library or if you modify it.

For example, if you distribute copies of the library, whether gratis or for a fee, you must give the recipients all the rights that we gave you. You must make sure that they, too, receive or can get the source code. If you link other code with the library, you must provide complete object files to the recipients, so that they can relink them with the library after making changes to the library and recompiling it. And you must show them these terms so they know their rights.

We protect your rights with a two-step method: (1) we copyright the library, and (2) we offer you this license, which gives you legal permission to copy, distribute and/or modify the library.

To protect each distributor, we want to make it very clear that there is no warranty for the free library. Also, if the library is modified by someone else and passed on, the recipients should know that what they have is not the original version, so that the original author's reputation will not be affected by problems that might be introduced by others.

Finally, software patents pose a constant threat to the existence of any free program. We wish to make sure that a company cannot effectively restrict the users of a free program by obtaining a restrictive license from a patent holder. Therefore, we insist that any patent license obtained for a version of the library must be consistent with the full freedom of use specified in this license.

Most GNU software, including some libraries, is covered by the ordinary GNU General Public License. This license, the GNU Lesser General Public License, applies to certain designated libraries, and is quite different from the ordinary General Public License. We use this license for certain libraries in order to permit linking those libraries into non-free programs.

When a program is linked with a library, whether statically or using a shared library, the combination of the two is legally speaking a *combined work*, a derivative of the original library. The ordinary General Public License therefore permits such linking only if the entire combination fits its criteria of freedom. The Lesser General Public License permits more lax criteria for linking other code with the library.

We call this license the "Lesser" General Public License because it does Less to protect the user's freedom than the ordinary General Public License. It also provides other free software developers Less of an advantage over competing non-free programs. These disadvantages are the reason we use the ordinary General Public License for many libraries. However, the Lesser license provides advantages in certain special circumstances.

For example, on rare occasions, there may be a special need to encourage the widest possible use of a certain library, so that it becomes a *de-facto* standard. To achieve this, non-free programs must be allowed to use the library. A more frequent case is that a free library does the same job as widely used non-free libraries. In this case, there is little to gain by limiting the free library to free software only, so we use the Lesser General Public License.

In other cases, permission to use a particular library in non-free programs enables a greater number of people to use a large body of free software. For example, permission to use the GNU C Library in non-free programs enables many more people to use the whole GNU operating system, as well as its variant, the GNU/Linux operating system.

Although the Lesser General Public License is Less protective of the users' freedom, it does ensure that the user of a program that is linked with the Library has the freedom and the wherewithal to run that program using a modified version of the Library.

The precise terms and conditions for copying, distribution and modification follow. Pay close attention to the difference between a "work based on the library" and a "work that uses the library". The former contains code derived from the library, whereas the latter must be combined with the library in order to run.

TERMS AND CONDITIONS FOR COPYING, DISTRIBUTION, AND MODIFICATION

0. This License Agreement applies to any software library or other program which contains a notice placed by the copyright holder or other authorized party saying it may be distributed under the terms of this Lesser General Public License (also called "this License"). Each licensee is addressed as "you".

   A "library" means a collection of software functions and/or data prepared so as to be conveniently linked with application programs (which use some of those functions and data) to form executables.

   The "Library", below, refers to any such software library or work which has been distributed under these terms. A "work based on the Library" means either the Library or any derivative work under copyright law—that is to say, a work containing the Library or a portion of it, either verbatim or with modifications and/or translated straightforwardly into another language. (Hereinafter, translation is included without limitation in the term "modification".)

   "Source code" for a work means the preferred form of the work for making modifications to it. For a library, complete source code means all the source code for all modules it contains, plus any associated interface definition files, plus the scripts used to control compilation and installation of the library.

   Activities other than copying, distribution and modification are not covered by this License; they are outside its scope. The act of running a program using the Library is not restricted, and output from such a program is covered only if its contents constitute a work based on the Library (independent of the use of the Library in a tool for writing it). Whether that is true depends on what the Library does and what the program that uses the Library does.

1. You may copy and distribute verbatim copies of the Library's complete source code as you receive it, in any medium, provided that you conspicuously and appropriately publish on each copy an appropriate copyright notice and disclaimer of warranty; keep intact all the notices that refer to this License and to the absence of any warranty; and distribute a copy of this License along with the Library.

   You may charge a fee for the physical act of transferring a copy, and you may at your option offer warranty protection in exchange for a fee.

2. You may modify your copy or copies of the Library or any portion of it, thus forming a work based on the Library, and copy and distribute such modifications or work under the terms of Section 1 above, provided that you also meet all of these conditions:

   a) The modified work must itself be a software library.

   b) You must cause the files modified to carry prominent notices stating that you changed the files and the date of any change.

   c) You must cause the whole of the work to be licensed at no charge to all third parties under the terms of this License.

   d) If a facility in the modified Library refers to a function or a table of data to be supplied by an application program that uses the facility, other than as an argument passed when the facility is invoked, then you must make a good faith effort to ensure that, in the event an application does not supply such function or table, the facility still operates, and performs whatever part of its purpose remains meaningful.

   (For example, a function in a library to compute square roots has a purpose that is entirely well-defined independent of the application. Therefore, Subsection 2d requires that any application-supplied function or table used by this function must be optional: if the application does not supply it, the square root function must still compute square roots.)

   These requirements apply to the modified work as a whole. If identifiable sections of that work are not derived from the Library, and can be reasonably considered independent and separate works in themselves, then this License, and its terms, do not apply to those sections when you distribute them as separate works. But when you distribute the same sections as part of a whole which is a work based on the Library, the distribution of the whole must be on the terms of this License, whose permissions for other licensees extend to the entire whole, and thus to each and every part regardless of who wrote it.

   Thus, it is not the intent of this section to claim rights or contest your rights to work written entirely by you; rather, the intent is to exercise the right to control the distribution of derivative or collective works based on the Library.

   In addition, mere aggregation of another work not based on the Library with the Library (or with a work based on the Library) on a volume of a storage or distribution medium does not bring the other work under the scope of this License.

3. You may opt to apply the terms of the ordinary GNU General Public License instead of this License to a given copy of the Library. To do this, you must alter all the notices that refer to this License, so that they refer to the ordinary GNU General Public License, version 2, instead of to this License. (If a newer version than version 2 of the ordinary GNU General Public License has appeared, then you can specify that version instead if you wish.) Do not make any other change in these notices. Once this change is made in a given copy, it is irreversible for that copy, so the ordinary GNU General Public License applies to all subsequent copies and derivative works made from that copy. This option is useful when you wish to copy part of the code of the Library into a program that is not a library.

4. You may copy and distribute the Library (or a portion or derivative of it, under Section 2) in object code or executable form under the terms of Sections 1 and 2 above provided that you accompany it with the complete corresponding machine-readable source code, which must be distributed under the terms of Sections 1 and 2 above on a medium customarily used for software interchange. If distribution of object code is made by offering access to copy from a designated place, then offering equivalent access to copy the source code from the same place satisfies the requirement to distribute the source code, even though third parties are not compelled to copy the source along with the object code.

5. A program that contains no derivative of any portion of the Library, but is designed to work with the Library by being compiled or linked with it, is called a "work that uses the Library". Such a work, in isolation, is not a derivative work of the Library, and therefore falls outside the scope of this License.

However, linking a "work that uses the Library" with the Library creates an executable that is a derivative of the Library (because it contains portions of the Library), rather than a "work that uses the library". The executable is therefore covered by this License. Section 6 states terms for distribution of such executables.

When a "work that uses the Library" uses material from a header file that is part of the Library, the object code for the work may be a derivative work of the Library even though the source code is not. Whether this is true is especially significant if the work can be linked without the Library, or if the work is itself a library. The threshold for this to be true is not precisely defined by law.

If such an object file uses only numerical parameters, data structure layouts and accessors, and small macros and small inline functions (ten lines or less in length), then the use of the object file is unrestricted, regardless of whether it is legally a derivative work. (Executables containing this object code plus portions of the Library will still fall under Section 6.)

Otherwise, if the work is a derivative of the Library, you may distribute the object code for the work under the terms of Section 6. Any executables containing that work also fall under Section 6, whether or not they are linked directly with the Library itself.

6. As an exception to the Sections above, you may also combine or link a "work that uses the Library" with the Library to produce a work containing portions of the Library, and distribute that work under terms of your choice, provided that the terms permit modification of the work for the customer's own use and reverse engineering for debugging such modifications.

You must give prominent notice with each copy of the work that the Library is used in it and that the Library and its use are covered by this License. You must supply a copy of this License. If the work during execution displays copyright notices, you must include the copyright notice for the Library among them, as well as a reference directing the user to the copy of this License. Also, you must do one of these things:

   a) Accompany the work with the complete corresponding machine-readable source code for the Library including whatever changes were used in the work (which must be distributed under Sections 1 and 2 above); and, if the work is an executable linked with the Library, with the complete machine-readable "work that uses the Library", as object code and/or source code, so that the user can modify the Library and then relink to produce a modified executable containing the modified Library. (It is understood that the user who changes the contents of definitions files in the Library will not necessarily be able to recompile the application to use the modified definitions.)

   b) Use a suitable shared library mechanism for linking with the Library. A suitable mechanism is one that (1) uses at run time a copy of the library already present on the user's computer system, rather than copying library functions into the executable, and (2) will operate properly with a modified version of the library, if the user installs one, as long as the modified version is interface-compatible with the version that the work was made with.

   c) Accompany the work with a written offer, valid for at least three years, to give the same user the materials specified in Subsection 6a, above, for a charge no more than the cost of performing this distribution.

   d) If distribution of the work is made by offering access to copy from a designated place, offer equivalent access to copy the above specified materials from the same place.

   e) Verify that the user has already received a copy of these materials or that you have already sent this user a copy.

For an executable, the required form of the "work that uses the Library" must include any data and utility programs needed for reproducing the executable from it. However, as a special exception, the materials to be distributed need not include anything that is normally distributed (in either source or binary form) with the major components (compiler, kernel, and so on) of the operating system on which the executable runs, unless that component itself accompanies the executable.

It may happen that this requirement contradicts the license restrictions of other proprietary libraries that do not normally accompany the operating system. Such a contradiction means you cannot use both them and the Library together in an executable that you distribute.

7. You may place library facilities that are a work based on the Library side-by-side in a single library together with other library facilities not covered by this License, and distribute such a combined library, provided that the separate distribution of the work based on the Library and of the other library facilities is otherwise permitted, and provided that you do these two things:

   a) Accompany the combined library with a copy of the same work based on the Library, uncombined with any other library facilities. This must be distributed under the terms of the Sections above.

   b) Give prominent notice with the combined library of the fact that part of it is a work based on the Library, and explaining where to find the accompanying uncombined form of the same work.

8. You may not copy, modify, sublicense, link with, or distribute the Library except as expressly provided under this License. Any attempt otherwise to copy, modify, sublicense, link with, or distribute the Library is void, and will automatically terminate your rights under this License. However, parties who have received copies, or rights, from you under this License will not have their licenses terminated so long as such parties remain in full compliance.

9. You are not required to accept this License, since you have not signed it. However, nothing else grants you permission to modify or distribute the Library or its derivative works. These actions are prohibited by law if you do not accept this License. Therefore, by modifying or distributing the Library (or any work based on the Library), you indicate your acceptance of this License to do so, and all its terms and conditions for copying, distributing or modifying the Library or works based on it.

10. Each time you redistribute the Library (or any work based on the Library), the recipient automatically receives a license from the original licensor to copy, distribute, link with or modify the Library subject to these terms and conditions. You may not impose any further restrictions on the recipients' exercise of the rights granted herein. You are not responsible for enforcing compliance by third parties with this License.

11. If, as a consequence of a court judgment or allegation of patent infringement or for any other reason (not limited to patent issues), conditions are imposed on you (whether by court order, agreement or otherwise) that contradict the conditions of this License, they do not excuse you from the conditions of this License. If you cannot distribute so as to satisfy simultaneously your obligations under this License and any other pertinent obligations, then as a consequence you may not distribute the Library at all. For example, if a patent license would not permit royalty-free redistribution of the Library by all those who receive copies directly or indirectly through you, then the only way you could satisfy both it and this License would be to refrain entirely from distribution of the Library.

If any portion of this section is held invalid or unenforceable under any particular circumstance, the balance of the section is intended to apply, and the section as a whole is intended to apply in other circumstances.

It is not the purpose of this section to induce you to infringe any patents or other property right claims or to contest validity of any such claims; this section has the sole purpose of protecting the integrity of the free software distribution system which is implemented by public license practices. Many people have made generous contributions to the wide range of software distributed through that system in reliance on consistent application of that system; it is up to the author/donor to decide if he or she is willing to distribute software through any other system and a licensee cannot impose that choice.

This section is intended to make thoroughly clear what is believed to be a consequence of the rest of this License.

12. If the distribution and/or use of the Library is restricted in certain countries either by patents or by copyrighted interfaces, the original copyright holder who places the Library under this License may add an explicit geographical distribution limitation excluding those countries, so that distribution is permitted only in or among countries not thus excluded. In such case, this License incorporates the limitation as if written in the body of this License.

13. The Free Software Foundation may publish revised and/or new versions of the Lesser General Public License from time to time. Such new versions will be similar in spirit to the present version, but may differ in detail to address new problems or concerns.

Each version is given a distinguishing version number. If the Library specifies a version number of this License which applies to it and "any later version", you have the option of following the terms and conditions either of that version or of any later version published by the Free Software Foundation. If the Library does not specify a license version number, you may choose any version ever published by the Free Software Foundation.

14. If you wish to incorporate parts of the Library into other free programs whose distribution conditions are incompatible with these, write to the author to ask for permission. For software which is copyrighted by the Free Software Foundation, write to the Free Software Foundation; we sometimes make exceptions for this. Our decision will be guided by the two goals of preserving the free status of all derivatives of our free software and of promoting the sharing and reuse of software generally.

15. BECAUSE THE LIBRARY IS LICENSED FREE OF CHARGE, THERE IS NO WARRANTY FOR THE LIBRARY, TO THE EXTENT PERMITTED BY APPLICABLE LAW. EXCEPT WHEN OTHERWISE STATED IN WRITING THE COPYRIGHT HOLDERS AND/OR OTHER PARTIES PROVIDE THE LIBRARY "AS IS" WITHOUT WARRANTY OF ANY KIND, EITHER EXPRESSED OR

IMPLIED, INCLUDING, BUT NOT LIMITED TO, THE IMPLIED WARRANTIES OF MER-
CHANTABILITY AND FITNESS FOR A PARTICULAR PURPOSE. THE ENTIRE RISK AS TO
THE QUALITY AND PERFORMANCE OF THE LIBRARY IS WITH YOU. SHOULD THE
LIBRARY PROVE DEFECTIVE, YOU ASSUME THE COST OF ALL NECESSARY SERVICING,
REPAIR OR CORRECTION.

16. IN NO EVENT UNLESS REQUIRED BY APPLICABLE LAW OR AGREED TO IN WRITING WILL
ANY COPYRIGHT HOLDER, OR ANY OTHER PARTY WHO MAY MODIFY AND/OR REDIS-
TRIBUTE THE LIBRARY AS PERMITTED ABOVE, BE LIABLE TO YOU FOR DAMAGES,
INCLUDING ANY GENERAL, SPECIAL, INCIDENTAL OR CONSEQUENTIAL DAMAGES ARIS-
ING OUT OF THE USE OR INABILITY TO USE THE LIBRARY (INCLUDING BUT NOT LIM-
ITED TO LOSS OF DATA OR DATA BEING RENDERED INACCURATE OR LOSSES SUS-
TAINED BY YOU OR THIRD PARTIES OR A FAILURE OF THE LIBRARY TO OPERATE WITH
ANY OTHER SOFTWARE), EVEN IF SUCH HOLDER OR OTHER PARTY HAS BEEN ADVISED
OF THE POSSIBILITY OF SUCH DAMAGES.

BSD License

The following is a BSD license template. To generate your own license, change the values of OWNER, ORGANIZATION and YEAR from their original values as given here, and substitute your own.

Note: The advertising clause in the license appearing on BSD Unix files was officially rescinded by the Director of the Office of Technology Licensing of the University of California on July 22 1999. He states that clause 3 is "hereby deleted in its entirety."

Note the new BSD license is thus equivalent to the MIT License, except for the no-endorsement final clause.<OWNER> = Regents of the University of California
<ORGANIZATION> = University of California, Berkeley
<YEAR> = 1998

In the original BSD license, the first occurrence of the phrase "COPYRIGHT HOLDERS AND CONTRIBUTORS" in the disclaimer read "REGENTS AND CONTRIBUTORS".

Here is the license template:

Copyright © <YEAR>, <OWNER>
All rights reserved.

Redistribution and use in source and binary forms, with or without modification, are permitted provided that the following conditions are met:

- Redistributions of source code must retain the above copyright notice, this list of conditions and the following disclaimer.
- Redistributions in binary form must reproduce the above copyright notice, this list of conditions and the following disclaimer in the documentation and/or other materials provided with the distribution.
- Neither the name of the <ORGANIZATION> nor the names of its contributors may be used to endorse or promote products derived from this software without specific prior written permission.

THIS SOFTWARE IS PROVIDED BY THE COPYRIGHT HOLDERS AND CONTRIBUTORS "AS IS" AND ANY EXPRESS OR IMPLIED WARRANTIES, INCLUDING, BUT NOT LIMITED TO, THE IMPLIED WARRANTIES OF MERCHANTABILITY AND FITNESS FOR A PARTICULAR PURPOSE ARE DISCLAIMED. IN NO EVENT SHALL THE REGENTS OR CONTRIBUTORS BE LIABLE FOR ANY DIRECT, INDIRECT, INCIDENTAL, SPECIAL, EXEMPLARY, OR CONSEQUENTIAL DAMAGES (INCLUDING, BUT NOT LIMITED TO, PROCUREMENT OF SUBSTITUTE GOODS OR SERVICES; LOSS OF USE, DATA, OR PROFITS; OR BUSINESS INTERRUPTION) HOWEVER CAUSED AND ON ANY THEORY OF LIABILITY, WHETHER IN CONTRACT, STRICT LIABILITY, OR TORT (INCLUDING NEGLIGENCE OR OTHERWISE) ARISING IN ANY WAY OUT OF THE USE OF THIS SOFTWARE, EVEN IF ADVISED OF THE POSSIBILITY OF SUCH DAMAGE.

ARTISTIC LICENSE

PREAMBLE

The intent of this document is to state the conditions under which a Package may be copied, such that the Copyright Holder maintains some semblance of artistic control over the development of the package, while giving the users of the package the right to use and distribute the Package in a more-or-less customary fashion, plus the right to make reasonable modifications.

DEFINITIONS

"Package" refers to the collection of files distributed by the Copyright Holder, and derivatives of that collection of files created through textual modification.

"Standard Version" refers to such a Package if it has not been modified, or has been modified in accordance with the wishes of the Copyright Holder.

"Copyright Holder" is whoever is named in the copyright or copyrights for the package.

"You" is you, if you're thinking about copying or distributing this Package.

"Reasonable copying fee" is whatever you can justify on the basis of media cost, duplication charges, time of people involved, and so on. (You will not be required to justify it to the Copyright Holder, but only to the computing community at large as a market that must bear the fee.)

"Freely Available" means that no fee is charged for the item itself, though there may be fees involved in handling the item. It also means that recipients of the item may redistribute it under the same conditions they received it.

1. You may make and give away verbatim copies of the source form of the Standard Version of this Package without restriction, provided that you duplicate all of the original copyright notices and associated disclaimers.
2. You may apply bug fixes, portability fixes and other modifications derived from the Public Domain or from the Copyright Holder. A Package modified in such a way shall still be considered the Standard Version.
3. You may otherwise modify your copy of this Package in any way, provided that you insert a prominent notice in each changed file stating how and when you changed that file, and provided that you do at least ONE of the following:

a) place your modifications in the Public Domain or otherwise make them Freely Available, such as by posting said modifications to Usenet or an equivalent medium, or placing the modifications on a major archive site such as **ftp.uu.net**, or by allowing the Copyright Holder to include your modifications in the Standard Version of the Package.

b) use the modified Package only within your corporation or organization.

c) rename any non-standard executables so the names do not conflict with standard executables, which must also be provided, and provide a separate manual page for each non-standard executable that clearly documents how it differs from the Standard Version.

d) make other distribution arrangements with the Copyright Holder.

4. You may distribute the programs of this Package in object code or executable form, provided that you do at least ONE of the following:

a) distribute a Standard Version of the executables and library files, together with instructions (in the manual page or equivalent) on where to get the Standard Version.

b) accompany the distribution with the machine-readable source of the Package with your modifications.

c) accompany any non-standard executables with their corresponding Standard Version executables, giving the non-standard executables non-standard names, and clearly documenting the differences in manual pages (or equivalent), together with instructions on where to get the Standard Version.

d) dmake other distribution arrangements with the Copyright Holder.

5. You may charge a reasonable copying fee for any distribution of this Package. You may charge any fee you choose for support of this Package. You may not charge a fee for this Package itself. However, you may distribute this Package in aggregate with other (possibly commercial) programs as part of a larger (possibly commercial) software distribution provided that you do not advertise this Package as a product of your own.

6. The scripts and library files supplied as input to or produced as output from the programs of this Package do not automatically fall under the copyright of this Package, but belong to whomever generated them, and may be sold commercially, and may be aggregated with this Package.

7. C or Perl subroutines supplied by you and linked into this Package shall not be considered part of this Package.

8. The name of the Copyright Holder may not be used to endorse or promote products derived from this software without specific prior written permission.

9. THIS PACKAGE IS PROVIDED "AS IS" AND WITHOUT ANY EXPRESS OR IMPLIED WARRANTIES, INCLUDING, WITHOUT LIMITATION, THE IMPLIED WARRANTIES OF MERCHANTABILITY AND FITNESS FOR A PARTICULAR PURPOSE.

MOZILLA PUBLIC LICENSE

Version 1.0

1.0. DEFINITIONS

1.1. "Contributor" means each entity that creates or contributes to the creation of Modifications.

1.2. "Contributor Version" means the combination of the Original Code, prior Modifications used by a Contributor, and the Modifications made by that particular Contributor.

1.3. "Covered Code" means the Original Code or Modifications or the combination of the Original Code and Modifications, in each case including portions thereof.

1.4. "Electronic Distribution Mechanism" means a mechanism generally accepted in the software development community for the electronic transfer of data.

1.5. "Executable" means Covered Code in any form other than Source Code.

1.6. "Initial Developer" means the individual or entity identified as the Initial Developer in the Source Code notice required by Exhibit A.

1.7. "Larger Work" means a work which combines Covered Code or portions thereof with code not governed by the terms of this License.

1.8. "License" means this document.

1.9. "Modifications" means any addition to or deletion from the substance or structure of either the Original Code or any previous Modifications. When Covered Code is released as a series of files, a Modification is:

   A. Any addition to or deletion from the contents of a file containing Original Code or previous Modifications.

   B. Any new file that contains any part of the Original Code or previous Modifications.

1.10. "Original Code" means Source Code of computer software code which is described in the Source Code notice required by Exhibit A as Original Code, and which, at the time of its release under this License is not already Covered Code governed by this License.

1.11. "Source Code" means the preferred form of the Covered Code for making modifications to it, including all modules it contains, plus any associated interface definition files, scripts used to control compilation and installation of an Executable, or a list of source code differential comparisons against either the Original Code or another well known, available Covered Code of the Contributor's choice. The Source Code can be in a compressed or archival form, provided the appropriate decompression or de-archiving software is widely available for no charge.

1.12. "You" means an individual or a legal entity exercising rights under, and complying with all of the terms of, this License or a future version of this License issued under Section 6.1. For legal entities, "You" includes any entity which controls, is controlled by, or is under common control with You. For purposes of this definition, "control" means (a) the power, direct or indirect, to cause the direction or management of such entity, whether by contract or otherwise, or (b) ownership of fifty percent (50%) or more of the outstanding shares or beneficial ownership of such entity.

2.0. Source Code License

2.1. The Initial Developer Grant.

The Initial Developer hereby grants You a world-wide, royalty-free, non-exclusive license, subject to third party intellectual property claims:

(a) to use, reproduce, modify, display, perform, sublicense and distribute the Original Code (or portions thereof) with or without Modifications, or as part of a Larger Work; and

(b) under patents now or hereafter owned or controlled by Initial Developer, to make, have made, use and sell ("Utilize") the Original Code (or portions thereof), but solely to the extent that any such patent is reasonably necessary to enable You to Utilize the Original Code (or portions thereof) and not to any greater extent that may be necessary to Utilize further Modifications or combinations.

2.2. Contributor Grant.

Each Contributor hereby grants You a world-wide, royalty-free, non-exclusive license, subject to third party intellectual property claims:

(a) to use, reproduce, modify, display, perform, sublicense and distribute the Modifications created by such Contributor (or portions thereof) either on an unmodified basis, with other Modifications, as Covered Code or as part of a Larger Work; and

(b) under patents now or hereafter owned or controlled by Contributor, to Utilize the Contributor Version (or portions thereof), but solely to the extent that any such patent is reasonably necessary to enable You to Utilize the Contributor Version (or portions thereof), and not to any greater extent that may be necessary to Utilize further Modifications or combinations.

3.0. Distribution Obligations

3.1. Application of License.

The Modifications which You create or to which You contribute are governed by the terms of this License, including without limitation Section 2.2. The Source Code version of Covered Code may be distributed only under the terms of this License or a future version of this License released under Section 6.1, and You must include a copy of this License with every copy of the Source Code You distribute. You may not offer or impose any terms on any Source Code version that alters or restricts the applicable version of this License or the recipients' rights hereunder. However, You may include an additional document offering the additional rights described in Section 3.5.

3.2. **Availability of Source Code.**

Any Modification which You create or to which You contribute must be made available in Source Code form under the terms of this License either on the same media as an Executable version or via an accepted Electronic Distribution Mechanism to anyone to whom you made an Executable version available; and if made available via Electronic Distribution Mechanism, must remain available for at least twelve (12) months after the date it initially became available, or at least six (6) months after a subsequent version of that particular Modification has been made available to such recipients. You are responsible for ensuring that the Source Code version remains available even if the Electronic Distribution Mechanism is maintained by a third party.

3.3. **Description of Modifications.**

You must cause all Covered Code to which you contribute to contain a file documenting the changes You made to create that Covered Code and the date of any change. You must include a prominent statement that the Modification is derived, directly or indirectly, from Original Code provided by the Initial Developer and including the name of the Initial Developer in (a) the Source Code, and (b) in any notice in an Executable version or related documentation in which You describe the origin or ownership of the Covered Code.

3.4. **Intellectual Property Matters.**

(a) *Third Party Claims.*

If You have knowledge that a party claims an intellectual property right in particular functionality or code (or its utilization under this License), you must include a text file with the source code distribution titled LEGAL which describes the claim and the party making the claim in sufficient detail that a recipient will know whom to contact. If you obtain such knowledge after You make Your Modification available as described in Section 3.2, You shall promptly modify the LEGAL file in all copies You make available thereafter and shall take other steps (such as notifying appropriate mailing lists or newsgroups) reasonably calculated to inform those who received the Covered Code that new knowledge has been obtained.

(b) *Contributor APIs.*

If Your Modification is an application programming interface, and You own or control patents which are reasonably necessary to implement that API, you must also include this information in the LEGAL file.

3.5. Required Notices.

You must duplicate the notice in Exhibit A in each file of the Source Code, and this License in any documentation for the Source Code, where You describe recipients' rights relating to Covered Code. If You created one or more Modification(s), You may add your name as a Contributor to the notice described in Exhibit A. If it is not possible to put such notice in a particular Source Code file due to its structure, then you must include such notice in a location (such as a relevant directory file) where a user would be likely to look for such a notice. You may choose to offer, and to charge a fee for, warranty, support, indemnity or liability obligations to one or more recipients of Covered Code. However, You may do so only on Your own behalf, and not on behalf of the Initial Developer or any Contributor. You must make it absolutely clear than any such warranty, support, indemnity or liability obligation is offered by You alone, and You hereby agree to indemnify the Initial Developer and every Contributor for any liability incurred by the Initial Developer or such Contributor as a result of warranty, support, indemnity or liability terms You offer.

3.6. Distribution of Executable Versions.

You may distribute Covered Code in Executable form only if the requirements of Section 3.1-3.5 have been met for that Covered Code, and if You include a notice stating that the Source Code version of the Covered Code is available under the terms of this License, including a description of how and where You have fulfilled the obligations of Section 3.2. The notice must be conspicuously included in any notice in an Executable version, related documentation or collateral in which You describe recipients' rights relating to the Covered Code. You may distribute the Executable version of Covered Code under a license of Your choice, which may contain terms different from this License, provided that You are in compliance with the terms of this License and that the license for the Executable version does not attempt to limit or alter the recipient's rights in the Source Code version from the rights set forth in this License. If You distribute the Executable version under a different license You must make it absolutely clear that any terms which differ from this License are offered by You alone, not by the Initial Developer or any Contributor. You hereby agree to indemnify the Initial Developer and every Contributor for any liability incurred by the Initial Developer or such Contributor as a result of any such terms You offer.

3.7. Larger Works.

You may create a Larger Work by combining Covered Code with other code not governed by the terms of this License and distribute the Larger Work as a single product. In such a case, You must make sure the requirements of this License are fulfilled for the Covered Code.

4.0. INABILITY TO COMPLY DUE TO STATUTE OR REGULATION

If it is impossible for You to comply with any of the terms of this License with respect to some or all of the Covered Code due to statute or regulation then You must: (a) comply with the terms of this License to the maximum extent possible; and (b) describe the limitations and the code they affect. Such description must be included in the LEGAL file described in Section 3.4 and must be included with all distributions of the Source Code. Except to the extent prohibited by statute or regulation, such description must be sufficiently detailed for a recipient of ordinary skill to be able to understand it.

5.0 APPLICATION OF THIS LICENSE

This License applies to code to which the Initial Developer has attached the notice in Exhibit A, and to related Covered Code.

6.0. VERSIONS OF THE LICENSE

6.1. **New Versions.**

Netscape Communications Corporation ("Netscape") may publish revised and/or new versions of the License from time to time. Each version will be given a distinguishing version number.

6.2. **Effect of New Versions.**

Once Covered Code has been published under a particular version of the License, You may always continue to use it under the terms of that version. You may also choose to use such Covered Code under the terms of any subsequent version of the License published by Netscape. No one other than Netscape has the right to modify the terms applicable to Covered Code created under this License.

6.3. **Derivative Works.**

If you create or use a modified version of this License (which you may only do in order to apply it to code which is not already Covered Code governed by this License), you must (a) rename Your license so that the phrases "Mozilla," "MOZILLAPL," "MOZPL," "Netscape," "NPL," or any confusingly similar phrase do not appear anywhere in your license and (b) otherwise make it clear that your version of the license contains terms that differ from the Mozilla Public License and Netscape Public License. (Filling in the name of the Initial Developer, Original Code or Contributor in the notice described in Exhibit A shall not of themselves be deemed to be modifications of this License.)

7.0. DISCLAIMER OF WARRANTY

COVERED CODE IS PROVIDED UNDER THIS LICENSE ON AN "AS IS" BASIS, WITHOUT WARRANTY OF ANY KIND, EITHER EXPRESSED OR IMPLIED, INCLUDING, WITHOUT LIMITATION, WARRANTIES THAT THE COVERED CODE IS FREE OF DEFECTS, MERCHANTABLE, FIT FOR A PARTICULAR PURPOSE OR NON-INFRINGING. THE ENTIRE RISK AS TO THE QUALITY AND PERFORMANCE OF THE COVERED CODE IS WITH YOU. SHOULD ANY COVERED CODE PROVE DEFECTIVE IN ANY RESPECT, YOU (NOT THE INITIAL DEVELOPER OR ANY OTHER CONTRIBUTOR) ASSUME THE COST OF ANY NECESSARY SERVICING, REPAIR OR CORRECTION. THIS DISCLAIMER OF WARRANTY CONSTITUTES AN ESSENTIAL PART OF THIS LICENSE. NO USE OF ANY COVERED CODE IS AUTHORIZED HEREUNDER EXCEPT UNDER THIS DISCLAIMER.

8.0. TERMINATION

This License and the rights granted hereunder will terminate automatically if You fail to comply with terms herein and fail to cure such breach within 30 days of becoming aware of the breach. All sublicenses to the Covered Code which are properly granted shall survive any termination of this License. Provisions which, by their nature, must remain in effect beyond the termination of this License shall survive.

9.0. LIMITATION OF LIABILITY

UNDER NO CIRCUMSTANCES AND UNDER NO LEGAL THEORY, WHETHER TORT (INCLUDING NEGLIGENCE), CONTRACT, OR OTHERWISE, SHALL THE INITIAL DEVELOPER, ANY OTHER CONTRIBUTOR, OR ANY DISTRIBUTOR OF COVERED CODE, OR ANY SUPPLIER OF ANY OF SUCH PARTIES, BE LIABLE TO YOU OR ANY OTHER PERSON FOR ANY INDIRECT, SPECIAL, INCIDENTAL, OR CONSEQUENTIAL DAMAGES OF ANY CHARACTER INCLUDING, WITHOUT LIMITATION, DAMAGES FOR LOSS OF GOODWILL, WORK STOPPAGE, COMPUTER FAILURE OR MALFUNCTION, OR ANY AND ALL OTHER COMMERCIAL DAMAGES OR LOSSES, EVEN IF SUCH PARTY SHALL HAVE BEEN INFORMED OF THE POSSIBILITY OF SUCH DAMAGES. THIS LIMITATION OF LIABILITY SHALL NOT APPLY TO LIABILITY FOR DEATH OR PERSONAL INJURY RESULTING FROM SUCH PARTY'S NEGLIGENCE TO THE EXTENT APPLICABLE LAW PROHIBITS SUCH LIMITATION. SOME JURISDICTIONS DO NOT ALLOW THE EXCLUSION OR LIMITATION OF INCIDENTAL OR CONSEQUENTIAL DAMAGES, SO THAT EXCLUSION AND LIMITATION MAY NOT APPLY TO YOU.

10.0. U.S. GOVERNMENT END USERS

The Covered Code is a "commercial item," as that term is defined in 48 C.F.R. 2.101 (Oct. 1995), consisting of "commercial computer software" and "commercial computer software documentation," as such terms are used in 48 C.F.R. 12.212 (Sept. 1995). Consistent with 48 C.F.R. 12.212 and 48 C.F.R. 227.7202-1 through 227.7202-4 (June 1995), all U.S. Government End Users acquire Covered Code with only those rights set forth herein.

11.0. MISCELLANEOUS

This License represents the complete agreement concerning subject matter hereof. If any provision of this License is held to be unenforceable, such provision shall be reformed only to the extent necessary to make it enforceable. This License shall be governed by California law provisions (except to the extent applicable law, if any, provides otherwise), excluding its conflict-of-law provisions. With respect to disputes in which at least one party is a citizen of, or an entity chartered or registered to do business in, the United States of America: (a) unless otherwise agreed in writing, all disputes relating to this License (excepting any dispute relating to intellectual property rights) shall be subject to final and binding arbitration, with the losing party paying all costs of arbitration; (b) any arbitration relating to this Agreement shall be held in Santa Clara County, California, under the auspices of JAMS/EndDispute; and (c) any litigation relating to this Agreement shall be subject to the jurisdiction of the Federal Courts of the Northern District of California, with venue lying in Santa Clara County, California, with the losing party responsible for costs, including without limitation, court costs and reasonable attorneys fees and expenses. The application of the United Nations Convention on Contracts for the International Sale of Goods is expressly excluded. Any law or regulation which provides that the language of a contract shall be construed against the drafter shall not apply to this License.

12.0. RESPONSIBILITY FOR CLAIMS

Except in cases where another Contributor has failed to comply with Section 3.4, You are responsible for damages arising, directly or indirectly, out of Your utilization of rights under this License, based on the number of copies of Covered Code you made available, the revenues you received from utilizing such rights, and other relevant factors. You agree to work with affected parties to distribute responsibility on an equitable basis.

EXHIBIT A.

The contents of this file are subject to the Mozilla Public License Version 1.0 (the "License"); you may not use this file except in compliance with the License. You may obtain a copy of the License at **http://www.mozilla.org/MPL/**

Software distributed under the License is distributed on an "AS IS" basis, WITHOUT WARRANTY OF ANY KIND, either express or implied. See the License for the specific language governing rights and limitations under the License.

The Original Code is _____.

The Initial Developer of the Original Code is _____.

Portions created by _____ are Copyright © _____. All Rights Reserved.

Contributor(s): _____.

THE APACHE SOFTWARE LICENSE

Version 1.1

Copyright © 2000 The Apache Software Foundation. All rights reserved.

Redistribution and use in source and binary forms, with or without modification, are permitted provided that the following conditions are met:

MIT LICENSE

Copyright © <year> <copyright holders>

Permission is hereby granted, free of charge, to any person obtaining a copy of this software and associated documentation files (the "Software"), to deal in the Software without restriction, including without limitation the rights to use, copy, modify, merge, publish, distribute, sublicense, and/or sell copies of the Software, and to permit persons to whom the Software is furnished to do so, subject to the following conditions:

The above copyright notice and this permission notice shall be included in all copies or substantial portions of the Software.

THE SOFTWARE IS PROVIDED "AS IS", WITHOUT WARRANTY OF ANY KIND, EXPRESS OR IMPLIED, INCLUDING BUT NOT LIMITED TO THE WARRANTIES OF MERCHANTABILITY, FITNESS FOR A PARTICULAR PURPOSE AND NONINFRINGEMENT. IN NO EVENT SHALL THE AUTHORS OR COPYRIGHT HOLDERS BE LIABLE FOR ANY CLAIM, DAMAGES OR OTHER LIABILITY, WHETHER IN AN ACTION OF CONTRACT, TORT OR OTHERWISE, ARISING FROM, OUT OF OR IN CONNECTION WITH THE SOFTWARE OR THE USE OR OTHER DEALINGS IN THE SOFTWARE.

APPENDIX B

PORTING

Back in The Good Old Days™, games were platform specific. You would write everything in assembly language (or raw machine code if you were a *Real* Programmer) and hit the hardware directly. Porting a game to another platform usually meant throwing away the original code and doing a complete rewrite. If you were lucky, you might be able to steal some graphics data from the original version if the graphics hardware was similar enough. You had to be platform specific if you wanted any sort of performance.

Since those days of nostalgia[1], two main advances have taken place that make porting games a much more viable prospect:

- The use of high-level languages
- Abstracted hardware interfaces

Although calling C and C++ "high-level languages" might be a subject of debate, they *are* high level in comparison to assembly language. Most important, code written on one platform has at least a running chance of being compiled for another. Other languages could provide the same benefits, but C and C++ are currently the predominant languages used for games.

Regarding the second point, it is simply not feasible to program directly to the hardware anymore. Even on the same platform, the variety of video, sound, and I/O hardware that may have to be supported is astronomical. So that responsibility must be delegated to the operating system, device drivers, and the interfaces they provide.

These facts mean that things are much better than they used to be, from a portability point of view. However, there is still a lot more to porting an application than simply recompiling it. Proprietary standards, closed formats, creative use of programming language features, and fundamental differences in platform capabilities still stand in your way.

The ideal game for porting has the following characteristics:

- It is well designed and cleanly structured. Clean code is *much* more portable than badly organized code.
- It uses open standards and cross-platform libraries wherever possible.
- It avoids platform or compiler-specific features.
- It has segregated any unavoidably platform-specific parts into separate files.

In contrast, the porting project from hell has the following characteristics:

- It has code that looks like spaghetti. There is no clear structure or separation of responsibility between modules.
- It uses closed, proprietary standards and APIs wherever possible. For extra credit, the program contains technologies covered by software patents and hefty license fees.
- It uses a programming language that's available only on the original platform or, failing this, makes extensive use of platform-specific language extensions.
- It contains masses of badly commented assembly code.

This appendix is somewhat biased toward porting an application from Windows to Linux because this is considered to be the most likely case. The good news is that the capabilities of the basic hardware will be pretty much identical. The bad news is that Windows games are rarely written with portability in mind. Well-structured original code is of immense help here; good programming practices such as abstraction and encapsulation inherently aid portability, even if that is not the original motivation for using these practices.

Porting Strategy

Starting a port can be a pretty daunting prospect. You have a bunch of source files written for an incompatible platform, possibly written by you, possibly written by others, probably badly documented. Where do you start?

Try Not to Fork the Codebase

If you misread the word *fork* in the title of this section, don't worry. The meaning doesn't change much.

There is a lot to be gained by trying to maintain a single codebase. That is, to make the porting changes while keeping the original version working. It's often tempting to diverge from the original by replacing old platform-specific bits with new platform-specific bits. Try to avoid this snafu by switching between the old and new versions using compile-time switches (#ifdefs). Better still, try putting platform-neutral code in place instead.

Here are some of the benefits of a shared codebase:

- Changes and fixes made on one platform will automatically be incorporated on the other(s).
- The original version will benefit from the scrutiny given to it during the porting process. Bug fixing, refactoring, and general tidying will improve the entire codebase, not just the new port.
- You can debug using tools on the original platform. Having extra debugging tools available is always a good thing.
- The codebase as a whole will become easier to port to additional platforms.

If active work is continuing on the original version, take care not to cause unnecessary breakage during the porting process. If possible, test your changes on the original platform as you go along. Most source control systems provide some sort of branching mechanism to help manage multiple streams of development. Potentially disruptive changes can be performed on a separate branch and merged into the main branch when they are judged to be well tested and stable. Of course, CVS, widely used in the Linux world, provides the required features.

Of course, sometimes you won't be able to share a codebase. Maybe the people in charge of the original version don't want you messing with their copy of the code, or maybe the platforms differ in such a radical way that a complete architectural rethink is required. Maybe the original codebase resides in a source control system without Linux support (Microsoft Sourcesafe, for example). In these cases, you have to maintain a separate Linux source repository, treating the original repository as a third-party package you have to track.

GETTING STARTED

As with so many things, the best approach is to just dive right in and start hacking away. Pick a file at random and try to compile it from the command line. A large number of the resulting errors are going to be trivial little things. Fix them. For bigger problems, use `#ifdef` to block out offending chunks of code, making sure that you leave some sort of `TODO:` comment or `NEEDS_WORK` marker that you can use `grep` to locate for later on. Replace problem functions with stubs that do nothing. Leave the big issues for later.

Go through all the files in this way. The goal at the moment is just to get the project to compile. You'll feel a sense of achievement wash over you as the compiler errors disappear. If you're lucky, you'll also be able to get successful linking.

You'll probably want to script up a makefile (or its equivalent). There is a strong likelihood that the original version of the game was built using an IDE (Integrated Development Environment) using proprietary project description files. For example, the Visual C/C++ IDE uses workspaces (`.DSW` files) containing one or more projects (described in `.DSP` files). Of course, these are of little or no use under Linux.

#ifdef Is Your Friend

The #ifdef statement is cool. There's a real temptation to just define a LINUX macro and have all your porting changes switched in with that. Instead, try to switch by feature availability and not by platform. Because most of the features you'll use are available on multiple platforms, you'll have much finer-grained control over your build configuration than if you use a blanket switch-by-platform approach. Here are some examples:

- If you are using a cross-platform library to aid your porting effort, the original codebase can benefit by having the extra configuration available. As an example, Windows NT doesn't (didn't?) have very good Direct3D support. Porting Direct3D game code to Linux using OpenGL gives you a Windows NT version essentially for free.
- A lot of the system calls provided by Linux are part of the POSIX standard. By switching these calls in using a macro called POSIX (for example) rather than LINUX, you'll be better placed to port to other POSIX-supporting platforms (the BSDs, for example).
- Even seemingly proprietary features can pop up in odd places. For example, there are a number of Win32 API implementations available for Linux/UNIX, such as the WINE project.
- Don't use a platform macro to switch in a compiler-specific feature. All compilers have predefined macros to let you identify them, so use these macros instead. Visual C/C++ is not the only Windows compiler available. GCC is not the only Linux compiler available.

Here are some useful compiler-defined macros:

Macro	Meaning
_WIN32	The Win32 API is available (defined by Visual C/C++).
_MSC_VER	Compiling on Microsoft Visual C/C++.
__GNUC__	Compiling on GCC.
__GNUG__	Compiling on GCC C++ compiler (G++). Implies __GNUC__.

The Harder Stuff

It's now time to start dealing with all the code you previously disabled using #ifdef preprocessor directive and stub functions.

At this point, you may have identified places in which some refactoring of the original code would help. Try to identify areas where separation of platform-dependent code from platform-independent code makes sense. Additionally, for particularly convoluted modules, refactoring just to make the code understandable can be worthwhile. Ideally, the refactoring would be done on the original platform so that you can keep the game running. This approach lets you test your changes to make sure that your changes haven't broken anything. Performing the changes on the target platform, where the game is not yet in a running state, requires a huge leap of faith. Untested code is almost always buggy code.

Often you'll have to make a decision between porting or rewriting a module. This can be a hard decision, and there is no magic method to help—except experience and familiarity with the code. A good rule of thumb is that if getting the existing code ported involves obfuscating it to any major degree, you are better off making sure that the interface is well defined, forking it off, and writing a new implementation.

FIRST LIGHT

"First light" is a magical moment. It is the first time you run the newly ported game and actually see something recognizable up on the screen. Of course, this is almost always immediately followed up by a screenful of random garbage and a horrible catastrophic crash.

It's still a memorable milestone.

Anyway, you're running Linux. Horrible catastrophic crashes are well behaved and easy to deal with, a nice example for the UK national railway operator, Railtrack, may like to follow.

COMPILER ISSUES

Although it took a long time to pin down, there is now an official C++ standard. However, implementing this standard accurately in a compiler is not trivial. Pity the poor compiler engineers; C++ is a complex language to implement. You'll be hard pressed to find a compiler that doesn't break or deviate from the standard in some way. The footpath of C++ is strewn with the dog-poo of standards violations.

If you are using C rather than C++, the situation is a lot better. The ANSI C standard has been in place for a while and has had time to settle. There are still a few new features being added here and there, and of course the compiler support for these additions is likely to be patchy.

At the time I am writing, Microsoft Visual C/C++ seems to be the predominant compiler for Windows. It can be a pretty good compiler, but it is somewhat idiosyncratic. It contains a lot of not-quite-standard behaviors that can trip up the porting process. It also supports some non-standard features such as compiler-level COM support.

For Linux, GCC is, of course, *the* compiler. GCC has traditionally been a pretty good C compiler but a really bad C++ compiler. Recently, however, a lot of effort has gone into improving GCC C++ code generation and adherence to standards. Although there are certainly additional improvements that could be made to GCC, it's now more or less on par with other C++ compilers.

The simple fact is that all current C++ compilers have quirks you'll have to work around. Make sure that you keep your compilers up to date and try to keep track of release notes and bug lists. For GCC, **http://gcc.gnu.org** is the site to watch.

GCC UPDATE INFORMATION: HTTP://GCC.GNU.ORG

The following sections describe some of the compiler differences you're likely to encounter.

Visual C/C++ Improper Scoping in for Loops

Visual C++ applies an incorrect scoping rule for variables declared in for statements such as the following:

```
for( int i=0; i<10; ++i )
{
    ... blah blah blah...
}
```

The C++ standard specifies that i should be placed within the scope of the loop body. The Visual C++ approach is to use an older scoping rule that places i in the next block up (that is, the block in which the for statement appears). If the variable is used solely by the loop, it won't cause problems. If the variable is reused further down, however, other compilers will choke. Conveniently, GCC displays a nice warning message explaining that the scoping rule has changed and that the later use of the variable is invalid.

GCC Code Size

GCC can produce quite large executables, especially if templates are involved. The large files can make debugging somewhat unwieldy at times. The size of the executable is not really a portability issue, but it can come as a bit of a surprise when moving code from, say, Visual C++.

Mixing Signed and Unsigned Types

Consider the following code snippet:

```
unsigned int foo = getvalue();
if( foo == -1 )
{
    ...do stuff...
}
```

It is comparing foo, an unsigned value, with -1, a signed value. GCC will complain that the types being compared differ, but Visual C++ seems to let it through without comment.

Assignment from void*

The C++ standard requires that you provide an explicit cast when assigning to a pointer type from a void*. Visual C++ adopts a pretty casual attitude to this sort of thing but GCC tends to complain loudly.

GCC Doesn't Complain About Missing Return Values

In the following piece of code, GCC doesn't complain that the non-WIN32 code path is reached without returning anything:

```
bool FileExists( const char* filename )
{
    bool exists;
#ifndef WIN32
    // linux/unix/posix version
    struct stat buf;
    exists = (stat( filename, &buf) == 0) ? true:false;
#else
    // windows version
    exists = (GetFileAttributes( filename ) != -1) ? true:false;
    return exists;     // BUG - should be after the ifdef
#endif
}
```

Turning on the -Wall switch fixes this behavior. In fact, it's good practice to keep -Wall on always.

This shouldn't be a big problem when porting to GCC, but it is easy to accidentally #ifdef out return statements during porting. The GCC compiler's silence means that it can go unnoticed.

GCC Doesn't Complain About Use of Uninitialized Variables

GCC doesn't seem to pick up on the use of uninitialized variables. For example, this following code compiles without warning on GCC:

```
int CalcAnswer()
{
    int i;
    i += 42;  /* !!! value of i is undefined! */
    return i;
}
```

Turning -Wall on doesn't seem to help.

GCC Is More Strict About Implicit Casting

Here is an example that uses overloaded functions:

```
int wibble( int i )
    { ... }

int wibble( float f )
    { ... }

int main( int argc, char* argv[] )
{
    long int x = 3;
    printf( "%d\n", wibble(x) );        // error under GCC
    return 0;
}
```

GCC considers the wibble(x) call to be ambiguous. It won't automatically cast i from long int down to the int value that's required to call wibble(int i).

Visual C++ automatically assumes that you meant to call wibble(int i). This can be a common problem when you're porting code to GCC, but luckily it's pretty trivial and easy to fix. Some well-placed casts in the call will do the trick, but the better solution is to tighten up the code to be more careful about data types in the first place.

Include Filenames

Windows filenames are not case sensitive and use a backslash as a path separator instead of a forward slash. This is not so much a compiler difference as an area in which underlying platform differences are exposed.

This example works fine under Windows:

```
#include <Sys\Stat.h>
```

For Linux, the statement must be changed to the following:

```
#include <sys/stat.h>
```

This variation will crop up regularly during porting; luckily, it is a trivial problem to fix. The fixed version will still compile under Windows because C and C++ compilers allow UNIX-style include filenames, even on non-UNIX platforms.

Struct Packing

Packing is where elements in a struct are forcibly stored in contiguous memory locations without padding, even if the resulting byte alignment is not optimal for the processor. It's generally an evil practice, but you may come across it.

To forcibly pack a struct, Visual C++ uses the #pragma pack(n) statement, where n is the byte alignment (1, 2, 4, 8, or 16):

```
#pragma pack(1)
struct foo
{
    char c;          // this would normally be padded
    int wibble;
    int pibble;
}
```

To forcibly pack a `struct`, GCC uses the `__attribute__` `((packed))` statement instead:

```
struct foo
{
    char c;          // this would normally be padded
    int wibble;
    int pibble;
} __attribute__ ((packed))
```

File System Issues

Most games have many data files—graphics, sound, level layout, and so on. Ideally, you want to retain compatibility with the data files from the original version of the game. However, if the game was written for Windows, you can guarantee that there will be trouble maintaining compatibility with the data files.

Since its creation, poor old Windows has had the huge albatross[2] called DOS hanging around its neck. Although great improvements have been made (particularly in Windows NT and Windows 2000), there are still a lot of file-related issues to be aware of when porting. The following sections describe some of these potential snafus.

Case Sensitivity

Linux filenames are case sensitive; Windows filenames are not. For example, the following filenames are all considered to refer to the same file in Windows, but Linux regards them as distinct:

```
Cloud.png
CLOUD.png
cloud.png
```

Windows programs are not, in general, very concerned about using the correct case. This is a shame because it means that the game will many times reference files by the wrong name (from the Linux point of view). This means more work for you.

The best solution to this problem is not always clear and will vary from project to project. Here are some options:

- Find every place in the game where files are referenced and make sure that the names correspond exactly to the names on disk. Remember that the game may reference data files that contain references to other files—it's not just the source code you must check. For this reason, this solution is not ideal. You want to keep data file changes to a minimum.

- If the file handling code is reasonably localized within the source, you could add a fix there by transforming all filenames to a specific pattern. For example, a file-open function could make lowercase all the filenames it is passed before trying to open them. The drawback with this method is that it assumes that the files on disk already conform to that specific naming pattern.

  You can always rename the files, but remember that this will break compatibility with the original data files. This is of special concern if your port is to be made available as a patch to the originally distributed version of the game.

  Of course, the file renaming can easily be performed automatically at install time.

- You can pass filenames through a function to match them up with real files. The function would have to perform a scan using a case-insensitive comparison. There are some potential speed issues with this method, but unless files are being opened at an extremely high rate, it shouldn't cause problems.

- Use a loopback device with a virtual VFAT partition within a file. This has a nice, smug, "look-what-you-can-do-in-Linux!" feel to it, but there are likely to be configuration problems. For example, the user may not be using a kernel with the correct file system support.

If users can name their own files (when saving games, for example), remember to take this into account. Users' file-naming inconsistencies can be an issue, particularly if they send files to one another. It's frustrating when a file saved by a player using the Linux version of the game cannot be loaded by a player using the original Windows version.

DRIVE LETTERS AND PATH SEPARATORS

Different operating systems use different path separators when specifying locations of files. Windows uses a backslash (\), UNIX-based OSes use a forward slash (/), and the MacOS uses a colon (:). Windows also uses a colon to denote the drive letter, typified by the (in)famous C:. Your filename-handling code must take these differences into account.

Sometimes, it'll be enough to search through all the source code and change backslashes to forward slashes. If you are porting from Windows, remember that all the Win32 file-handling API calls are just as happy with forward slashes as they are with backslashes, so you can do the replacement without breaking the original version.

Another approach is to write a translation function that converts filenames to a UNIX style and then to make sure that you call it from all the appropriate places. Such a function might be desirable if the original data files contain many Windows-style filenames. However, if filenames are exposed to the player at all, you'll want to be careful to present filenames in only the native form.

A common construct for composing filenames takes a form like this:

```
string spritefile = gfxdir + '\\' + "Wibble.spr";
```

Of course, you can search the source looking for this sort of thing, changing the \\ to / as you go, but if filenames appear often, you'll probably be better off writing a name composition function that hides the platform specifics. Consider this example:

```
string spritefile = JoinPath( gfxdir, "Wibble.spr" );
```

This method has the following benefits:

- Encapsulation of platform-specific details (always a good thing).
- Easier to improve robustness. What if gfxdir in this example already has a trailing separator? By adding a check in JoinPath(), you automatically make all the filename composition occurrences more bulletproof.

LINE TERMINATION

Text files present a classic portability issue: different platforms use different end-of-line (EOL) sequences. In the following chart, LF means "line feed" (0x0A '\n') and CR means "carriage return" (0x0D '\r').

Platform	End-of-Line Sequence
UNIX-based	LF
Windows/DOS	CR followed by LF
MacOS	CR

Of course, C and C++ use '\n' (LF), and I/O functionality in the standard libraries supports on-the-fly translation if files are opened in text mode.

The best thing to do is to make sure that your file-reading functions are flexible. Allowing any EOL convention to be used means you will have less trouble swapping files between systems. Ideally, you'll want to write out any text files using the native standard (that is, LF on Linux), but to maintain compatibility, you might need to output an explicit CR/LF pair.

FILE ATTRIBUTES AND HOME DIRECTORIES

Although Windows does have some support for multiple user accounts, most (all?) Win32 games assume that the system is for a single user. If games have any sort of user-profile support, they inevitably ignore any features provided by the OS and instead implement it themselves.

The Windows user typically runs with the Windows equivalent of root access and therefore has read/write access to all game files. This contrasts strongly with file security on UNIX-based systems in which the user usually has write access only within his home directory. This security difference can cause problems if the game requires write access. Under Windows, the game assumes that it can always write. Under Linux, the game will be in for a rude shock. Here are some solutions:

- Allow installation only within a home (or otherwise publicly writable) directory. This is not a very elegant solution because the standard Linux installation points for games are /usr/games/ and /usr/local/games/.
- Allow installation (as root) to somewhere sensible and have the installation process change the permissions on any files or directories the game needs to write to. This is probably workable, but it's not really "The Linux Way" and raises security issues.
- Force the user to play the game with root permissions. This solution reeks of unspeakable evil[3]. Don't even consider it.
- Separate the game files into two groups: read-only and read/write. Install the read-only files in /usr/games or /usr/local/games and store the writable files in the user's home directory. This is the One True Answer. With this solution, you can easily support multiple users, each with his own in-game preference settings and saved games. Whenever the game starts, you can check the user's home directory to see whether he has played before. If not, you can create a fresh profile by copying a template set of files from the read-only part of the installation. An easy way to do this is to use a shell script "wrapper" to launch the game.

ASSEMBLY LANGUAGE

Games are usually performance-critical applications, often employing hand-tuned assembly language to speed up hot spots. Porting this assembly to Linux can be fiddly because the GNU tools use a different syntax than the Microsoft tools. Note that the assumption here is that the port is being done from Windows to Linux on the 32-bit i386 architecture (or IA32, as Intel now likes to call it). With the same processor, porting assembly is mainly an exercise in translating the code into the expected syntax. Porting assembly between different processors will almost always require a rewrite.

Hopefully, all the assembly routines will still have the equivalent C source code available for you to use. If you have the source code, you can at least get the game up and running. If there is no C equivalent, it may be worth writing it as your first step—especially if you are porting to another processor.

The GNU tools use the AT&T assembly syntax rather than the Intel syntax used by the Microsoft tools. However, there are other assemblers available for Linux. Of particular note is NASM, the NetWide Assembler. It uses the more traditional Intel syntax and so provides an easier target for code originating on Windows.

The following sections describe some of the differences between Intel and AT&T syntax.

OPERAND ORDER

Intel syntax uses instructions of the following form:

```
op dest,src
```

AT&T reverses the source and destination operands:

```
op src,dest
```

If you have done a lot of programming using one syntax, the other can take some getting used to.

REGISTER NAMING

AT&T syntax prepends a percent symbol (%) to register names: %eax, %ebx, and so on. Intel syntax uses unadorned register names.

OPCODE NAMING AND OPERAND SIZE

AT&T syntax adds b, w, or l to the opcode name to denote 8-bit, 16-bit, and 32-bit instructions respectively. Where the instruction size is clear from the operand, you are allowed to use the plain opcode name. For example, add %eax,%ebx is obviously a 32-bit operation. The explicit specification of size must be used whenever the size of the operands is ambiguous. For example, use incl foo to increment the 32-bit variable at memory location foo.

IMMEDIATE VALUES

Immediate values are prefixed with a $ in AT&T syntax. For example, the following are considered to be reads from memory locations:

```
movel 100,%eax
movel wibble,%ebx
```

However, the following statements copy immediate values (the address of wibble in the second case):

```
movel $100,%eax
movel $wibble,%ebx
```

ADDRESSING MODES

AT&T addressing modes take the following form:

```
offset(base,index,scale)
```

In this syntax, scale can be 1, 2, 4, or 8. Any unused term can be omitted.

ENDIANESS

No guide to porting would be complete without a section on endianess. Little-endian processors (for example, i386 or Alpha) store multi-byte numbers with the least significant byte first. Big-endian processors (such as PowerPC, MIPS, and Sparc) store the most significant byte first.

The 32-bit hex value 0x12345678 is stored in memory on a big-endian machine like this:

```
0x12, 0x34, 0x56, 0x78
```

That same value would be stored on a little-endian machine like this:

```
0x78, 0x56, 0x34, 0x12
```

In most code, you won't care which byte ordering the processor uses. The problems start when you want to share values with processors using the other convention. File formats and network protocols are the usual suspects; they are places where numbers sneak out of the code into the world beyond.

The solution is to define and use conventions. Network protocols, for example, traditionally send and receive values in "network byte order" which is big-endian. Implementing this on a little-endian machine requires code that translates values into the host format (by reversing the byte order). The BSD sockets API provides functions to handle this translation:

Function	Description
htonl()	Host order to network order (long int)
htons()	Host order to network order (short int)
ntohl()	Network order to host order (long int)
ntohs()	Network order to host order (short int)

A similar approach can be used on binary file formats. The ordering convention on disk should be independent of the processor used. If the game being ported has only ever run on the one platform, then it probably just writes values out in whatever ordering the original processor uses. In this case, the choice of convention has been made for you already; if you want to retain data file compatibility, you have to go along with it. Porting to a processor with different endianess involves going through the file and network code with a fine-tooth comb, looking for values that need translation.

Keep in mind that Linux is not an i386-specific operating system. The large range of architectures it runs on is one of its most insanely cool features, and it's well worth your time to maintain support for all these architectures!

WINDOWS ISSUES

As well as the differences between compilers and operating systems, there are also several differences in the way you program for each of them. Windows has a habit of forcing developers to do things the "Microsoft Way."

WinMain() AND MESSAGE LOOPS

The entry point for Win32 applications is the WinMain() function instead of the more traditional main(). Its prototype is shown here:

```
int WINAPI WinMain( HINSTANCE hInstance,
    HINSTANCE hPrevInstance,
    LPSTR lpCmdLine,
    int nCmdShow );
```

Most of the arguments passed in are pretty irrelevant. The lpCmdLine parameter holds any arguments that were passed in during process creation, such as a raw version of argc/argv. In fact, the Microsoft C runtime library also provides a "cooked" version of lpCmdLine in the form of __argc and __argv. nCmdShow holds an enumerated value with the desired visibility state of the application (which is usually ignored).

WinMain() typically initializes the application, opens a window, and then drops into a message loop. The message loop waits for incoming messages (user input, timers, window repaint requests, and so on) and dispatches them to the WindowProc handler of the window using the Win32 DispatchMessage() call. WindowProc usually takes the form of a large case statement that switches on message type.

When porting a Windows game to Linux, you'll have to replace WinMain() and the message loop. Most of the logic should carry over onto whatever framework you are using—be it raw X or an extra library layer (SDL, for example). You may have to shuffle things around a bit, but because this will vary from project to project, there are no concrete rules.

TIMERS

Most games are driven using a function that performs a single game update. This function must be called at regular intervals to keep the game running. Under Windows, this call might be made as part of the message loop in WinMain(), or it might be called from the WindowProc in response to a timer message.

Here are some of the common timing mechanisms used in Windows:

- SetTimer() **and** WM_TIMER. The SetTimer() call specifies a frequency at which Windows sends WM_TIMER messages to be processed by the message loop. This mechanism is very easy to implement, but the timer is of too low a resolution to be useful for most games.
- **Multimedia timers.** These higher-resolution timers are set up using timeSetEvent(). A callback will be called at the specified frequency that often simply sends a user-defined (WM_USER+x) message to the message loop.
- **Separate timer thread.** An extra thread is created to send regular tick notifications to the main thread. Like the multimedia timer method, this notification is often done by sending a user-defined Windows message to the message loop. In fact, the multimedia timers are implemented in Windows using a timer thread.
- Sleep(). This call causes the current process to wait for the specified number of milliseconds. Often this call is used as part of the main loop: sleep for an interval, perform a game update, process any pending window messages, repeat.
- QueryPerformanceCounter(). This call polls the high-performance tick counter on the processor. This is the most accurate timing function available in Windows.

THE REGISTRY

Most Windows programs store configuration information in the Windows Registry, a hierarchical tree structure that holds named values. Applications usually store their settings in the following Registry keys:

```
HKEY_LOCAL_MACHINE\Software\[vendorname]\[app name]\...
HKEY_CURRENT_USER\Software\[vendorname]\[app name]\...
```

HKEY_LOCAL_MACHINE is for global settings across the entire machine; each user has his own HKEY_CURRENT_USER branch. In practice, however, most Windows games don't bother supporting any user account features in the OS, so the use of these two branches can often be somewhat fuzzy.

A configuration file is the obvious alternative implementation. You can change all the game code that accesses the Registry so that it instead uses a configuration file. Alternatively, you can implement a subset of the Windows Registry API (which reads and writes to a file). Unless the game accesses the Registry a *lot*, the former option is probably the better one.

HUNGARIAN NOTATION

Microsoft uses a naming scheme known as Hungarian Notation, which involves prefixing identifiers with a type tag. Windows uses Hungarian Notation extensively in its APIs and type definitions and, by osmosis, many Windows programs have also adopted the convention. If you haven't yet come across it, Hungarian Notation can be a little unsettling.

Here are some example variable names:

Variable Name	Meaning
cbSize	A byte count
fSuccess	A flag
hwndParent	A window handle
lpszFile	A pointer to a string (the l indicates a "long" or "far" pointer, a throwback to 16-bit days)

Some people love Hungarian Notation, others find it aesthetically offensive. Regardless of which camp you fall into, you'll probably have to read it.

GRAPHICS ISSUES

Porting graphics code from Windows is generally regarded as "The Biggie"—the main barrier to running Windows code under another OS. The main reason for this is DirectX, the collection of Microsoft APIs designed for games. DirectX is a closed system that is specific to Windows. However, if the original Windows code is well structured, it may not be as hard to port as you think.

DirectDraw

DirectDraw is the 2D component of DirectX. It is a reasonably thin abstraction, providing access to the frame buffer and features such as hardware accelerated blitting.

Porting from DirectDraw to another API can actually be quite straightforward because most DirectDraw concepts map well to other APIs. Most 2D APIs work in terms of manipulating surfaces. Here is a short list of some basic surface operations:

- Accessing surface memory (between lock/unlock guards)
- Blitting pixel data between surfaces
- Surface memory management (allocating surfaces in either main system memory or in video memory)
- Double buffering, page-flipping

The main thing is to understand your target API and to understand the intent of the original DirectDraw calls.

DOS Frame Buffer

DOS games traditionally use the frame buffer by directly accessing hardware registers or by using low-level BIOS or VESA calls.

Actual pixel manipulation is done by accessing video memory. This is made more complicated by the need for bank switching, a process by which video memory can be accessed only through a memory window that may have to be moved around to access the entire frame buffer. This is why 320x200x8-bit (mode 13h) was so popular; it used a small-enough section of memory to be accessible through a single 64K window without the complications of bank switching.

Many DOS extenders provide mechanisms to map the frame buffer into a single linear area of memory. The VESA interface also provides linear frame buffers on some hardware.

Games using linear frame buffers correspond nicely to the display surfaces presented by most modern graphics APIs and shouldn't cause too many porting headaches. Code using bank switching might require a little more reworking.

The hardware access under DOS also means that more esoteric hardware features could be used. Probably the most (in)famous example is ModeX, in which each byte accesses four pixels. A latch register sets which of those four pixels is affected. The benefit of ModeX was that it allowed you to squeeze multiple frames into a single 64K memory window, which in turn opened up the option of hardware page flipping and smooth scrolling techniques. ModeX code will definitely require some porting work.

Direct3D

Access to accelerated 3D hardware in DirectX is provided by Direct3D. The only real option when porting this code to Linux is to rewrite the 3D code using OpenGL.

If the original code was well designed, the incidence of Direct3D may be quite localized, which will help a lot. Many games use an API-neutral high-level layer to deal with aspects such as object geometry, spatial partitioning, culling, and so on. This layer is built on top of an API-specific low-level back end that actually pushes polygons out to the video card. If you provide a replacement low-level layer, the rest of the code will be happy.

Then again, there's a reasonable chance that the original code was badly written and that the raw Direct3D API is exposed in code and data structures all over the place. In this case, you'll probably just have to rewrite the whole shebang. Joy.

Because Direct3D and OpenGL are both trying to expose the same set of hardware features, there is some degree of agreement between the two APIs—they both encapsulate the same concepts. Indeed, recent versions of the Direct3D API have been moving noticeably toward the style of interface provided by OpenGL. This is a really Good Thing, and will make your porting task easier.

The following sections address some of the differences and similarities between OpenGL and the Direct3D API.

COORDINATE SYSTEMS

OpenGL uses a right-handed coordinate system while Direct3D uses a left-handed system. However, the OpenGL ModelView matrix can be fudged to produce a left-handed system by scaling Z by –1. The following example takes the existing Direct3D coordinate system and, by simply applying the glScale() function, transforms it into an OpenGL system:

```
glMatrixMode( GL_MODELVIEW );
glLoadIdentity();
// want left-handed coordinate system
glScalef( 1.0, 1.0, -1.0 );
// now transform as usual...
```

POLYGON WINDING

Direct3D identifies front-facing polygons as polygons that have their vertices listed in clockwise order. In OpenGL, the default assumption is that front-facing polygons are defined in counter-clockwise order. This behavior can be changed using glFrontFace():

```
void glFrontFace( GLenum mode )
```

In this syntax, mode is GL_CW for clockwise and GL_CCW for counter-clockwise.

TEXTURE MANAGEMENT

Textures in OpenGL are very opaque objects. Once you've created a texture and passed it in, the rest is handled for you. You don't have to worry about juggling video memory requirements or using the transfer mechanisms to shuffle texture data out from system memory or any other potentially hardware-specific operations. These things are left up to the driver.

The earlier versions of Direct3D assumed that the programmer would require complete control of texture management details—essentially, each application could provide its own custom texture management. Although more recent versions of Direct3D provide automatic texture management in a style similar to OpenGL, porting code written using the older systems could pose some challenges.

OpenGL Extensions

At first glance, you may think Direct3D has some features that are missing from OpenGL. In fact, most of these features are actually provided as OpenGL extensions. Extensions take the form of new functions or new enumerants to existing functions. A runtime query must be performed to determine whether the OpenGL driver supports the required extensions.

A good example is multitexturing, in which the hardware can perform multiple rendering passes in one go. Most consumer 3D cards these days have this capability. In OpenGL, multitexturing is exposed with the ARB_multitexture extension.

In general, if Direct3D provides a hardware feature that is missing from the base OpenGL specification, there will be an OpenGL extension to support it.

The OpenGL Web site at **http://www.opengl.org** maintains up-to-date information about extensions. Of course, the hardware manufacturers themselves usually have extension information available to encourage you to support the new features on their latest and greatest chipset.

Sound Issues

Unless the original sound code was written using a cross-platform API, you'll be looking at a complete rewrite for these sections of the original game. The good news is that sound code is usually quite well encapsulated. Most games have a very well-defined set of sound requirements: play a sound effect, start a music track, change the volume, and so on. Porting the sound code is a matter of retaining the interface seen by the rest of the game while replacing the implementation.

DirectX provides audio support through the DirectSound API. It's quite a low-level interface, centered around managing sound buffers containing waveform data. This contrasts somewhat with the file-centric Linux approach to audio generation, which involves streaming waveform data out to an audio device.

Networking Issues

Winsock

The Winsock API provides a Windows implementation of the familiar BSD sockets library. But it has some quirks that can make porting tricky.

FILE AND SOCKET HANDLES

The "everything-is-a-file" approach of UNIX means that file handles and socket handles are usually interchangeable. Windows tends not to allow you to treat sockets as files. Where UNIX file and socket handles are usually just integers, Winsock defines the data type SOCKET to represent socket handles.

Where a UNIX program might use read() to pull data in from a socket, the Windows equivalent has to use the socket-specific recv() (or WSARecvEx()). Fortunately, this difference falls in your favor because socket-specific calls such as recv() also work in UNIX.

INCLUDE FILES

Winsock is included in your code using winsock.h or winsock2.h. The winsock2.h header is for version 2 of the Winsock API, which now seems to be more or less standard. BSD sockets on UNIX require various include files, depending on the features being used.

RETURN CODES

Although Winsock and BSD sockets share a similar basic set of error conditions, the way those conditions are communicated differs. Most socket calls return a 0 to indicate success. On failure, Winsock returns SOCKET_ERROR instead of the more traditional -1. Additionally, Winsock uses INVALID_SOCKET to denote a bogus socket handle value where BSD socket calls again use -1.

The Winsock header files define SOCKET_ERROR as -1 and INVALID_SOCKET as ~0 (which, from a bitwise point of view, is also -1). So Winsock *does*, in fact, use the same return codes as BSD sockets, but the naming is different.

If an error occurs, you'll often need to know more: "What type of error? What happened? Can I recover? Should I panic yet?" BSD sockets use the standard errno variable used by other file-handling calls. As a consequence of Winsock sockets not being real file handles, errno doesn't work. Instead, WSAGetLastError() provides the same functionality. The codes returned are pretty much the same set as those used by errno, except that they have been given a WSA prefix. For example, WSAECONNRESET corresponds directly to ECONNRESET.

Different Calls

Winsock provides most of the standard calls present in BSD sockets. Most of these calls also have one or more Winsock-specific versions. Sometimes, the Winsock versions provide significant extra functionality; other calls appear to be present merely for the sake of consistency. For example, `recv()` and `WSARecvEx()` are almost identical, but `select()`, `WSAAsyncSelect()`, and `WSAEventSelect()` all work differently.

Some differences between Winsock and BSD sockets are a consequence of the non-file handle aspect of Winsock sockets. We've already seen the way that the BSD `errno` functionality is provided by `WSAGetLastError()`. Following are some other examples of the differences between Winsock and BSD sockets:

- The BSD-style `close()` call in the Microsoft C runtime library won't work with Winsock sockets. Sockets should instead be closed using the `closesocket()` call.
- Winsock provides `ioctlsocket()` to replace the BSD `ioctl()` call.

DirectPlay Is Evil

Some Windows games use DirectPlay for their network requirements. Like all the DirectX components, DirectPlay is a proprietary API. This wouldn't be too bad—you can always port to another API— except that DirectPlay also imposes a proprietary network protocol. This means that the people playing your Linux port will not be able to play with people running the Windows version of the game. It's a bad situation, and unless the protocol is opened up by Microsoft (or by someone with good reverse-engineering skills!), you're out of luck. The best you can do is to persuade programmers and game players not to support DirectPlay unless it is freed by Microsoft.

DirectPlay is a prime example of why proprietary protocols are a Bad Thing™.

Useful Links

The Mozilla project has a good section on portable coding in C++. It is pretty comprehensive, and you'll want to pick and choose from the advice given:

```
http://www.mozilla.org/hacking/portable-cpp.html
```

Wilfredo Sánchez of Apple has written a paper documenting some of the issues facing the development of OSX. His paper is an interesting read, and many of the same sorts of issues (and solutions) facing OSX crop up when you're porting games to Linux:

> "The Challenges of Integrating the UNIX and Mac OS Environments"
> http://www.mit.edu/people/wsanchez/papers/USENIX_2000/

DJGPP, a DOS port of GCC, has an FAQ that contains some information on dealing with assembly language syntax:

> DJGPP FAQ, section 17.2: "Converting Between Intel ASM Syntax and AT&T Syntax"
> http://www.delorie.com/djgpp/v2faq/index.html

For porting sockets code:

> Winsock Programmers FAQ
> http://www.cyberport.com/~tangent/programming/winsock/

> UNIX Socket FAQ
> http://www.lcg.org/sock-faq/

A D3D/OpenGL feature comparison:

> http://www.xmission.com/~legalize/d3d-vs-opengl.html

The NASM home page:

> http://www.web-sites.co.uk/nasm

FOOTNOTES

1. It ain't what it used to be.
2. Any flavor you like.
3. "Once you start down the dark path, forever will it dominate your destiny. Consume you, it will!"

APPENDIX C

REFERENCES

ell, my friends, it's been fun. But all good things must come to an end, and here it is. Before I leave you to the chaos that is game development, I'll give you some tips: Read the Web sites and buy the books listed in this section. They have helped me, and I'm sure they'll help you in your quest to be the next big thing in the game development community.

WEB SITES

In the big white world of the Internet, there are literally millions of Web sites dedicated to helping game developers. Some are good, most aren't, but here are some of the more useful resources online.

GAMEDEV.NET

HTTP://WWW.GAMEDEV.NET

Probably the best resource for amateur developers (even the guys who own the GamaSutra site [the CMP group] agree with me on this one), this site features everything from daily news to references and message boards. Created by amateur developers for amateur developers, this site contains everything someone new to game programming needs. Also on offer is the GDNet mail service (**http://www.gdnmail.com**), a free Web mail system so that people will know you're a game programmer.

GAMASUTRA

HTTP://WWW.GAMASUTRA.COM

This site is well funded with support and regular articles from some of the biggest names in game development. The site features regular post-mortems of hit games, industry opinions, and a message board that draws some of the best developers out there. It's definitely worth a look (if you have a fast Internet connection).

FLIPCODE

HTTP://WWW.FLIPCODE.COM

Although Flipcode offers many services to the game development community, it does draw a slashdot-esque troll community as well. But don't let that put you off because this site features some advanced articles and various other things worth searching for. Flipcode is part of the FutureGaming network.

Happy Penguin

HTTP://HAPPYPENGUIN.ORG

This site offers Linux game development news and resources. The site includes links to just about every Linux game known to exist (and it generates plenty of references to SourceForge). The site also has links to how-to articles on getting various games (such as Starcraft) working under WINE (**http://winehq.org**).

Indrema Developer Network

HTTP://IDN.INDREMA.COM

This site is the gateway to the developer's side of the upcoming Linux-based console, the L600. Although this site is a touch on the slow side, it consists of more mailing lists than you can shake a big pointy stick at. It's the perfect resource for anyone who wants to break into the world of console programming and has regular input from the Indrema executives.

Linux Games

HTTP://LINUXGAMES.COM

I'm not sure what this site is. Part of me is convinced it's a site aimed at developers, while the other part thinks it's more of a gamer's site. It offers a good mix of the two sides of game development for Linux and is definitely worth a look (even if the administrators do post e-mails there without the author's permission :/).

Linux Game Developer Resource Centre

HTTP://SUNSITE.AUC.DK/LGDC

Hosted on one of the most powerful Web server networks out there (the Sunsite network), the LGDC offers a brilliant collection of links and articles, as well as occasional interviews with big names in the Linux community. Just about everyone who is anyone in the Linux games community subscribes to the mailing list (which has been victim to the occasional mail bomb resulting from what may have been my mail account being deleted *nervous grin*), although the message traffic is kinda slow. Overall, this site is definitely worth a look.

Books

No library is complete without any books; hell, it's not even a library. It's just a room with some empty shelves. To help you fill those shelves, here are some useful guides to the various aspects of game programming, as well as some other references.

OpenGL Super Bible (The Red Book)

A must for any 3D programmer, this book covers everything from transformations to bump mapping. Anyone who has done 3D programming has read this book or has had it recommended to him.

OpenGL Reference (The Blue Book)

A printed version of the OpenGL man pages. The only reason for buying this book is if you prefer hardcopy references to the system help and don't have a fast printer. I don't recommend this title for the OpenGL newbie because it doesn't contain much in the way of tutorials.

Graphics Programming Black Book

By Michael Abrash (Coriolis)

ISBN 1-56710-174-6

This is the graphics programmer's bible. In addition to amusing anecdotes of Abrash's life, this book covers everything from anti-aliasing to to-the-metal optimization techniques. Although it requires some effort to apply the assembly code in this book to Linux systems (which uses a different syntax), it's still a very handy reference to have, but it's not cheap. You do get what you pay for, however, because it is probably the ultimate game programmer's reference.

Game Architecture and Design

By Andrew Rollings and Dave Morris (Coriolis)

ISBN 1-56710-425-7

This book covers every aspect of game design, from team assignments to interface planning. It is a must for any team leader/lead programmer—as well as a useful guide for anyone who wants to break into the industry—because it gives helpful tips and case studies of the way things work on the inside. Although I personally disagree with some of the business models contained in this title, it is nonetheless a good read, and it was written by two people with a long career in the game industry.

TCP/IP Illustrated (Volume 2)

By Richard W. Stevens

Written by the late TCP/IP networking guru, this book (the second of three) covers all the network calls—with full source code—that you could ever need if you decide to do any heavy network coding.

Linux Device Drivers

By Alessandro Rubini (O'Reilly)

ISBN 1-56592-292-1

If you want to do low-level stuff under Linux, understanding how the kernel works and how it prioritizes tasks is essential. This book will help you find out how things are done under the hood. Although just diving into the kernel is one useful approach, this book gives you some guidance on where to look for the things that can help you squeeze every ounce of performance out of your code. In addition, the book offers some useful tips on writing your own modules (if you ever feel masochistic).

Game Development Series

Various Authors (Prima Publishing)

ISBN (various)

The book you are holding is just one of a growing series of game development books from Prima. Although this is the only Linux-specific book in the series to date, the series covers other topics including isometric programming (written by Ernest Pazera, a good friend of mine from GameDev.Net) and dedicated OpenGL books. The series is a must for any game programmer, amateur, or professional (but then, I'm biased; I get paid royalties).

MAGAZINES

There are a few good game development magazines in the world, but those that are stand out from the crowd like a sore thumb on Viagra.

GAME DEVELOPER MAGAZINE

HTTP://WWW.GDMAG.COM

From the same people who brought you GamaSutra comes *Game Developer Magazine*. (They gave me a free T-shirt at ECTS—that's how you buy my support: Clothes.) This magazine is pretty much a paper version of the Web site, filled to the brim with useful techniques and trade news. Free to professional developers in the United States.

DEVELOP

The UK version of *Game Developer Magazine, Develop* was rereleased in November after being bought by the people who print *MCV*. Free to professional developers in the United Kingdom.

EDGE

HTTP://WWW.FUTURENET.COM

Printed by Future Publishing (based in my hometown of Bath in the United Kingdom), this magazine is more suited to gamers with an interest in the development side of things, although it does feature an extensive job section as well as articles from professionals. You can also find out what Peter Molyneux is up to every month because he's sure to be in every magazine somewhere (instead of finishing *Black & White*).

NEWSPAPERS

Where would we be without updates on the industry? As well as the Web, many companies prefer to issue press releases to the traditional press before making the information available to Web sites. These newspapers sometimes have the news before the Net, and are vital resources for keeping an eye on the state of the industry.

COMPUTER TRADE WEEKLY

CTW is filled to the brim with industry news, ranging from who hired who to what games retailers should be placing on the shelves. If you're into the business side of game development, this newspaper is definitely for you. Free for developers in the United Kingdom.

MCV

MCV is filled to the brim with industry news, ranging from who hired whom to what games retailers should be placing on the shelves. If you're into the business side of game development, this newspaper is definitely for you. Free for developers in the United Kingdom. (deja-vu?)

COMPUTER WEEKLY

Computer Weekly is a weekly publication for the entire IT industry, not just games. Free to U.K. IT professionals, it has a decent job section covering both U.K. and international positions, with the occasional games-related job sneaking in.

COMPUTING

Like *Computer Weekly*, *Computing* magazine is not strictly aimed at the games industry, but it does keep you up-to-date on the current state of the IT industry as a whole. It has the added bonus of being the only newspaper in the United Kingdom to feature a *Dilbert* comic strip every week.

NEWSGROUPS

The best newsgroups are usually contained within the **rec.games.*** and **comp.games.*** groups. Note that many people prefer mailing lists to newsgroups because of the lack of spambots there. If you're interested in finding out what the enemy is working on, a useful group is **ms.directx.***, which discusses many things about just about every aspect of the games industry.

MAILING LISTS

The obvious mailing list you should belong to is the LGDC mailing list (**http://sunsite.auc.dk**). This list tends to be very quiet at times and very busy at others (especially when my ex-employer's mail server starts flooding it).

Indrema and CollabNET also run a few Indrema-related lists for various subjects, ranging from the Indrema-specific certification discussions to a list for getting groups of developers together for working on common ideas. You can subscribe to all of these lists at the IDN Web site (**http://idn.indrema.com**).

APPENDIX D

GLOSSARY

A

ALSA (Advanced Linux Sound Architecture). A set of sound drivers for Linux that supports OSS emulation.

B

BeOs. A multimedia operating system.

Blender. A freeware 3D modeling and visualization package; the latest version includes a game engine.

BSD. A version of UNIX distributed under the BSD license.

BSD Sockets. A TCP/IP programming API.

C

Client. A program that connects to a server. A game running under X Windows is an example of a client program.

Console. a) The text mode interface on Linux. b) A home entertainment system.

Copyleft. An alternative to traditional copyright. It is associated with lower restrictions on redistribution. Also a vendor of Linux T-shirts and other related merchandise.

CVS (Concurrency Versioning System). A system that enables users to share and edit source.

D

Debian HURD. A UNIX-like system, similar to Linux, which uses a modularized microkernel instead of a monolithic kernel.

DRM (Digital Rights Management). A system designed to prevent software piracy on the Indrema L600 console.

DV Linux. A special distribution of Linux designed to make sure that Indrema games run on a standard Linux box running DV Linux.

E

Eric S. Raymond. Founder of OpenSource.org and acknowledged guru of the OpenSource movement.

F

Free Software Foundation. An organization to promote the use of free software (specifically the GNU licenses).

FreeBSD. *See* BSD.

Freshmeat. A directory of software for Linux, located at **http://www.freshmeat.net**.

G

GameDev.Net. An online reference for game developers of all levels, located at **http://www.gamedev.net**.

GDNet. *See* GameDev.Net.

GNU Public License. The most widely used OpenSource license. Commonly referred to as the GPL.

H

HSR (Hidden Surface Removal). A technique used in 3D graphics to work out what needs to be drawn.

HUD. Heads-up display.

I

IDN (Indrema Developer Network). A resource for people interested in Indrema development, located at **http://idn.indrema.com**.

IES (Indrema Entertainment Systems). Creators of the Linux-powered L600 console.

Indrema. *See* IES.

J

Joystick. A type of input, frequently used for games.

K

Kernel. The core of an operating system. The kernel controls access to the hardware.

L

Lesser GNU Public License. An OpenSource license designed for use with libraries.

Linux. A free OpenSource operating system originally created in 1991. Linux is used on millions of PCs and servers worldwide. It is the "official" operating system of China.

LOD (Level of Detail). A technique in 3D graphics similar to MIP-mapping. The further away an object is, the lower the quality.

Loki. A company that makes a living porting commercial games to Linux.

M

Minix. A free UNIX operating system on which Linux was initially based.

MIP-mapping. A technique to keep the quality of a scaled image high. Instead of scaling the image, you "render" different versions of it at different sizes.

MMORPG (Massively Multiplayer Online Role Play Game). A large multiplayer environment played over the Internet.

N

Neverwinter Nights. An upcoming MMORPG from the creators of *Baldours Gate.* This game will be available for various platforms, including Linux and BeOS.

O

OpenAL (OpenSource Audio Library). An OpenGL-based sound API by Loki.

OpenBSD. *See* BSD.

OpenGL. A 3D graphics API originally created by SGI. It is available for just about every operating system going.

OpenLobby. An OpenSource lobbying API for games.

OpenSource. A software distribution model that encourages the sharing of source code, knowledge, and skills.

OSS (Open Sound System). A sound driver for Linux.

P

Pretty Poly. An OpenSource modeling package.

Q

Quake. The first next-generation, 3D, first-person, shoot-em-up game. *Quake* is now OpenSourced under the GNU Public License.

R

Richard M. Stallman. Founder of the GNU Project and head of the Free Software Foundation.

S

SDL (Simple DirectMedia Layer). A DirectX-like API that runs on various platforms, including Linux, BeOS, and Win32.

Server. A program to which a client connects. An X Windows server is an example of a server.

SourceForge. An online source repository for OpenSource projects, located at **http://www.sourceforge.net**.

SVGAlib. A console graphics library.

T

TCP (Transport Control Protocol). A subset of TCP/IP.

TCP/IP. The protocol used on the Internet as well as on most networks on the planet.

Tux. The accepted Linux penguin mascot created by Larry Ewing.

U

UDP (User Datagram Protocol). A subset of TCP/IP.

W

Win32. The Windows 9x/NT/2k/ME programming library.

WINE (WINE Is Not an Emulator). A program that emulates the Win32 API for Linux. Several games can run under WINE. For more information, see **http://www.winehq.org**.

X

X Consortium. The group that defines the X Windowing protocol.

X Windowing System. A distributed user interface system, commonly referred to as X.

Xbox. The new console being produced by Microsoft; it is due for release in the third quarter of 2001.

XFree86. An OpenSource implementation of the X Windowing protocol. Originally intended for the x86 series of processors, XFree86 has been ported to other platforms.

APPENDIX E

What's on the CD-ROM

The CD-ROM that accompanies this book contains both binaries and source code (when available) for SDL, OpenAL, IESDK, PrettyPoly, Mesa3D, SVGAlib, and source code only for Linux Kernel versions 2.2.18, 2.4.0, and 2.4.1. The CD-ROM also has all the sample files that the author used throughout the book.

RUNNING THE CD-ROM WITH WINDOWS 95/98/2000/NT

To make the CD user-friendly and take less of your disk space, no installation is required to view the CD. This means that the only files transferred to your hard disk are the ones you choose to copy or install. You can run the CD on any operating system that can view files; however, not all the programs can be installed on all operating systems.

1. Insert the CD into the CD-ROM drive and close the tray.
2. Go to My Computer or Windows Explorer and double-click the CD-ROM drive.
3. Most of the files contained on the CD can be viewed with WINZIP.

RUNNING THE CD WITH LINUX

To make the CD user-friendly and take less of your disk space, no installation is required to view the CD. This means that the only files transferred to your hard disk are the ones you choose to copy or install. You can run the CD on any operating system that can view files; however, not all the programs can be installed on all operating systems.

1. Insert the CD into the CD-ROM drive and close the tray.
2. Either make sure that automount is running, or mount the CD by issuing the mount command from a shell prompt.
3. Change to the root directory of the CD, usually /mnt/cdrom.
4. Most of the files contained on the CD will need to be uncompressed and un-tarred with the following commands:

```
gunzip filename
tar -xvf filename
```

1NDEX

Home •
News
Strategy Guides
Forums
Game Worlds

More Than
Just Strategy

Strategy:

Over 250 Fast Track Guides with many
more to come — new online strategy
every week.

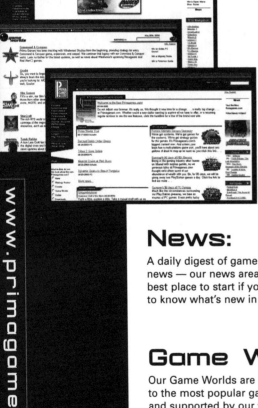

News:

A daily digest of game industry
news — our news area is the
best place to start if you want
to know what's new in games.

Game Worlds:

Our Game Worlds are dedicated
to the most popular games
and supported by our wealth
of Fan Site Affiliates.

www.primagames.com

PRIMA GAMES.COM

Gamedev.net

The most comprehensive game development resource

- The latest news in game development
- The most active forums and chatrooms anywhere, with insights and tips from experienced game developers
- Links to thousands of additional game development resources
- Thorough book and product reviews
- Over 1000 game development articles!
  Game design
  Graphics
  DirectX
  OpenGL
  AI
  Art
  Music
  Physics
  Source Code
  Sound
  Assembly
  And More!

Gamedev.net

License Agreement/Notice of Limited Warranty